OSTEOARCHAEOLOGY
IN HISTORICAL CONTEXT

Sidestone Press

OSTEOARCHAEOLOGY IN HISTORICAL CONTEXT

CEMETERY RESEARCH FROM THE LOW COUNTRIES

edited by
Roos van Oosten, Rachel Schats & Kerry Fast

URBAN GRAVEYARD PROCEEDINGS 3

Published by Sidestone Press, Leiden
www.sidestone.com

Lay-out & cover design: Sidestone Press
Cover illustration: Laurens van Maren

ISBN 978-90-8890-833-0 (softcover)
ISBN 978-90-8890-834-7 (hardcover)
ISBN 978-90-8890-835-4 (PDF e-book)

Contents

Immigrants in Vlaardingen

Archaeological research at a cemetery, 1000-1050

Tim de Ridder

Introduction

The subject of this paper[1] is an excavation carried out in early 2002 in Vlaardingen at the Gat in de Markt (Hole in the Market) site (Fig. 1). The section of the burial area that was investigated is part of the cemetery of the Vlaardingen Grote Kerk and is situated south of the church. The history of the church goes back to the early 8th century. *C.* 1000, the church and cemetery were probably within the ringfort of Count Dirk III. The burials excavated in 2002 were exceptionally well preserved and were dated from a short period, 1000-1050. This was the time when Vlaardingen developed into a centre of the county, which was later Holland. This chapter centres on the question of what new information on medieval Vlaardingen and its residents did the investigation of this cemetery produce. To answer that question, I will first provide some background information on medieval Vlaardingen before discussing the results of the excavations at the Gat in de Markt site in more detail.

Background information

The following section presents a brief history of the church associated with the cemetery and of the relation between the counts of Frisia[2] and Vlaardingen. This is followed by a short discussion of the main developments in Vlaardingen in the 11th and 12th centuries and, finally, of later perceptions of Vlaardingen at this time.

---

1 This text is based on a paper on medieval burial grounds presented during a conference at the Cultural Heritage Agency of the Netherlands (RCE), December 12, 2013. The text is a synthesis of several previously published preliminary reports and articles. References to these publications are given in the footnotes. English translation by GrondTaal (Gerre van der Kleij). The author is grateful to Gerre van der Kleij for her critical remarks.

2 Frisia was the name of an area extending along the entire Dutch coast from the Zwin in Zeeland in the south to the Vlie in the north. The county of Frisia's core was the area that today makes up the Dutch provinces of Noord-Holland and Zuid-Holland.

Fig. 1: The church mound in Vlaardingen. At the right of the photo, the undeveloped area of the Gat in de Markt site where the edge of the medieval cemetery was identified in early 2002. Photo collection municipal archives, Vlaardingen Municipality.

The development of Vlaardingen into Count Dirk III's power base

In 726/727 the missionary Willibrord gifted a small church and some associated land to his own proprietary monastery at Echternach in Luxemburg.[3] The deed of donation states:

> *The clergyman Heribald gave me and placed into my hands a [or the] church in the shire of Marsum, where the Meuse flows into the sea, with all that pertains to it, in addition, a piece of marshland suitable for grazing sheep. The above mentioned and recorded items I, Clemens Willibrord, donate and I transfer them to the above mentioned house of God, Echternach.*[4]

Although this text fragment does not explicitly mention Vlaardingen, historians are, nonetheless, of the opinion that it refers to the Vlaardingen church. In a later period, the Vlaardingen church was at the centre of a dispute with the monastery at Echternach, which claimed ownership of it. In light of its ties with Echternach, it is assumed that the Vlaardingen church is in fact the church mentioned in the 726/727 deed.[5] This would make the Vlaardingen church one of five mother

3 A proprietary monastery or church was an establishment that was the personal property of a member of the nobility (e.g., king or count) or higher clergy (e.g., a bishop). Usually the proprietor was also entitled to the foundation's revenues and could appoint its senior clergy.

4 Nieuwenhuijsen & De Ridder 2012, 164, translation from the Latin.

5 Dijkstra 2011, 282.

churches in the future county of Holland.[6] According to a document allegedly drafted in 1083 by someone at Egmond Abbey,[7] Count Arnulf (998-993) donated the church and all that belonged to it to the abbey. If this were the case, the county's connection to Vlaardingen would go back at least as far as Arnulf's reign. That the connection between that dynasty and Vlaardingen went back to that period is manifest from events that took place after 993. Shortly after the murder of Count Arnulf in that year, his widow, Lutgardis of Luxemburg, settled in Vlaardingen with her young children, and by 1018 Count Dirk III, Arnulf's son, had evidently established a significant power base in Vlaardingen.[8] From his stronghold there, he was intercepting vessels sailing between England and Tiel and charging a toll. To his contemporaries this constituted piracy, for toll collection required the emperor's permission, which Dirk III did not have. In addition, Count Dirk III was claiming a share of the yield from local farmers as taxation even though a significant portion of the land they were farming was not his. Dirk III's high-handedness stirred up resentment among land owners (including the Bishop of Utrecht) and Tiel merchants, who in turn complained to Count Dirk III's liege lord, the German Emperor Henry II. During the Imperial Diet of April 6, 1018, the emperor organized a punitive expedition to Vlaardingen to depose Dirk III. On the morning of July 29, 1018 things came to a head as a large fleet sailed from Tiel towards Vlaardingen. Although the imperial army outnumbered Dirk's forces several times over, the battle was decided in the count's favour, who was aided by the local population.

The count's victory in the Battle of Vlaardingen strengthened his hold over the county while weakening the influence of the Bishop of Utrecht, and he was able to maintain his control over the reclamations in his territory and thereby increase his revenues. If the battle had been lost, the county would have lost its autonomous status as well, and its revenues would have gone to other rulers. It is because of this that Dirk III has entered the history books as one of the founding fathers of Holland. For Vlaardingen, the event inaugurated a period of prosperity; the settlement expanded to become one of the chief towns[9] of a county, which from 1101 onwards was called Holland.[10] The Annals of Berthold, for example, state:

> *King Rudolph, however, celebrated Whitsunday [May 27, 1078] at Goslar with great splendour, gathering about him not a few noblemen from Saxony and Thuringia, and when he had taken counsel with them there he organized an*

---

6 Four other mother churches in Holland were established at Velsen, Oegstgeest, Heiloo, and Petten. A mother church could in its turn establish daughter churches and chapels. Daughter foundations of the Vlaardingen church were Schie, Harg (later Kethel), Berkel, and Schiedam.

7 The document was probably drafted in the 12th century, but some scholars argue that it was based on authentic information. See Nieuwenhuijsen & De Ridder 2012, 187.

8 Nieuwenhuijsen & De Ridder 2012, 193.

9 In 1206 the Loon War ended. William, Count of Holland, was forced to order all his vassals and *ministeriales* to pay homage to the Count of Loon and to swear an oath of allegiance to him. The towns of Dordrecht, Vlaardingen, Leiden, and Haarlem were specifically mentioned, suggesting that these were Holland's chief towns at the time. See De Ridder 2001; De Boer & Cordfunke 1997, 60; Van Maanen 2017, 18.

10 Henderikx 2001, 63.

expedition against King Henry [IV]. With him were envoys from Philip, the king of France, and from Vlaardingen as well as a large number from Lorraine, and also from the king of Hungary.[11]

What emerges from this fragment is that Vlaardingen was counted among the larger European territories. The first Vlaardingen coinage dates from the same period; the Swedish numismatic collection in Stockholm contains a coin with the word 'Comes' on one side and on the reverse 'Flardi-ga', which together could be read as 'Count of Vlaardingen'.[12]

Vlaardingen's downfall

Vlaardingen remained one of the chief towns of the county of Holland until at least the early 13th century. Its decline began in the mid 12th century, when, on December 21, 1163, a disastrous flood caused the collapse of the dykes near Vlaardingen over a length of several kilometres. Much of Vlaardingen was covered with a thick layer of clay. Unfortunately for Vlaardingen, those same floods created much more favourable conditions for Dordrecht, and that town rapidly eclipsed Vlaardingen in importance. Nevertheless, in 1273 Vlaardingen received a charter that was based on earlier privileges, probably acquired in the early 13th century.[13] While a charter is often the harbinger of a prosperous future, in the case of Vlaardingen it represented the final echo of a glorious past. While other Holland towns were burgeoning, Vlaardingen stagnated. By *c.* 1400 it had become one of the smallest of the Holland towns.

Meanwhile, the water's assault on Vlaardingen continued. Until the 16th century, flood waters regularly reached the foot of the church mound of the Grote Kerk, and in 1494 the river washed away a 15-rod section of the dyke that protected the church mound in the south. The people of Vlaardingen lamented their fate, for they could still remember a time when the land in front of the dyke had been dry and even supported 'streets and houses'. And more had been lost as well. Fruin, a 19th-century professor in history at the University of Leiden wrote, 'as has been observed and is still the case regarding the dead who were buried here in the past in hollowed-out trees, that all of that has now been destroyed by the water'.[14]

By the 16th century, Vlaardingen's decline had reached a point where other towns questioned Vlaardingen's status as a chartered town.[15] Indeed, with its 2,500 residents and without town walls or gates, Vlaardingen in the 16th century

11 *Bertholdi Annales* in Nieuwenhuijsen & De Ridder 2012, 64. Berthold von der Reichenau (d. 1088?) was a German Benedictine monk.

12 Nieuwenhuijsen & De Ridder 2012, 209.

13 Van Maanen (2017, 19) suggests that the oldest elements of the Vlaardingen charter were granted by Count William I (1175-1222), from which he also deduces that the count thus intended to bind the four main settlements to himself. Van Maanen further states that the question whether Dordrecht or Geertruidenberg holds the oldest charter remains unsettled.

14 Fruin 1876, 244. Hollowed out trees is a reference to tree-trunk coffins.

15 In 1545, Hans die Cuyper, a Vlaardingen brewer, became embroiled in a legal dispute with other towns. A summons was issued against the brewer by Dordrecht, Delft, Leiden, Amsterdam, and Gouda, then leading towns, that invoked the *Ordre*, or decree, by the sovereign, Emperor Charles V, according to which only chartered towns were allowed to practice certain trades including brewing. However, Vlaardingen was a chartered town, and the plaintiffs' case was rejected, and they were ordered to pay the costs of the trial. See Ter Brugge & De Ridder 1996, 5.

resembled a largish village rather than a proper town. Its pre-eminent position in the 11th and 12th centuries had been entirely forgotten.

Perception and hypotheses

The floods not only had a negative physical impact on Vlaardingen but also rendered its importance during the 11th and 12th centuries invisible. This led later historians to assert that the Battle of Vlaardingen had in fact taken place near Dordrecht.[16] Also Rotterdam municipal archaeologist Hoek, who carried out extensive research in Vlaardingen, assumed, partly on the basis of historical sources, that the old settlement had mostly been washed away and moreover that the church had had to be relocated.[17] Hoek based the latter assumption in part on a small-scale excavation inside the Grote Kerk in 1967 (Fig. 2), which led him to conclude that the church mound had been raised in the mid-12th century in order to build the Grote Kerk. He situated its predecessor south of the Grote Kerk.

Fig. 2: 1967 excavation inside the Grote Kerk. Photo BOOR, collection archaeology, Vlaardingen Municipality.

16 In the 18th century, the *Rymchronyk* surfaced, allegedly written in the 12th century by an Egmond monk, Klaas Kolyn. The work contained a rhymed history of Holland, and among other things, it recounted how Count Dirk III built his stronghold at Dordrecht and collected tolls there. The much respected historian Jan Wagenaar endorsed this version and therefore logically assumed that the Battle of Vlaardingen had also taken place near Dordrecht. Later Wagenaar himself came to the conclusion that the *Rymchronyk* was a forgery. By then, however, the idea that the Battle of Vlaardingen had in fact been a Battle of Dordrecht had become firmly entrenched and proved to be a tenacious and recurrent theme in histories of Holland. Nieuwenhuijsen, De Ridder & Luth 2017, 60.

17 Hoek 1973, 134. For a description of the older plan of Vlaardingen, see De Ridder 2002.

Excavations at the Gat in de Markt site

Introduction

Since the 1980s, an L-shaped plot in the centre of Vlaardingen had lain undeveloped, but after two decades concrete plans finally materialized to build on this Gat in de Markt site. Archaeological research at this location began at the end of 2001 (Fig. 3).[18] The excavation was a stone's throw away from the Grote Kerk and south of the church mound. Research at this location was an opportunity to test Hoek's hypotheses that Vlaardingen's settled area had extended further south and that the church and its cemetery had been relocated.

The flood of 1494 had exposed tree-trunk coffins at the edge of the mound, and so the presence of a burial ground at that location was noted as a distinct possibility. In the summer of 2001, prior to the archaeological research, amateur archaeologist Piet Heinsbroek conducted a bore-hole survey at the site, and at a depth of several metres, he encountered a layer of wood about one meter thick. The present author, who by chance was present, suspected that the wood was oak, which raised the possibility that the auger had hit a tree-trunk coffin. However, the archaeological investigation initially failed to produce any evidence of a cemetery at the location. It was only towards the end of the official excavation that graves were uncovered, at a depth of approximately three metres.

In a trench approximately 6 x 5 m, 45 burials were uncovered of which 41 could be lifted. All burials seemed to have taken place within a short period of time, 1000-1050.[19] The graves thus give us an unprecedented glimpse of Vlaardingen society during the period when the town developed into one of the count's main power bases. One of the graves was found in a later stratum, dated to the late 12th/early 13th century; this grave was situated between a 13th-century moat and the slope of the late-12th-century dyke,[20] outside the contemporary medieval cemetery.

Spatial organization

Our research at the Gat in de Markt site yielded new information on the spatial changes that occurred in relation to the church and other buildings in the 10th and 11th centuries. For example, it became apparent that the land surface had been raised considerably *c.* 1000, just before this plot became a burial ground. In the process, what was possibly a moat was moved a short distance south. The cemetery itself was surrounded by a ditch approximately one meter wide with a wattle fence between the ditch and the cemetery. If the slightly curving ditch would be extended, we would end up with a roughly circular area that also encompassed the present church building. It seems reasonable to assume that the excavated cemetery from

---

18 Van Loon & De Ridder 2006.

19 The chronology is based on a combination of radiocarbon and tree-ring analysis and on its stratigraphic position relative to other strata and features.

20 This dyke protected Vlaardingen from the Meuse and Merwede. Its oldest phase probably dates from shortly after 1134. After the disastrous flood which hit Vlaardingen in 1163, a large section of the dyke was moved further inland. As a result, the dyke abutted the church mound before continuing north, along the course of the present Hoogstraat.

1000-1050 was associated with a church. Since the present Grote Kerk (built in the 18th century) is situated within the circular enclosure, it seems safe to conclude that the *c.* 1000 church was also situated within the circle. Moreover, there is no evidence to indicate that the church was moved after 1000. We may therefore assume that the *c.* 1000 church and its predecessors stood approximately where the

Fig. 3: Excavation of the Gat in de Markt site. Visible in the background is a corner of the Vlaardingen town hall with a statue of Count Dirk III overlooking the excavation of his contemporaries. Photo collection archaeology, Vlaardingen Municipality.

present Grote Kerk is located. This hypothesis is supported by subsequent borehole surveying in and around the Grote Kerk that produced human bone fragments and wood (probably from coffins) pre-1000.[21] Interestingly, this section of the cemetery did not remain in use very long; it was last used *c.* 1046.[22] We know that between 1046 and 1049 Vlaardingen once again became a battlefield, and sources from 1047 describe Rijnsburg and Vlaardingen as exceptionally strong fortifications. In the case of Vlaardingen, it is assumed that this refers to a ringfort, in which the church was located.[23] Vlaardingen's fortifications seem to have been strengthened in or before 1047, and it is possible that this reinforcement took in some of the cemetery area, which was situated where the bank of the ringfort is assumed to have been. The edge of the cemetery and the possible bank was also the location of the dyke that was built between 1164 and 1170. Perhaps by that time the location had already been elevated, given the hypothetical presence of the former bank. Because of later disturbances it was impossible to test this during the archaeological investigations.

Grave types

In total, 41 burials were lifted. All were oriented east-west and in all but one, the heads were pointing west. The single exception was a burial in which the head pointed east; in all other respects this grave was similar to the others. There was some variation in the construction of the graves and coffins. Of the 45 graves, 23 were coffin burials, no wood was found in 10, six contained wood remains, four were grave pits with a lid, and two were lined pits with a lid. Fig. 4 and Table 1

Type	Description
I	Coffin grave. The sides and ends of the coffin are made of planks with pegged tenon joints. The bottom consists of slats, each tapering to a peg joining it to the side planks.
II	Coffin grave. The same as Type I, with the difference that the two coffin ends are not plank boards but two slats.
III	Pit grave. A pit that has no wooden lining or a coffin but has a wooden lid.
IV	Pit grave. A pit with all walls lined with loose wooden planks and with a lid, but these are not joined.
Tree-trunk coffin	A coffin carved out of a tree truck, with a lid.

Table 1: Grave types.

Lid type	Description
A	Made of a single plank
B	Made of two joined planks, usually a wide and a narrow one
C	Made of three or more planks, either loose or joined.

Table 2: Lid types.

21 Van Dasselaar 2013.

22 The terminus date is based on tree-ring analysis.

23 Nieuwenhuijsen, De Ridder & Luth 2017, 39. At several locations around the church it was possible to establish that it was surrounded by an unusually wide (>10 to at least 30 m) body of water, possibly a moat.

show the various grave types, Table 2 lists the lid types, and Table 3 lists the various combinations of grave and lid types.[24]

The lids may also have been used as biers to transport the deceased; this would explain the frequent presence of one or two separate pieces of timber found in association with a lid.

Table 3: Number of graves per type. Nineteen graves could be assigned to a specific type. The other 26 were too disturbed to allow for classification with any certainty.

Type	
I-A	5
I-B	5
II-A	2
III-A	1
III-B	2
III-C	1
IV-A	1
IV-B	1
Tree-trunk coffin	1
Total	19

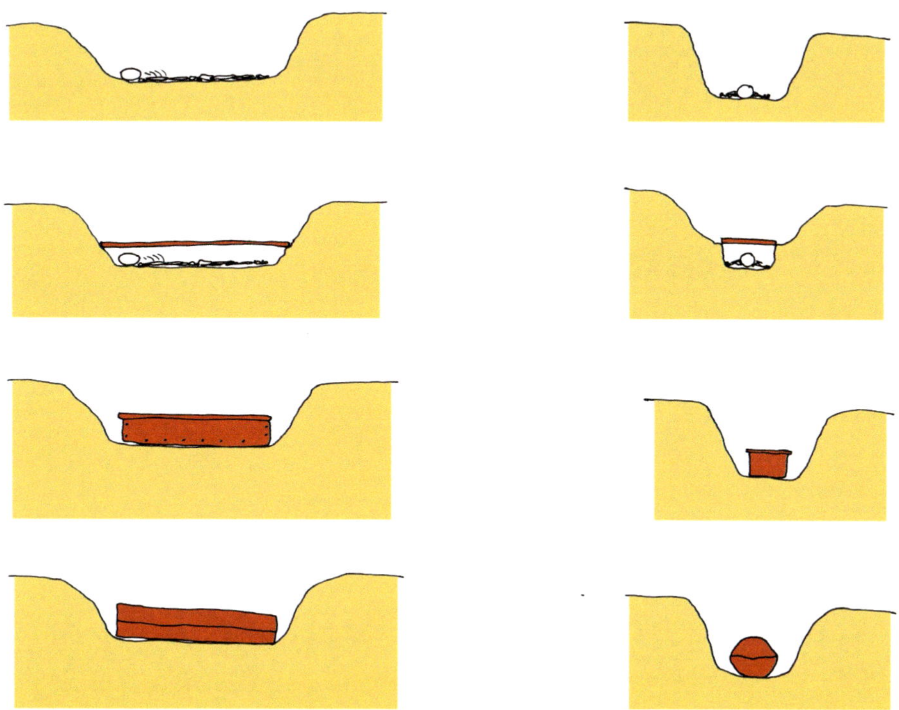

Fig. 4: Different grave types uncovered at the Gat in de Markt site. From top to bottom: a pit grave, a pit grave covered by wooden planks, a coffin grave, a tree-trunk coffin. Drawing collection archaeology, Vlaardingen Municipality.

24 Vredenbregt & De Ridder 2004.

Fig. 5: A slat-bottomed coffin. Most of the skeleton has been lifted, only the skull is still in situ. Photo collection archaeology, Vlaardingen Municipality.

Fig. 6: Imprint of a skeleton in the wood of a coffin lid. Photo collection archaeology, Vlaardingen Municipality.

The graves were situated approximately three meters below the surface. The weight of the soil had pressed the slat-bottom coffins vertically down into the soil below (Fig. 5). As a result, the skeletons in many cases had been pressed up against their wooden lid, and occasionally bones protruded through the lid. In one instance, the entire length of the skeleton had been pushed into the lid (Fig. 6).

Grave contents

The state of preservation of the graves was excellent; even the straw that had been used to cover the bodies in many graves still looked fresh (Fig. 7). That rules out the possibility that the deceased were wearing garments of leather or wool, for under these conditions such materials would certainly have been preserved. In one of the children's graves, the muddy imprint of a textile fragment was clearly visible. In the same grave a blackish substance was observed covering the straw layer, suggesting that the body had been packed in straw and then wrapped in fabric (Fig. 8). Since the fabric itself had not been preserved it was probably linen, a plant-based material that decays quickly. Some medieval illustrations show bodies sown inside sacks for burial (Fig. 9). Perhaps the Vlaardingen dead

Fig. 7: Straw on a skull. Photo collection archaeology, Vlaardingen Municipality.

Fig. 8: Burial of a young boy with muddy imprints of textile on top of and next to the straw. Photo collection archaeology, Vlaardingen Municipality.

were buried in linen sacks in a similar fashion. The straw analysis showed that it consisted of stem fragments of oats (*Avena sativa*) and reed (*Phragmites australis*) mixed with threshing waste and shoreline plants.[25] None of the graves contained grave goods.

The wood from the graves

All the coffin wood was removed and subsequently analysed. All of it turned out to have been recycled, except for the tree-truck coffin. Some of the wood was originally construction timber, evinced by a number of tongue-and-groove planks (Fig. 10). Other wood came from decommissioned vessels built in the Viking style, as indicated by the clinker-built construction and the presence of rivets (Fig. 11). Tree-ring analysis indicated that the oldest ship's timber dated from 918 (± 6) and the most recent from 1045/1046. In total, remains of three vessels constructed in the Viking style were identified. The reference curve indicated that one of the vessels came from the northern Netherlands or northern Germany. This vessel had been built *c.* 967 (± 6) and it was therefore approximately 50 years old when parts of it were recycled in a grave shortly after 1043. Tree-ring analysis further showed the other ship fragment came from a vessel built in England *c.* 1009 (± 6) and re-used for funerary purposes shortly after 1043. This vessel was therefore much younger when it ended up as coffin wood in a Vlaardingen inhumation. It may have been a vessel of a similar type as one found at Hedeby, Denmark and known as Hedeby 3.2 (Fig. 12).

---

25 Brinkkemper, Van Loon & De Ridder 2006, 5.

Fig. 9: Images of corpses sown into sacks, from the Getijdenboek van Parijs, Ariès 1983, p. 107.

Fig. 10: A reconstruction drawing showing planks slotted into beams to make walls. Drawing M.J.A. de Haan, source Dijkstra 1998, p. 26, Fig. 13.

Fig. 11: Planks used as a grave cover from a Danish Viking ship built in England shortly after 1008. Photo collection archaeology, Vlaardingen Municipality.

The ship fragments could be easily identified by their clinker-built construction of overlapping planks riveted together. The chinks between the planks still contained oakum which analysis showed to consist of cow hair and sheep's wool (Fig. 13). The pollen trapped in the hairs was analysed as well; the cows in question had grazed in a semi-open landscape dominated by willow, which suggests a tidal marsh or foreshore. The oakum material definitely did not originate in Vlaardingen, which was surrounded by an open landscape and slightly further inland by alder carr.

The burials

Age and sex distribution

All skulls were wrapped in foil while still in the field to prevent any loss of small elements such as teeth. The skeletal material was analysed by physical anthropologist Mike Groen.[26] The data presented below is derive from this

26 Groen & De Ridder 2007.

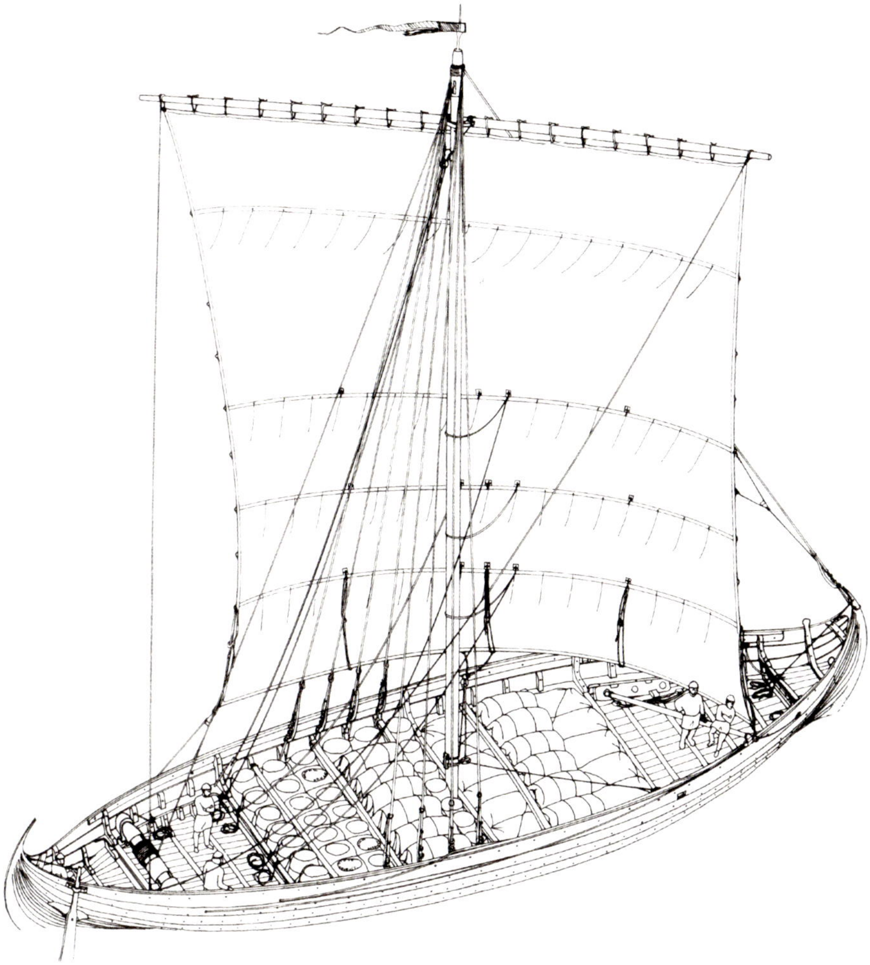

Fig. 12: Drawing of the Viking ship Hedeby, probably a 20m freighter. Drawing Sune Villum-Nielsen, source: Crumlin-Pedersen 1997, p. 103, Fig. 4.36.

Fig. 13: Oakum consisting of twisted cow hair and sheep's wool. Photo collection archaeology, Vlaardingen Municipality.

research. Fifteen adults (six females [22%]; nine males [15%]) and 26 subadults (63%) were buried in the cemetery. Of the subadults, 15 were younger than five when they died, eight were between five and 10, while 3 were between 10 and 20 years old when they died.

The average age at death of the women was 48.4 years (standard deviation 10.46) and that of the men 46.4 years (standard deviation 13.50). Only three of the adults were between 20 and 40 years old when they died.

Location	Source	Date *(c.)*	Source	Women	Source	Men
Vlaardingen		1000-1050	Trotter & Gleser 1958	163.1 (N=6)	Trotter 1970 & Breitinger 1937	177.7 (N=7)
Church of St. Salvator Abbey, Susteren, Limburg	Baetsen 1998	800-1100	Trotter & Gleser 1952, 1958	162.9 (N=30)	Trotter & Gleser 1952, 1958	174.4 (N=13)
St. Nicholas Shambles parish church, London	White 1988	1000-1200		157.5 (N=?)		172.8 (N= ?)
St. Andrew, monastic complex, York	Stroud 1993	1000-1200	Trotter 1970	approx. 158 (N=30)	Trotter 1970	approx. 172 (N=43)
Oosthoek, monastic grange, Hellevoetsluis, Netherlands	Smits 1999; see also Carmiggelt 2017	1250-1300	Trotter & Gleser 1952, 1958	161.2 (N=33)	Trotter & Gleser 1952, 1958	172.4 (N=55)

Table 4: Average stature (cm) of comparable burial populations from approximately the same period.

Adults

The adults were in good to excellent health, as indicated by their comparatively tall stature.[27] The women were on average 163.1 cm tall (standard deviation 3.67) while the average height of the men was 174.7 cm (standard deviation 5.02) to 1.77 cm (standard deviation 3.33). Both sexes were taller than their contemporaries elsewhere, at least at the time of the analysis (2005).[28]

Source of table: Groen & De Ridder 2007, 36

A large portion of the Vlaardingen adult skeletons showed symptoms of diffuse idiopathic skeletal hyperostosis (DISH). DISH is a metabolic disorder causing ossification on the right side of the spine. It is sometimes associated with type II diabetes and obesity. Because there is a link between these two and a diet rich in sugar and carbohydrates, DISH is often regarded as an affluence-related disorder. One female skeleton showed signs of gout, another disorder often associated with an affluent lifestyle.

Traces of joint disorders were observed on both male and female skeletons, more specifically osteoarthritis and degenerative disc disease (DDD), degeneration of the intervertebral discs of the spine. DDD primarily occurs at an advanced age and is slightly more common in men than in women. Two of the male Vlaardingen skeletons displayed a mild form of vertebral osteoarthritis (vOA) (a condition that affects the axial facet joints) in the cervical vertebrae, while two other males suffered from a medium form of peripheral osteoarthritis (pOA) in the acromioclavicular joints. These forms of osteoarthritis may be related to activities using mainly neck and shoulder muscles and carried out mostly by males.[29]

---

27 Stature was determined on the basis of long-bone measurements. The methods used for the conversion to body length were Trotter & Gleser 1958 for females and Trotter 1970 and Breitinger 1937 for males.

28 Groen & De Ridder 2007, 36. Interestingly, 11th- and 12th-century shoes excavated elsewhere in Vlaardingen proved to be surprisingly large as well, the average being a size 40 (about 254 mm); Goubitz & Ter Brugge 1996.

29 Groen & De Ridder 2006, 43; Larsen 2003, 176-177.

All skulls were measured. Interestingly, the shape of the skulls varied significantly, a possible indication that this was not a closed population but rather one that included many individuals from elsewhere.

Children

Approximately 19% of the children showed signs of deficiency-related illnesses such as rickets and cribra orbitalia (porosity and pitting in the orbital vaults). Rickets is associated with vitamin-D deficiency while anaemia is one possible cause of cribra orbitalia. The prevalence of deficiency-related illnesses in the Vlaardingen subadult population is low compared to what has been observed in other burial populations, nor were the cases as severe as elsewhere.

Signs of trauma

All signs of trauma observed on the skeletons of women and children in Vlaardingen (mainly wrist fractures) can be explained as the result of accidents. With regard to the male skeletons, the situation is different. Rib and nose fractures were observed as well as injuries to the cranial vault on male skeletons. Such fractures are associated with violence, and since these men were contemporaries of Count Dirk III, their trauma may be the result of injuries suffered in the Battle of Vlaardingen. However, there was no indication of the more common trauma associated with battle wounds. Injuries sustained during battle could be expected to have been inflicted with a sharp object like a spear or a sword,[30] but none of the observed injuries matched such weapons. Yet another type of trauma commonly associated with warfare are parry fractures, for example, a sword blow to the head or the fracture of the distal end of the ulna occurring

Fig. 14: Skull of a 40-50-year-old male who sustained two hard blows to the head. Photo collection archaeology, Vlaardingen Municipality.

30 For example, Alpert of Metz mentioned that the Frisians fought by throwing javelins while their adversaries wielded swords. Nieuwenhuijsen & De Ridder 2012, 40.

when a person raises an arm to parry a blow to the head. But this type of trauma was not observed either. Three skulls, however, showed clear signs of an impact with a hard, blunt object (Fig. 14). While obviously not cuts from a sword, could these be the result of a sword blow to a head protected by a helmet? All in all, there were no convincing indications that the Vlaardingen males participated in the Battle of Vlaardingen. In addition, historical sources of that encounter state that only the imperial army suffered fatalities. Although the sources may be exaggerated, the number of victims injured or killed on the Vlaardingen side was probably limited.

Chronology

The excavated Vlaardingen burials came from a period of approximately 50 years.[31] Although that is very short, we wanted to further subdivide this period on the basis of grave depth and overlap. It turned out that the cemetery had been extended once, probably *c.* 1025. Not all burials could be attributed with certainty to a specific phase (either pre- or post-1025), but 12 individuals could be assigned to phase 1 and 22 to phase 2. Only women and children were interred in phase 1 while in phase 2 adult males, children, and a small number of women were buried. Also of note was the fact that during phase 1, the average age at death for the children was 6.5 years while during phase 2 it was 3.5 years. However, due to the small sample size these observations may not be statistically significant.

Tree-trunk coffin

The one tree-trunk coffin was found in the top layer of the section of the cemetery where burial ceased *c.* 1050 (Fig. 15). It is therefore likely that the tree-trunk coffin was interred shortly before that date. The wood of the coffin contained only about 55 rings. Unfortunately, this is not enough for a reliable tree-ring date. Unusually, the coffin lid was largely preserved. The lid of the coffin included a small oak plank board 43 x 16 x 3 cm (Fig. 16) over the spot where the deceased's breast would have been. It may have been a repair, but it is also possible that it covered a hole in the lid, much like tree-trunk coffins found in the German town of Seppenrade. Here coffins longer than 1.9 meters featured a hole above the deceased's face in the shape of a rectangle, a star, or two small round holes. These graves dated from the 10th century.[32] However, no Dutch parallels have been identified. The Vlaardingen tree-trunk coffin contained the skeleton of a man who was approximately 1.74 meters tall and 52-61 years old when he died.[33]

---

31 One grave was dated 12th-13th century. It was situated outside this section of the cemetery and is not discussed here.

32 Zeischka 1983, 46, 47.

33 Groen & De Ridder 2005. Because of the unusual nature of the find, the Vlaardings Museum decided to give this ancient Vlaardingen resident a face. Physical anthropologist Maja d' Hollosy made a reconstruction of 'tree-trunk coffin man' (Fig. 17 and 18), and novelist Karin de Roos brought him back to life in her book *Dubio*, set in Vlaardingen in the year 1018. A few other Vlaardingers were also given faces (Figs. 19-22).

Fig. 15: A nearly intact tree-trunk coffin. Photo collection archaeology, Vlaardingen Municipality.

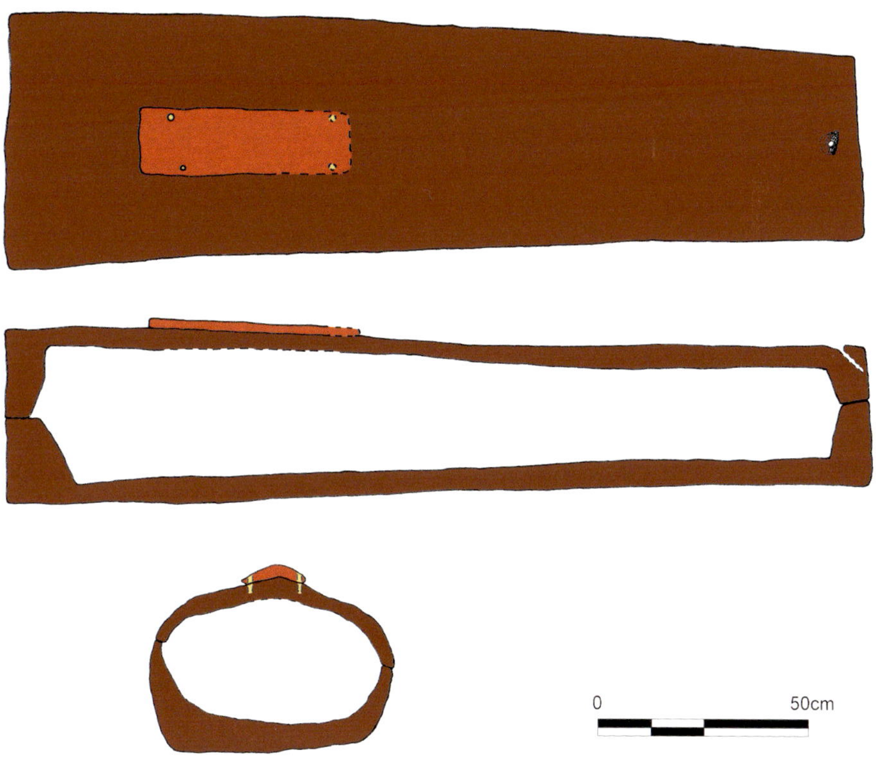

Fig. 16: Sketch of the tree-trunk coffin: top-, side-, and end views. Drawing collection archaeology, Vlaardingen Municipality.

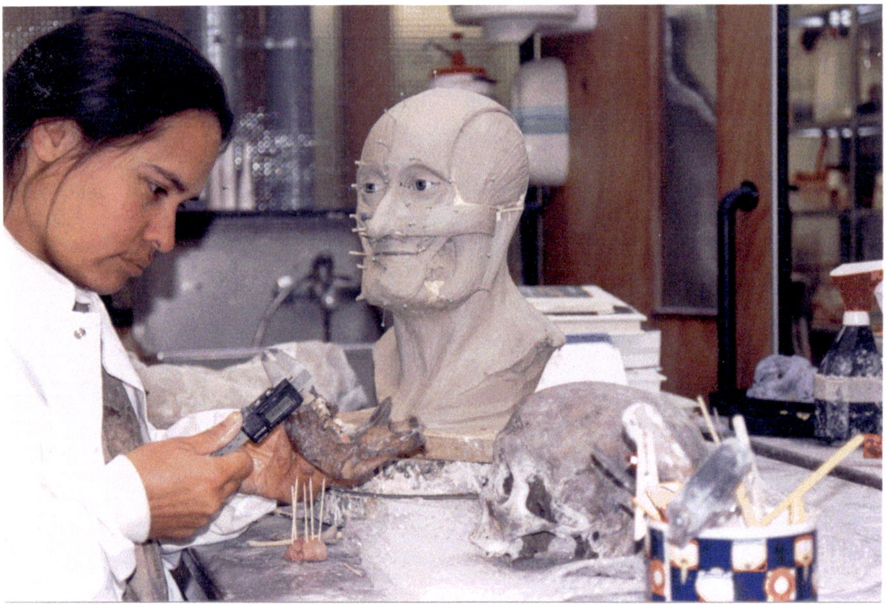

Fig. 17: Maja d' Hollosy working on the facial reconstruction of the 'tree-trunk coffin man' commissioned by Vlaardingen Museum. Photo collection Maja d' Hollosy.

DNA analysis

The excellent preservation of the Vlaardingen burials raised the question whether such preservation might also extend to their DNA. A pilot study carried out in late 2005 revealed that the 1000-year-old bone material still contained human DNA, at that time the oldest human DNA in the Netherlands. Twenty-five skeletons qualified for a DNA study; molars were used for sampling. The DNA study had two foci, one was its public appeal and the other its scientific pursuit.[34] The scientific study was part of PhD research into modern human evolution undertaken by Eveline Altena (Fig. 23). The study's public appeal lay in the fact that efforts were made, unique in the Netherlands at the time, to establish a direct family connection between the skeletal remains and individuals alive today so as to make people more aware of their medieval roots. This specific research project was undertaken in collaboration with Professor Peter de Knijff and Eveline Altena at the Forensic Laboratory for DNA Research, Leiden University Medical Center.

The study was based on the premise that the Y-chromosome, which is passed from father to son, mutates approximately once every 50 generations. Since we wanted to bridge a gap of only 30 generations, the likelihood of spontaneous mutations having occurred during the period in question was small. In order to further increase the chance of a DNA match, any men who volunteered for the study were required to document their descent from a 16th-century Vlaardingen resident (Fig. 24). The genealogical data were checked by Vlaardingen municipal archivist Harm Jan Luth. Eighty-eight men were selected and donated a sample

34 De Ridder *et al.* 2008.

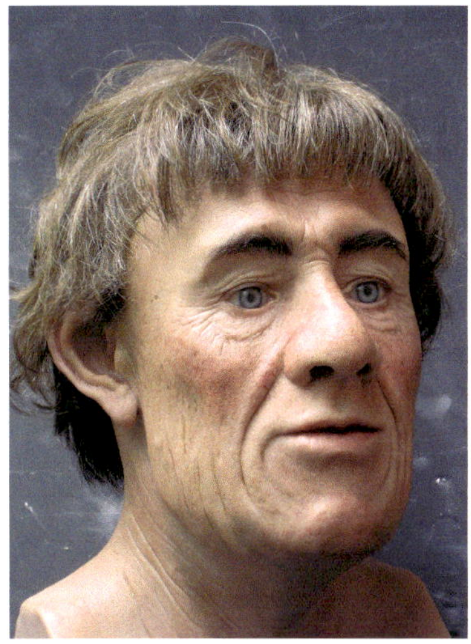

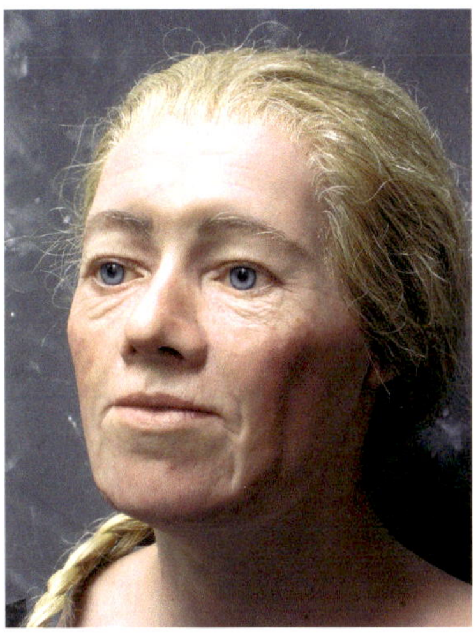

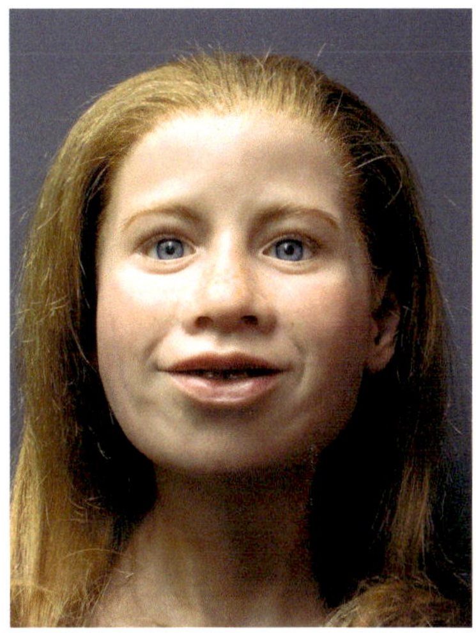

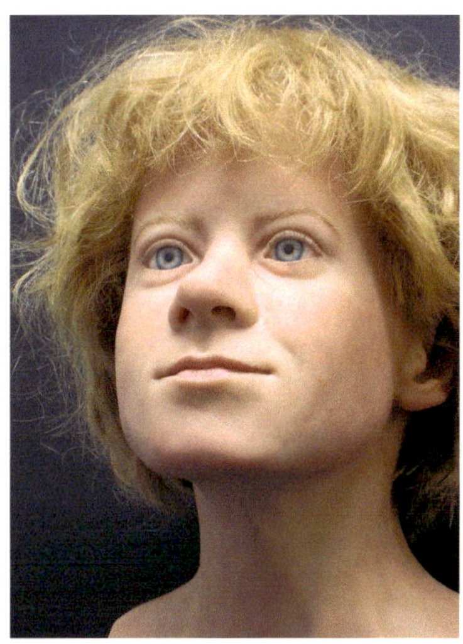

Fig. 18 to 22: Reconstructions of 11th-century Vlaardingen residents: 'tree-trunk coffin man' (Fig. 18), a 40-50-year-old man (Fig. 19), a 41-49-year-old woman (Fig. 20), an 8-year-old girl (Fig. 21), and a 5/6-year-old boy (Fig. 22). Photos collection Vlaardingen Museum (Fig. 18) and Vlaardingen Municipality (Fig. 19-22).

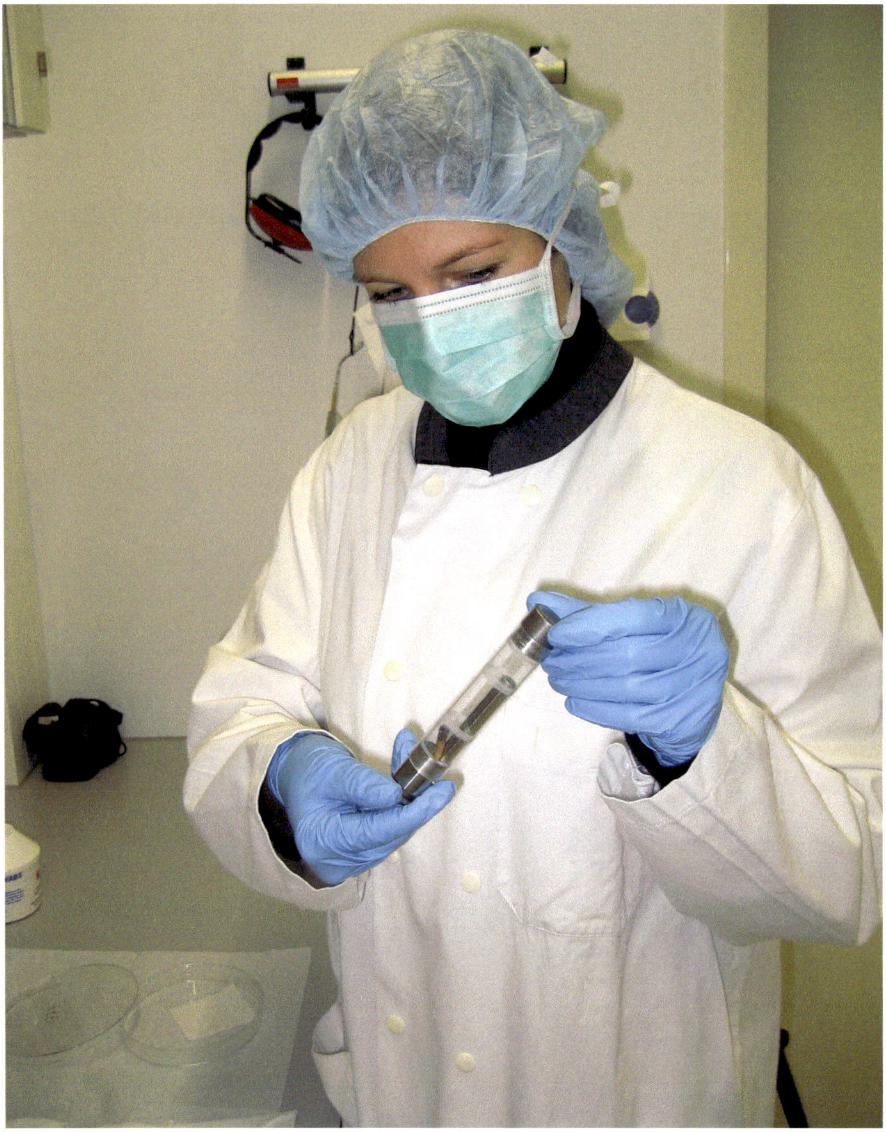

Fig. 23: Eveline Altena of the Forensic Laboratory for DNA Research, Leiden, examining DNA samples. Photo collection archaeology, Vlaardingen Municipality.

from their oral mucous membrane (Fig. 25). One interesting additional outcome of the analysis was that the DNA of two large Vlaardingen families, Drop and Bot, differed by only one mutation, which means that the families presumably share a common Vlaardingen ancestor. The most spectacular result, however, was the match between DNA from an 11th-century skull and that of a modern Rotterdam dentist, Eduard Zuiderent (Fig. 26). For the first time in the Netherlands, a direct link was established between archaeologically obtained DNA and living individuals. The project has since sparked similar projects in other towns, for example, Oldenzaal and Vlissingen.

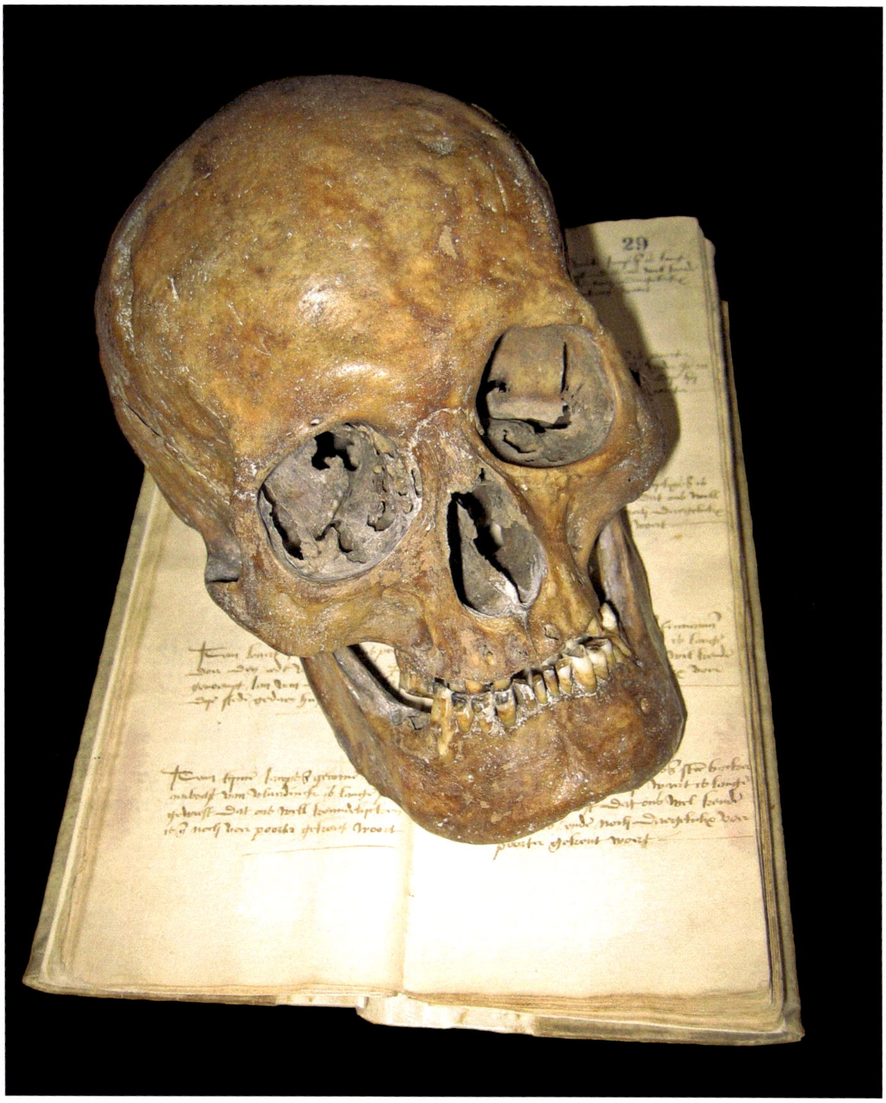

Fig. 24: One of the skulls from the Gat in de Markt site and the 16th-century register of Vlaardingen poorters, or burghers. Photo collection archaeology, Vlaardingen Municipality.

Fig. 25: Municipal archaeologist Tim de Ridder taking a sample from the inside of the mouth of a male participant as part of the search for the first Vlaardinger. Photos collection archaeology, Vlaardingen Municipality.

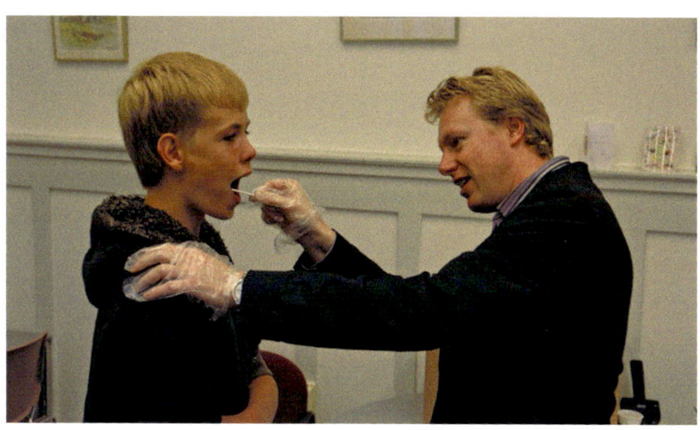

Fig. 26: Eduard Zuiderent being interviewed by Dutch commercial television channel RTL4, just after Mayor Tjerk Bruinsma announced that Zuiderent's DNA was a perfect match with that of an 11th-century skull. Photo collection archaeology, Vlaardingen Municipality.

Isotope analysis

The bone material was submitted to isotope analysis to obtain information on the medieval Vlaardingen diet and on the deceased individuals' possible origins.[35] With regard to diet, samples from 31 individuals were analysed for nitrogen ($^{15}N/^{14}N$) and carbon ($^{13}C/^{12}C$) isotopes. The results show that the diet of these Vlaardingen residents was based on C3-terrestrial food.[36] The ^{15}N scores showed an unusually wide spread, suggesting diets ranging from largely vegetarian to almost exclusively animal-based. Among the animal products, fish, both freshwater and sea, was a significant component of the diets. It was not possible given this highly heterogeneous sample to identify subgroups associated with a particular age, sex, or origin.

Twenty-six individuals were sampled for oxygen isotope analysis ($^{18}O/^{16}O$), and 10 individuals were sampled for strontium analysis ($^{87}Sr/^{86}Sr$). Oxygen isotope analysis revealed that four individuals were not local. Two children, one women, and one men could be assigned to southwest England, Ireland, southern Norway, and Normandy. Two more individuals were identified as non-local on the basis of strontium analysis. One was a 30-40-year-old male who likewise did not originate in Vlaardingen but who was an outsider even within this group of outsiders. For

---

35 Van de Locht & Kars, 2008a, 2008b; Kootker 2018.

36 'Terrestrial' refers to land-based food sources, such as cultivated crops.

Fig. 27: Using ground-penetrating radar inside the Grote Kerk. Photo collection archaeology, Vlaardingen Municipality.

Fig. 28: Core samples being taken inside the Grote Kerk. Photo collection archaeology, Vlaardingen Municipality.

now, his origins remain a mystery. The 'tree-trunk coffin man' also turned out to be non-local; he came from either York, Scotland, or Germany. In other words, of the 26 individuals analysed, at least 6 came to Vlaardingen from elsewhere.

Since fish was demonstrably part of the Vlaardingen diet, C14 samples were taken of three skeletons to account for potential reservoir effects[37] and analysed by Ricardo Fernandes of the Leibniz-Laboratory for Radiometric Dating and Isotope Research. All three produced a result that was 130 to 245 years older than the actual calendar date. This confirms that C14 dates of a population of fish-eaters will indeed be in error, showing too old a date.

Research in and around the cemetery

The 2002 excavations were followed by more research at several locations around the church mound. In 2007, the interior and surroundings of the Grote Kerk were tested with ground-penetrating radar (Fig. 27),[38] revealing the presence of two concentric circles at a depth of several metres below the church. If Count Dirk III had a motte-and-bailey castle, these features could be its moats. A subsequent borehole survey in and around the church (Fig. 28) failed to detect the circles archaeologically, but it did encounter wood fragments and human remains at a depth of three metres and below. Several wood fragments were radiocarbon dated to the 8th and 9th centuries. This supports the hypothesis that the Vlaardingen church was never moved and dates back to the early 8th century. The same survey also indicated that the former tidal creek of Vlaarding was situated much further west than was previously thought, and that a branch of it flowed between the church and the settlement. Apparently the church with its cemetery was situated within Dirk III's stronghold, which may in fact have been a ringfort, not a motte-and-bailey (Fig. 29). This is similar to other ringforts such as Rijnsburg (where it has been suggested that the church was within the ringfort) and Zutphen and Deventer (both where is was demonstrably so).

Synthesis

Research at the Gat in de Markt site revealed the presence of 45 graves from which 41 complete or partial skeletons could be retrieved, dating from the period 1000-1050. In 19 cases it was possible to establish the type of coffin or burial. The comparatively large number of children (26) buried was unusual. Child burials tend to be low-status, which raises the question as to the status of the adult burials in the same area. Important individuals were usually buried inside or near the church; perhaps the excavated individuals who were buried at the edge of the cemetery occupied less prominent positions in local society. That would make the excellent state of health of the adults all the more remarkable.

The relatively high proportion of skeletons displaying signs of affluence-related illnesses suggests that these individuals led comfortable lives. Isotope analysis showed that a significant proportion of them, not only adult males but

37 Individuals who have a diet high in fish, ingest large quantities of 'old' carbon, which results in an older C14 date than the actual calendar date.

38 Van der Roest & Van Loon 2007.

Fig. 29: 2018 reconstruction drawing of Vlaardingen in the year 1018. The drawing shows the church and its cemetery inside Dirk III's presumed ringfort. Image Ulco Glimmerveen, commissioned by and based on information provided by Vlaardingen Municipality. Collection archaeology, Vlaardingen Municipality.

also women and children, were not local. It seems that Vlaardingen in 1000-1050 attracted a fair number of immigrants. The many fractures observed on the male skeletons point to frequent small-scale conflicts. Perhaps we can draw a parallel with merchants from the town of Tiel. Alpert of Metz, a monk who between 1021 and 1024 wrote a detailed account of the Battle of Vlaardingen, also reported on the lifestyle of the Tiel merchants. Perhaps the Vlaardingen merchants cultivated similar habits. In the words of Alpert:

> *Here however, not to speak ill of them but out of sincere compassion, I wish to dedicate a few words to the habits and customs in which those at Tiel set themselves apart from other trade towns. They are rough folks who are, one might say, unaccustomed to any form of discipline. In their sentencing they do not follow customary law but instead their own home-made rules, and they claim that the right to do so was granted to them and guaranteed by the emperor, in a charter. (...) Early in the morning they are engaged in drunken revels, and whosoever in the loudest voice utters lewd witticisms to make the common rabble laugh and encourages them to drink wine is held in high esteem among them (...) and on important feast days they can be said to almost solemnly abandon themselves to drunkenness.*[39]

Conclusions and new questions

Although only a small section of the cemetery (approximately 5 x 6 m) was investigated, it nonetheless, offers us a keyhole through which we may catch a glimpse of Vlaardingen 1000-1050. The results provide important information on

39 Nieuwenhuijsen & De Ridder 2012, 35.

the layout of the old settlement and the location of the old church. The medieval settlement of Vlaardingen has not disappeared, as older publications suggest, but is still there in the soil, and its church was never moved. Analysis of the burials revealed much about the population of the period. The adults were somewhat taller than their contemporaries elsewhere and they were well nourished. A remarkable outcome of the isotope analysis was the observation that not only some of the men but also some of the women and children did not come from Vlaardingen but came from south-west England, Ireland, southern Norway, and Normandy. It seems entire families migrated to Vlaardingen. Perhaps there is a connection between the fragments of vessels built of English timber discovered in coffins and these new arrivals in Vlaardingen. Further research will hopefully shed more light on how we should view these data on immigrants in a broader context.

Only a small section of the cemetery was excavated. What does that mean for the representativeness of the results with regard to the Vlaardingen settlement as a whole? Is the large number of non-local individuals a coincidence or is it an accurate reflection of the Vlaardingen population at that time? If the latter, was Vlaardingen an exception in this regard or was this a more widespread pattern? Opportunities for further research in Vlaardingen itself are limited. There are no activities planned that might allow further research at the burial site. However, there are definitely opportunities for further testing. Vlaardingen could be compared to contemporary burial grounds along the North Sea coast; isotope analysis in particular may yield important new information in this regard. Furthermore, other historical and archaeological sources could be examined for information to indicate whether or not populations were indeed highly dynamic.

Bibliography

Ariès, Ph., 1983: *Het beeld van de dood*, Nijmegen. Translated by J. Holierhoek, *Images de l'homme devant la mort.*

Baetsen, S., 1998: Het menselijk skeletmateriaal van het Salvatorplein te Susteren, Amersfoort (unpublished report ROB Amersfoort).

Breitinger, E., 1937: 'Zur Berechnung der Körperhöhe aus den langen Gliedmaßenknochen', *Anthropologischen Anzeiger* 14, 249-274.

Brinkkemper, O., C. van Loon & T. de Ridder (eds.), 2006: *Gat in de Markt 1.101. Het botanisch onderzoek*, Vlaardingen (VLAK-verslag 15.4).

Buitenhuis, H. & D.C. Brinkhuizen, 2006: *Gat in de Markt 1.101. Het dierlijk botmateriaal*, Vlaardingen (VLAKverslag 15.5).

Carmiggelt, A.H., 2017: 'Monniken, lekenbroeders en loonarbeiders. Een 13de-eeuwse begraafplaats in Hellevoetsluis', in: R.M.R. van Oosten, R. Schats, N. Arts & H.M.P. Bouwmeester *De stad en de dood. Archeologische perspectieven*, Leiden (Urban Graveyard Proceedings 1), 27-44.

Crumlin-Pedersen, O., 1997: *Viking-age ships and shipbuilding in Hedeby/Hathabu and Schleswig*, Schleswig & Roskilde (Ships and boats from the North. Volume 2).

De Boer, D.E.H. & E.H.P. Cordfunke, 1997: *Graven van Holland. Portretten in woord en beeld*, 2nd edition. Zutphen.

De Ridder, T., 2001: *Van donk tot stad. Water, vriend en vijand*, Vlaardingen (VLAK-overdruk 3, eerder gepubliceerd in het Historisch Jaarboek Vlaardingen).

De Ridder, T., 2002: 'Waar ligt het oude Vlaardingen? Een nieuw model voor een oude stad', *Terra Nigra* 155, 36-53.

De Ridder, T., K. Vlierman & A.H.L. Vredenbregt, 2004: 'Vikingen in Vlaardingen. De betekenis van de resten van gesloopte Vikingschepen in elfde-eeuwse Vlaardingse begravingen', *Westerheem* 53/4, 142-154.

De Ridder, T., E. Altena, P. de Knijff, A.H.L.Vredenbregt & H.J. Luth, 2008: 'De zoektocht naar de oer-Vlaardinger', in: T. De Ridder, E. Altena, N. Arts, G. Groeneweg & M. Lockefeer (eds.), *Westerheem, Special 2008: DNA en archeologie*, 28- 38.

Dijkstra, J., 1998: *Archeologisch Onderzoek in de binnenstad van Tiel juni t/m september 1996. Lokaties Koornmarkt en Tol-Zuid*, Amersfoort (Rapportage Archeologische Monumentenzorg 57).

Dijkstra, M.F.P., 2011: *Rondom de mondingen van Rijn & Maas. Landschap en bewoning tussen de 3e en 9e eeuw in Zuid-Holland, in het bijzonder de Oude Rijnstreek,* Leiden: Sidestone Press.

Fruin, R., 1876: *Enqueste ende informatie upt stuck van der reductie ende reformatie van den schiltaelen, voertijts getaxeert ende gestelt geweest over de landen van Hollant ende Vrieslant*, Leiden: Brill.

Goubitz, O. & J. ter Brugge, 1996: 'Vlaardingen. Het waaigat 1990/'91. Leder, textiel, haar, touw en hoor', *Westerheem* 45/4, 208-224.

Groen, W.J. & T. de Ridder, 2007: *Gat in de Markt 01.101. Het menselijk botmateriaal uit de periode 1000-1050*, Vlaardingen (VLAK-verslag 15.3).

Henderikx, P.A., 2001: 'De bisschop van Utrecht en het Maas-Merwede-gebied in de elfde en twaalfde eeuw', in: B. van Bavel *et al.*, *Land water en bewoning. Waterstaats- en nederzettingsgeschiedenis in de Zeeuwse en Hollandse delta in de Middeleeuwen*, Verloren, Hilversum, 38-67.

Hoek, C., 1973: 'De Middeleeuwen', in: T. Vos-Dahmen von Buchholz (ed.), *Van steurvisser tot stedeling, Flenio*, 118-146.

Larsen, C.P., 2003: *Bioarchaeology: Interpreting behaviour from the human skeleton*, Cambridge University Press, Cambridge.

Kootker, L., 2018: Vlaardingen-onderzoek 2008, unpublished report, Amsterdam.

Nieuwenhuijsen, K. & T. de Ridder, 2012: *Ad Flaridingun, 2012: Vlaardingen in de elfde eeuw*, Hilversum: Uitgeverij Verloren.

Nieuwenhuijsen, K., T. de Ridder & H.J. Luth-Mulders, 2017: 'Graven in Vlaardingen. Gebeurtenissen rondom de Slag bij Vlaardingen in 1018', *Historisch Jaarboek* Vlaardingen 2017, 9-91.

Smits, E., 1999: 'Het onderzoek van het menselijk skeletmateriaal,' in: T.A. Carmiggelt, T. Goossens & A.J. Guiran (eds.), *Een 13e-eeuwse begraafplaats te Hellevoetsluis bij de Uithof Oosthoek van de Vlaamse Cisterciënzerabdij ter Doest*, Rotterdam (BOORrapport 47) 76-90.

Stroud, G., 1993: 'The human bones', in: G. Stroud & R.L. Kemp (eds.), *Cemeteries of the church and priory of St. Andrew, Fishergate*, York: Council for British Archaeology (The Medieval Cemeteries 2/The Archaeology of York 12) 160-241.

Ter Brugge, J.P. & T. de Ridder, 1996: *Archeologisch en historisch onderzoek van de Fransen- en de Kuiperstraat*, Vlaardingen (Archeologische Rapporten nr. 2).

Trotter, M., 1970: 'Estimation of stature from intact limb bones', in: T.D. Stewart (ed.), *Personal identification in mass disasters*, Washington DC: National Museum of Natural History/Smithsonian Institution, 71-97.

Trotter, M. & G.C. Gleser, 1958: 'A re-evaluation of estimation of stature based on measurements of stature taken during life and of long bones after death', *American Journal of Physical Anthropology* 16, 79-123. https://doi.org/10.1002/ajpa.1330160106

Van Dasselaar, M., 2012: *Archeologisch onderzoek Stadshart te Vlaardingen. Inventariserend veldonderzoek met boringen, verkennende en waarderende fase*, Nieuwerkerk aan de IJssel: Archeomedia (Archeomedia Rapport A11-009-I).

Van Dasselaar, M., 2013: *Archeologisch onderzoek aan de Markt te Vlaardingen, Grote Kerk. Inventariserend veldonderzoek met boringen*, Nieuwerkerk aan de IJssel: Archeomedia (Archeolmedia Rapport A13-076-I).

Van de Locht, R. & H. Kars, 2008a: *Stabiele stikstof en koolstof isotopen als indicatie voor paleodieet in Middeleeuws Vlaardingen*, Amsterdam (Instituut voor Geo- en Bioarcheologie, IGBA Rapport 2008-04).

Van de Locht, R. & H. Kars, 2008b: *Herkomstbepaling door middel van Strontium en Zuurstof isotopen van 11de eeuwse Vlaardingers*, Amsterdam (Instituut voor Geo- en Bioarcheologie, IGBA Rapport 2008-10).

Van der Roest, P.B. & C. van Loon, 2007: *Markt 01.125. Het geofysisch onderzoek*, Vlaardingen (VLAK-verslag 45).

Van Loon, C. & T. de Ridder, 2006: *Gat in de Markt 1.101. Basisverslag*, Vlaardingen (VLAKverslag 15.1).

Van Maanen, R., 2017: 'Het oudste stadsrecht van Holland', in: Verslaglegging over het symposium 'De dageraad van Holland, 1000-1300', May 12, 2017, PDF 36 pages, www.zuidholland.nl.

Vredenbregt, A.H.L. & T. de Ridder (eds.), with a contribution by K. Vlierman, 2004: *Gat in de Markt 1.101. Houtgebruik in 11e-eeuwse graven*, Vlaardingen (VLAK-verslag 15.2).

White, W.J., 1988: 'The human bones: skeletal analysis', in: W.J. White (ed.), *Skeletal remains from the cemetery of St. Nicholas Shambles, City of London*, London: London & Middlesex Archaeological Society, London, 28-55.

Zeischka, A., 1983: Seppenrade, Ausgrabung einer münsterländischen Dorfkirche 1976/77. Denkmalpflege und Forschung in Westfalen, no. 5. Bonn.

Digging up the dead in Eindhoven

The choir and churchyard of St. Catharine's, 1200-1850

Nico Arts

Introduction

Medieval Eindhoven is one of the small new towns in the northeastern part of the Duchy of Brabant (now Southern Netherlands). The town was founded early in the 13th century by duke Hendrik I of Brabant (1190-1235). Town rights were granted in 1232 which is possibly the year in which the construction of the new town was completed. From its birth onward Eindhoven remained small. This situation changed in the 19th century when industry settled which last century caused a boomtown. Contemporary Eindhoven is not known as an old town. The Second World War bombings, the post-war demolition policy and the nature of nowadays buildings left little of the idendity of the medieval town and its countryside. Actually, only the medieval street pattern remained and in some places also the archeological subsoil.

Prior to construction projects in 1985 a series of rescue excavations was started, often on places where there are now deep underground car parks. So far about 46,500 m^2 has been excavated, that is some 17% of the medieval town surface. One of the smallest excavations, also the most complex, was the choir part with bordering graveyard of St. Catharine's, the only medieval church in town. Early in 2002 this excavation started with a small trial trench. The skeleton of a 9-11 years old child was found and the existence of DNA was discovered in one of his teeth, what was exceptional in Dutch archaeology at the time. According to DNA it was a boy and both this discovery and the forensic facial reconstruction of the medieval child received much publicity. Eventually this resulted in an extensive excavation in 2005-2006. The main reason for the dig was to collect more DNA samples as there was a fear that DNA, which was hopefully still preserved in unexcavated skeletons, would dissolve by sharp fluctuations in the ground water table caused by nearby deep construction works. Another reason was that, even though it was acknowledged that the site was of great archaeological importance, a long-term

Fig. 1: Town plan of Eindhoven in circa 1557-1568 (detail) by Jacob van Deventer (circa 1505-1575). Collection Royal Library of Belgium, Brussels (inv.nr. KP. Ms. 22090 nr. 30; 410 x 293 mm).

guarantee to protect the site as an archaeological monument was not very credible. More substantive the excavation was also expected to provide more knowledge on the lives of former townsmen and their burial customs in the course of the centuries. This paper provides a summary of the results of this research.[1]

The medieval church and churchyard of Eindhoven

Medieval Eindhoven has a strategic location in the natural landscape: on the end of an elongated sand ridge between two stream valleys where the stream called Gender ends up in the Dommel. On this spot two already existing through roads came together close to a 11th/12th century motte castle. In the beginning the town

1 Most of this paper is based on a Dutch language book on the results of the excavation of Catharine's church (Arts ed. 2013), with some additional data and interpretations. Shortly after the 2002 and 2005-2006 excavations public accounts were published (Arts 2002; 2003; Arts & Nollen 2006). The photos in this paper were made by Ruud Balk (Fig. 4), René Bogaerts (Fig. 10, 11) and Laurens Mulkens (Fig. 5, 12-17, 19-21); René Bogaerts also digitalized the plans (Fig. 4, 6-11).

constituted of only a rectangular market field surrounded by timber houses with elongated yards. In the 14th century the town was provided with moats and earthen ramparts. From that time onwards the town had dimensions of circa 400 x 750 m and a surface of only 27 hectares (Fig. 1). Such small medieval towns were common at the time. Starting at the end of the 14th century the history of Eindhoven was haunted by wars and crises. In 1486 the town was largely destroyed and in 1554 a domestic accident resulted in a large town fire. During the Eighty Years' War (1568-1648), the revolt of the Netherlands independence from Spain, the town repeatedly suffert by violence.

The oldest more or less accurate population counts date from the 15th century. In 1438 Eindhoven had a population of circa 990, but in 1496 the number of inhabitants was decreased with 32% to circa 670. In 1526 and 1567 the population increased to around 900.[2] In 1687 the population was almost doubled to 1726 (547 females, 408 males and 771 children). During the eighteenth century the population rose a bit with 1785 (in 1736) and 1837 (in 1792) inhabitants.[3] The large imbalance between females and males in 1687 is particularily remarkable, the underlying cause is unknown.

During the first century of existence the dead were buried in a graveyard just outside the first phase of town development. Later a church was built on that graveyard. There are not many parallels for the construction of a late medieval church on an already existing late medieval graveyard.[4] The oldest written record of the church dates from 1340.[5] This church, devoted to Saint Catharine, remained the only one in town. With dimensions of 56 x 27 m it was a comparatively small brick building with a lumpish tower in the west and (in the post-medieval period) three choirs in the east (Fig. 2). The roof was covered with slate. The building was used for religious purposes, to bury the dead and as a public meeting venue. In the 17th century, probably earlier, the church and its graveyard were surrounded by a brick wall. During the iconoclasm in August 1566 much of the interior was destroyed. In 1648 the church was closed for catholics and was confiscated by the reformed community, but catholics were allowed to continue to bury the dead in the graveyard as well in the church. In 1793 burying in the church was stopped. In 1810 the building was renovated and put into service again for catholics but due to the increasing population of Eindhoven the church became too small. In 1858 the graveyard was abolished and a new plot north of the town moat was established as burial ground. In 1860 the old building was demolished and in 1860-1867 a much larger and still existing new church was build on the site. The only parts which remained unbuilt were the medieval choir and parts of the graveyard.

---

2 These numbers are based on hearth (house) counts (Cuvelier 1912, 478-483; Van der Hammen & Sassen 1894) with during the late middle ages an average of 4 individuals per house (Blockmans, Pieters, Prevenier & Van Schaik 1980, 42).

3 Melssen 1979, XVI-XVII (the year 1687); Van der Hammen & Sassen 1894 (the years 1736, 1792).

4 Archaeological examples are nearby St. Martin's in Luijksgestel (southern Netherlands), St. Martin's in Wharram Percy and St. Peter's in Barton-upon-Humber (northern England) (Gilchrist 2012, 201; Theuws 2018, 34-35).

5 The best information on historical records of the church and churchyard is Melssen 2009 (summarized in Melssen 2013).

Fig. 2: View of St. Catharine's church from the northeast in 1738. Coloured pen drawing by Jan de Beyer (1703-1780). Collection Regional Historical Centre Eindhoven (inv. nr AVC nr. 0023812; 168 x 145 mm).

It is plausible that the graveyard was used predominantly for the townsmen of Eindhoven for each village in the surrounding countryside had its own church with graveyard. During the post-medieval centuries each year a few dozen to 88 death were buried in Eindhoven. With an annual death rate of about 3.5 to 4.0 % it is roughly estimated that in 1200-1850 all together some 55,000 dead were buried in the church and on the graveyard of Eindhoven.[6] No records survived on the number of plague victims. In the 16th century seven years with plague are mentioned and during the 17th century about ten. In 1637-1640 the costs to bury in church were 14 penny (stuiver) for an adult and 7 for a child. On the graveyard these rates amounted half. In the church many dead were buried under a tombstone. Probably on the graveyard there were not many funeral monuments, but a stone cross (in 1510), 'a stick on the grave' (in 1668) and on graves of reformed dead crucifixes with 'bid voor de ziele' ('pray for the souls', in 1699) are mentioned in records.[7] In order to allow more graves, both the interior of the

---

6 The annual death rate in towns in medieval England is estimated to be 3.5% (Bassett, Dyer & Holt 1992, 2) and in late medieval Flanders 4.0% (Van Oosten & Schats 2018, 7 note 1). It is supposed that the death rate in Eindhoven was about similar.

7 Melssen 2009; 2013.

church and the graveyard were heightend periodically with sand. During the post-medieval period almost all dead were wrapped in a shroud and buried in a timber coffin, sometimes with on the head a 'crown' (in 1695).[8]

Excavations

The small 2002 trial excavation was in a trench of 3.2 x 8.5 m. This test aimed to investigate if there were any foundations left of the medieval church, which could be an inspiration for a planned renovation of the area. It was also hoped to find human remains which should further increase the existing archaeological and archival knowledge on the former town inhabitants. However, due to decalcification the sandy soils of the region generally are unsuitable to preserve skeletal remains. Nevertheless, the excavation produced well preserved human remains. In the topsoil also foundations of the choir, part of a vault and part of the basis of an altar (all brick) were found. In order to investigate whether bones were also preserved in deeper levels, one grave in front of the altar foundation was excavated. This grave was one of the few whose contours were completely visible in the narrow trial trench. On the bottom of the grave pit the skeleton of a child was found with a length of circa 105 cm, with on the chest a worn Venetian groat with a weared eye. Apparently, this exotic coin was used in a lenghty period as a pendant or, through the image of San Marco, as a pilgrim badge. In the eye the remains of a silk thread were preserved. Due to wear it was not possible to date the coin more precisely than 1192-1423, but potsherds in the grave filling are older than 1325/1350 and later a calibrated radiocarbon date resulted in 1282-1392.[9] The special location for the grave of a child (in the choir and in front of the altar) and the exotic grave good led to the assumption that this was a child of a local elite. Its dentition indicated an age of 9-11 years. The question was whether the child was a girl or a boy. Therefore, it was examined if the sex could be determined by DNA. This proved to be the case: it was a boy, which was then nicknamed 'Marcus van Eindhoven' because of the image of San Marco on the coin and the town where he was found. The discovery of archaeological DNA and the forensic facial reconstruction were news items on the Dutch national televison news as well as in the children news program (Fig. 3). The day following the broadcast the author of this paper was phoned by Peter de Knijff, forensic geneticist at the Leiden University Medical Centre. He told that archaeological DNA could also be of importance for medical research, in particular in relation to the origin of certain DNA mutations protecting humans against diseases such as plague and HIV. Peter asked if there would be any more DNA samples available to be excavated. In the city council of Eindhoven this led to a debate on what to do with an archaeological site with medieval human DNA. A debatable point was the highly fluctuating groundwater table in the area as a result of deep building projects at that time, which might dissolve the DNA. Two years later the city council decided to conduct a complete excavation of the site. The overall costs of the excavation, analysis and publication amounted 2.5 million euro which was financied by the city council, a regional municipal partnership, the province North-Brabant and the

---

8 It is not mentioned whether the ones with a 'crown' were reformed or catholics (Melssen 2009).

9 GrA-39119: 650±25 BP.

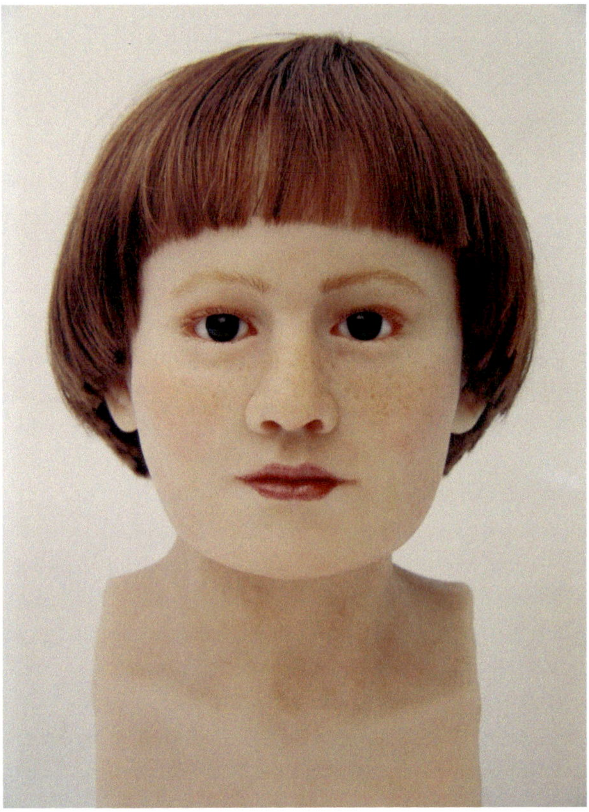

Fig. 3: Facial reconstruction made in 2002 by Maja d'Hollosy (Amsterdam) of the 9-11 years old boy who died circa 1300, nicknamed 'Marcus van Eindhoven'.

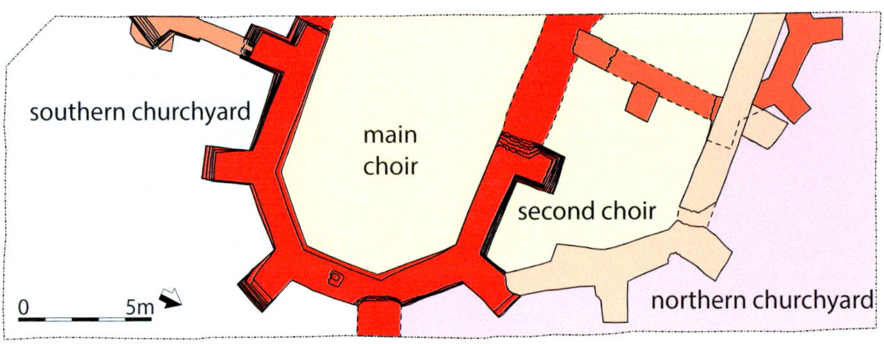

Fig. 4: Spatial layout of the excavated area.

science department of the national government. Also a grant was received from a large funeral company with its headquarters in Eindhoven.

The excavation, which took place six days a week in March 2005-August 2006, was limited to the eastern part of the former church with bordering graveyard, covering 376 m2 which is 5.5% of the surface of the church site (including graveyard) (Fig. 4).[10] Unexcavated parts of the medieval church and most of the

10 Melssen 2009 (chapter IV p. 3) mentions a surface of 6800 m^2 in 1571.

Fig. 5: The excavation in progress, July 2005.

graveyard are underneath the church that was built in 1860-1867. A more than hundred-man team with archaeologists, physical anthropologists, field assistants, students, volonteers and educational guides did the field work and the cataloguing and investigation of the results. The nearby field headquarter and the excavation itselves were accesible daily for the public. All together almost 100,000 local and foreign visitors visited the work including the Dutch queen, the Dutch Minister of Science and the eminent British archaeologist Don Brothwell (1933-2016).

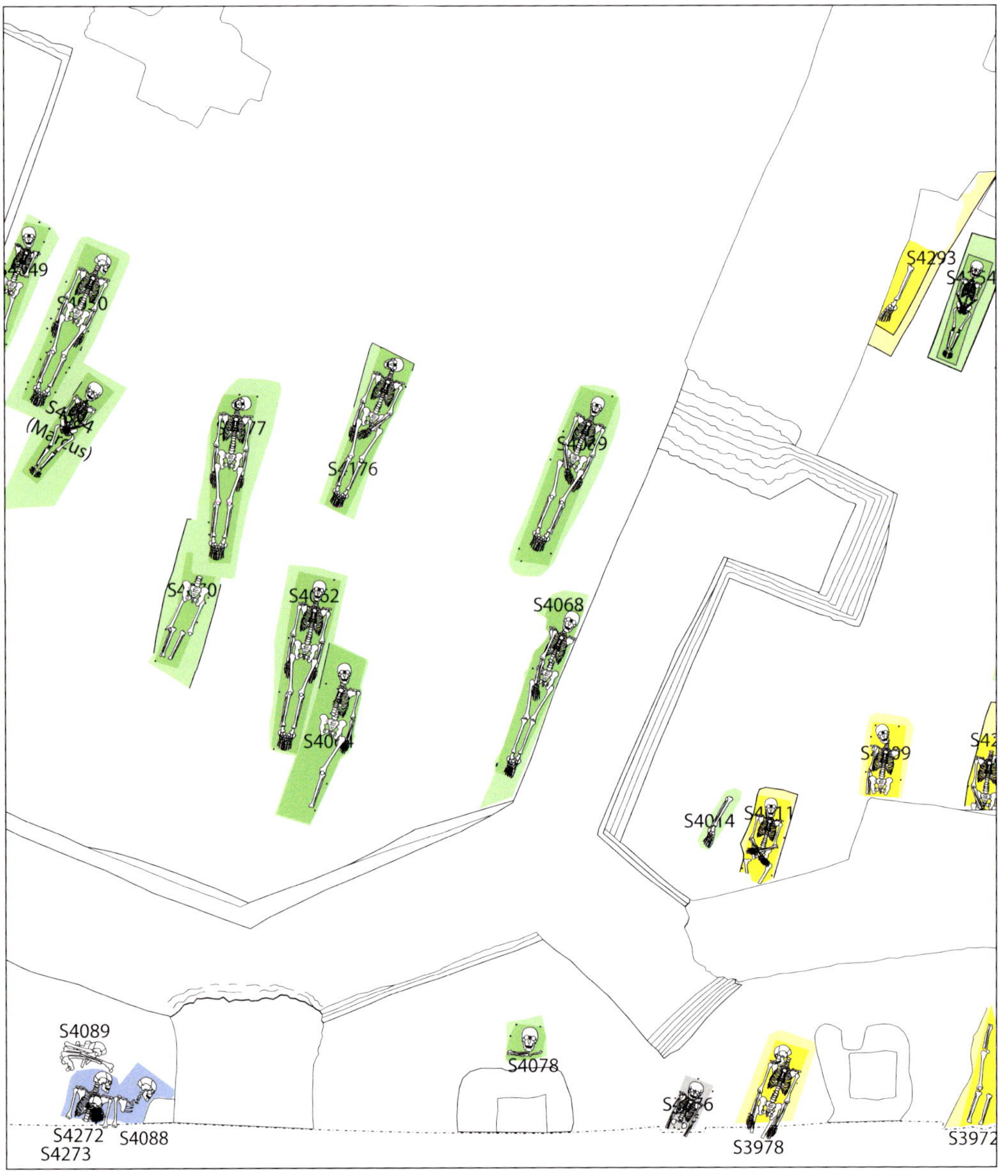

Fig. 6: Example of one of the floor plans (layer 14).

During the excavation all removal of sand was done with shovels, trowels, wooden spatulae and brushes, no mechanical diggers were involved (Fig. 5).[11] The sand removed from the filling of each grave was sieved (mesh size 1 or 4 mm). The various brick foundations indicated five building phases of the church choir ranging between the 14th and 17th/18th century.[12] The oldest brick foundation belongs to the main choir which most probably dates from the second half of the

11 Nollen 2013a.
12 Nollen 2013b.

14th century. This foundation transects a number of grave pits which therefore must be older. Obviously, the choir was built on an already existing graveyard.

All together 754 mostly well-preserved primary burials and the bones of at least 303 secondary burials were uncovered.[13] Primary burials are skeletons, or parts of it, which were still in situ in an anatomical composition. Secondary burials are isolated bones from previous burials which were disarticulated during construction works for extensions of the church building or the digging of new grave pits and sometimes, but not always, were reburied in charnel pits. All charnel pits found during the excavation are post-medieval.

The primary burials were spread over the whole excavated area, no limits of the graveyard were found.[14] The burials were in a 1.8 meters thick layer, often disturbed in the process of interring successive dead. In order to get some insight in this chaos the excavation was conducted in 19 levels (Fig. 6). On the basis of 26 radiocarbon dated skeletons, 5 optically stimulated luminescence datings of brick foundations, the dating of pottery sherds which unintentionally dropt into grave fillings from the soil above, coin finds and a Harris-matrix most primary graves could be organized in four periods: 1200-1350 (N=82), 1350-1500 (N=134), 1500-1650 (N=141) and 1650-1850 (N=260), the remaining 162 (22%) remained undated.[15]

Burial customs

Given the Christian tradition the church had a west to east orientation with the tower in het west and the choir in the east. In the same tradition almost all dead were buried more or less with the same orientation with the head in the west (Table 1). Seven individuals were buried the other way around, for one it was north to south and one undated individual was buried standing (see below).[16] One of the seven individuals with east to west orientation, who were probably all religious, was buried in a brick vault. It was a 65-78 years old male from the 17th of 18th century (a reverend?) with next to him the remains of a 70 years old female (his wife?), buried west-east, as well as the remains of at least four young children.

The graves of adult females and adult males are spread proportionally over the whole excavated area but more males (20%) than females were buried in the choir (which dates after 1350).[17] Most individuals were in coffined but generally the timber itself was completely decayed. Mostly contours of coffins were recogizable by the remains of iron nails with sometimes small pieces of timber of oak or pine preserved in the rust. All coffins are tapered with a somewhate wider head end (45-60 cm) than the foot end (35-45 cm). No information is available on the design of the lids. Several coffins had specials: coffins with iron handles, coffins with lime smeared at

---

13 The minimum number of individuals in secondary burials was defined using the most common skeletal element, in this case the left femur.

14 Nollen 2013c.

15 Arts & Nollen 2013; Arts & Van den Broek 2013; Johns & Wallinga 2013; Nollen 2013c; Pelsdonk 2013.

16 Buried east-west: 5 individuals in the southern churchyard (1x 1200-1350, 1x 1350-1500, 2x 1500-1650 and 1x 1650-1850) and 2 individuals in the main choir (both 1650-1850); buried north-south: 1 individual in the second choir (undated).

17 Nollen 2013c.

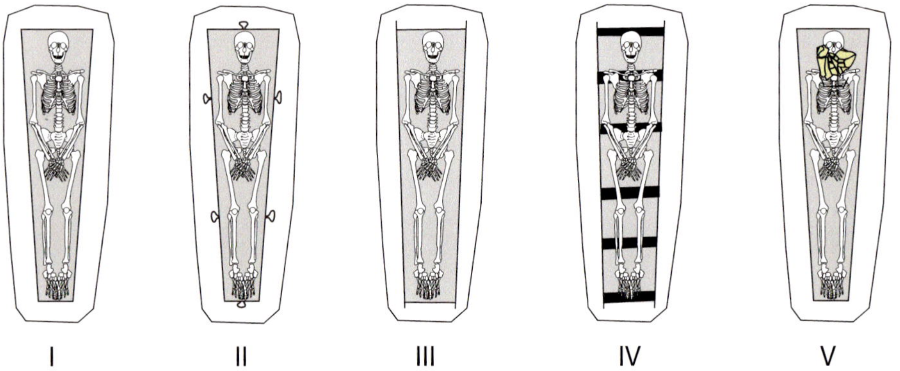

Fig. 7: Types of coffins: I ordinary, II with handles, III with protruding parts at the ends, IV with a ladder-looking bottom, V with a glass pane in the lid.

the interior, one coffin with a glass pane in the lid, one coffin with a ladder looking bottom and one coffin with protruding parts at the ends (Fig. 7).

All coffins with handles were inside the church, dating 1500-1650 (N=2) and 1650-1850 (N=11). Noteworthy are coffins with lime which were all found on the graveyard outside the church, dating 1350-1500 (N=3), 1500-1650 (N=10) and 1650-1850 (N=11) (Fig. 8). Additionally, there were another 17 coffins with met only minor fragments of lime. Lime is a means to prevent infection. The corpses who were buried in such coffins probably were feared, possibly they were plague victims. In a 17th century document it is written that plague victims were buried in St. Catharine's graveyard.[18]

Almost all individuals were on their back, usually with folded hands (type I, N=208), with hands along the body (type II, N=155), with hands on the upper legs (type III, N=32) or with hands on the chest (type IV, N=14). Six individuals were on the side (type V) and two on the abdomen (type VI) (Fig. 9). Possibly types V and VI can be explained because the coffin arrived incorrectly in the grave pit by accident. Information on the position of the hands of the remaining 334 individuals was not available because of the incompletness of skeletons. Throughout the ages a chronological pattern is not discernable.

During the investigation of parasite-samples from four coffins from the earliest period (1200-1350) also a relatively high number of pollen of heather was found, which would seem to indicate that the dead were buried in the coffin on a bed of heather.[19] Probably for such beds also straw was used which completely decayed, but in one coffin oblong round imprints in lime with a diameter of 2.5 mm were recognized, dating from 1500-1650. In death straw had the ritual meaning of a stake or a repellent against evil spirits or as a symbol of the usual way to sleep on during life.[20] Straw was also scattered on the road to the graveyard which meant to prevent the dead to return home.[21]

18 Melssen 2009.
19 Heather used as linings or as pillows is also reported in England (Gilchrist 2008, 137).
20 Fahrenfort & Van de Graft 1947, 27; Hirsch 1921, 84-85.
21 Hirsch 1921, 86.

Fig. 8: Floor plan of part of the southern graveyard showing coffins with lime. Possibly the deceased buried in such coffins were plague victims.

Six burials are deviant. The upper body (skull, torso and arms) of an about 60 years old female (undated) was buried standing with folded arms; the lower part of the body (hips and legs) was absent (Fig. 10). A 10-12 years old boy (1600-1650) was buried without coffin in a pit with the head and shoulders upright against the wall of the pit and with outstreched arms (Fig. 11). One adult individual (sex could not be determined) had a 3-5 years old male child on the chest, dating

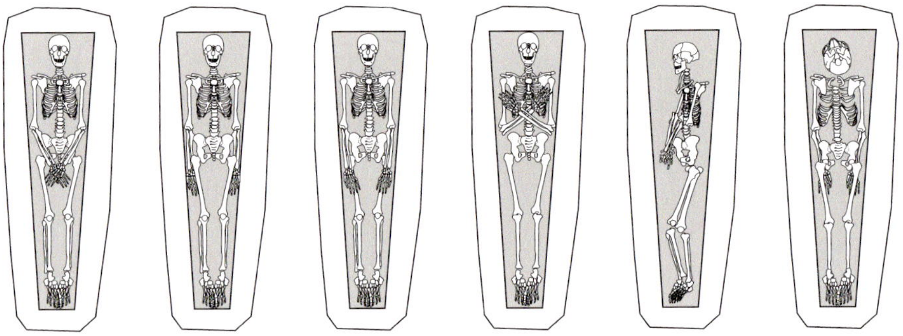

Fig. 9: The variety of positions of the deceased: on the back, usually with folded hands (type I), with hands along the body (type II), with hands on the upper legs (type III) or with hands on the chest (type IV), on the side (type V), on the abdomen (type VI).

Fig. 10: Upper body (torso and arms) of an about 60 years old female who was interred standing with folded arms; the lower part of her body (hips and legs) was absent. The skull is not on this photo.

Fig. 11: A burial without coffin: a 10-12 years old boy (1600-1650) interred in a pit with the head and shoulders upright against the wall of the pit and with outstreched arms.

Fig. 12: Adult individual (sex could not be determined) with a 3-5 years old male child on the chest (1650-1850).

Fig. 13: Bottom of a grave with a series of long human bones carefully arranged across, with the coffin placed on top (1600-1800).

1650-1850 (Fig. 12). A 40-49 years old male had directly on the place of the coffin lid the coffin of a 3-5 years old male child, dating 1675-1725. In both cases the adult and child were clearly interred simultaniously. This also applies for two adult males in one grave. Finally, at the bottom of one grave dating 1600-1800 a series of long human bones had been carefully arranged across the bottom of the grave, with the coffin placed on top (Fig. 13).

period	main choir	second choir	northern churchyard	southern churchyard
west-east:				
1650-1850	15	31	75	19
1500-1650	9	23	12	15
1350-1500	33	28	29	6
1200-1350	20	21	18	9
undated	23	45	26	20
southwest-northeast:				
1650-1850	0	5	54	22
1500-1650	1	1	8	37
1350-1500	3	0	8	4
1200-1350	1	0	3	3
undated	0	4	13	9
northwest-southeast:				
1650-1850	0	0	16	6
1500-1650	1	3	6	1
1350-1500	1	4	3	0
1200-1350	0	2	2	1
undated	1	1	8	0

Table 1: The orientation of burials per period (absolute numbers of individuals).

The small finds

Next to the brick foundations and human bones the site produced 69.274 small finds.[22] Additionally 433 animal bones were found.[23] There are five explanations for the presence of the finds (Table 2): (1) objects which were intentionally deposited during funeral rites and other rituals, (2) rubble of the church building and its interior, (3) domestic waste in the sand which was used for heighten the graveyard and the inside of the church, (4) toys and games, and (5) objects which came into the site naturally. The latter are skeletal remains of mice which were sieved from the contents of human skulls, also several frog bones are present. The presence of quite a lot of toys and games suggests that the graveyard was also used as a playground for old and young: 271 stoneware marbles (mostly fragments), a lead bullroarer, a bone play pastern, a bone die, a lead ballcross and several engraved slates. Using a graveyard for games is also reported elsewhere.[24]

The use of the site as a graveyard produced the largest diversity of objects including the remains of 30,997 iron coffin nails. The finds of 102 coins, 4 jetons and 7 tokens makes this site the one with largest concentration of coins, jetons and tokens in town. The same is true for many other church compounts

22 Including several stone age artefacts and a few pottery sherds older than the 13th century (Arts & Van den Broek 2013).

23 Esser 2013.

24 Fahrenfort & Van de Graft 1947, 30; Gilchrist 2012, 193.

elsewhere.[25] Most coins, jetons and tokens are believed to be associated with the use of the site as graveyard or for other rituals. Though many are not found in the context of a grave pit, some might be in the site as a result of the intercutting and truncation of graves, brought into the site with sand yielding domestic waste which was used to heighten the graveyard and the interior of the church, hidden for other ritual purposes or simply might be lost. Often these are called 'death coins', which usually are quite worn. They have different meanings: during afterlife the death remained in possession of a part of his properties; coins on the eyes aimed to prevent the return of the soul; coins used as entrance fee for heaven and coins with the image of a cross were believed to have an invocatory function against the devil.[26]

Five lead tokens, dating 1450-1550, have the image of a sword or/and a wheel which are symbols for St. Catharine with one also bearing the name 'Catherien'. Most probably these are tokens for the poor specially made for St. Catharine's church at Eindhoven (Fig. 14). Probably the poor who attended a mass in the church received such a token to buy for instance a bread or some peat. A similar token is known from an other site in the town of Eindhoven and one from a nearby site in the countryside, but elsewhere they are unknown.[27]

Graveyards reveals diversity in local practice and ritual. As far as it concerns Eindhoven 63 primary burials (8.4%) out of 754 had small finds. For instance, St. Rombout's cemetery in Mechelen (Belgium) has 535 individuals (12.9%) out of 3617 with grave goods.[28] Of ten excavated medieval graveyards in England with altogether 4272 graves only 91 (2%) yielded grave goods.[29]

In Eindhoven grave goods are divided in items which are associated with a shroud (buttons, hooked fastener, pins, needles, nests; in 36 graves, all postmedieval), personal ornaments (earrings; in 1 grave, postmedieval) or devotional and other ritual items (crucifixes, beads, coins, tokens, floral wreaths; in 27 graves, medieval and postmedieval) (Table 3). Most beads were part of various kinds of Catholic praying-beads (Fig. 15, 16). Four graves included one or more beads of jet and one grave also a bead of amber. Beads of jet and amber are apotropaic materials believed to posses occult natural power to guard against evil forces.[30]

The richest grave in Eindhoven is that of a 10-12 years old boy dating 1600-1650, buried in a pit without a coffin. One can guess what deeper meaning is hidden in this interment. Also the most exotic grave good (a Venetian coin) was in the grave of a male child (9-11 years), dating 1275-1325. Both were buried outside the church on the graveyard. Perhaps the graves with silk cords (dating 1275-1325 and 1500-1700) represent modest representations of elite burials.[31]

---

25 For example, Alkmaar (Bitter 2002, 259-267, 321-323) and Baden and elsewhere in Switzerland (Doppler 2008).
26 Dezutter 1975, 198-201; Fahrenfort & Van de Graft 1947, 28; Hirsch 1921, 35-37.
27 Pelsdonk 2003.
28 Van de Vijver, Kinnaer & Depuydt 2018, 267; see also Van Bulck 2017.
29 Excluding priests' burials: Gilchrist 2012, 277-282.
30 Gilchrist 2008, 139.
31 Hirsch 1921, 34.

Fig. 14: Two of the five lead tokens dating 1450-1550 with the image of a sword or/and a wheel, which are symbols for St. Catharine.

The only gendered associations of grave-goods are bone buttons (in 9 male graves, all dating 1650-1850) and floral wreaths (in 3 female graves, dating 1436-1626 and 1650-1850). However, sometimes it was believed that buttons might prevent the depart of the soul.[32] Each time the remains of which are believed to be floral wreaths is a green stain on the frontal bone as a result of completely perished copper wires used to fix flowers or leaves (Fig. 17). This was a widespread ritual from the 15th century onwards.[33] In the Netherlands a floral wreath was typical for the unmarried after death having an apotropaic meaning for the dead against evil powers.[34] In Germany marriage was believed to be essential for everybody and for the unmarried dead the floral wreath symbolized the crown for the bride as a form of a *rite de passage*.[35]

Such as is the case with grave goods there is also intra-site variety in the design of the coffin and the coffin lid. In Eindhoven almost all medieval and post-medieval dead were interred in tapered coffins, most probably with flat lids. There is no evidence on the occurence of roofed lids, which symbolize a house for the dead. Flat lids and roofed lids were used simultaneously but it is stated that roofed lids were more common in the middle ages and flat lids became standerdised later (Fig. 18).[36]

Except the interments with typical catholic grave-goods (beads, a crucifix) no differences are distinguishable between catholics and reformed burials.

The human remains

Over the centuries on the graveyard the burial space was used and reused intensively which resulted in a complicated stratigraphy. No evidence was found on clearing old graves to give way for new graves. The few excavated charnel pits seem to be the result of the reburial of bones found during the construction of foundations for extensions of the church building.

---

32 Fahrenfort & Van de Graft 1947, 26.
33 Bamberger 2001; Nooijen 2016, 140-142; Williams 2016, 189-192.
34 Hirsch 1921, 42.
35 Bamberger 2001, 99.
36 Fahrenfort & Van de Graft 1947, 25; Van Spelde & Hoogland 2018, 314.

Fig. 15: Bone pendants of a praying-bead (N=26) sieved from the contents of a grave of a male older than 20 years dating 1650-1850.

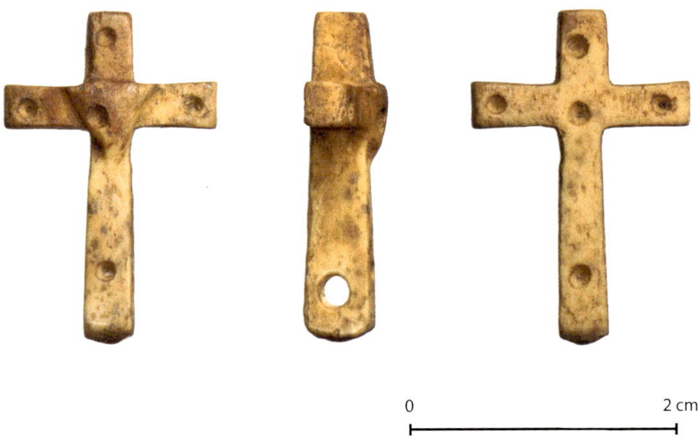

Fig. 16: Bone crucifix (part of a praying-bead) from a grave of a 40-49 years old male dating 1500-1650.

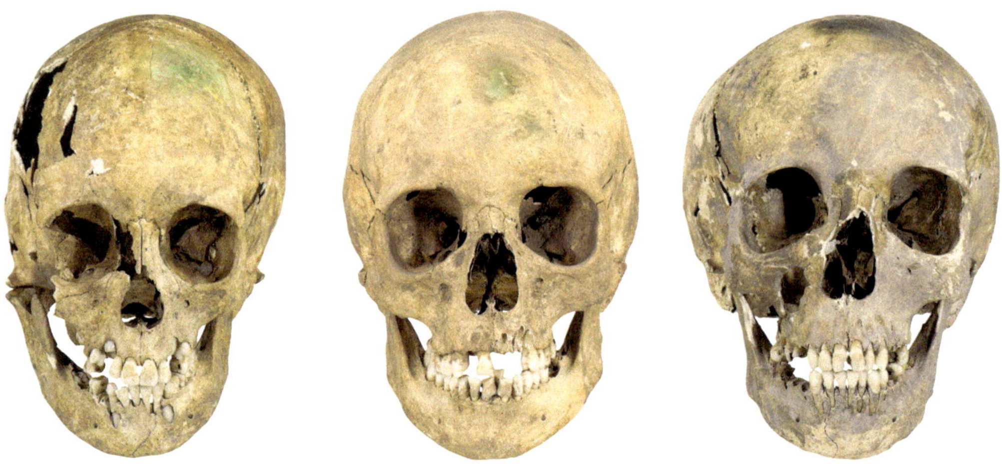

Fig. 17: Green stains on frontal bones, the only remains of floral wreaths with copper wires. Left: a young female (9-10 years, radiocarbon dated 1436-1626), middle and right: two females (both 20-29 years and 1650-1850).

Despite the usually poor conditions for preserving bones on the local sandy soils, most skeletal remains were preserved extremely well. Probably this is due to the runoff of numerous pieces of construction debris rich in lime. The nature of conservation was less perfect for the older remains. For the completness of skeletons the opposite trend was observed: the skeletons dating from the youngest period (1650-1850) were often less complete.

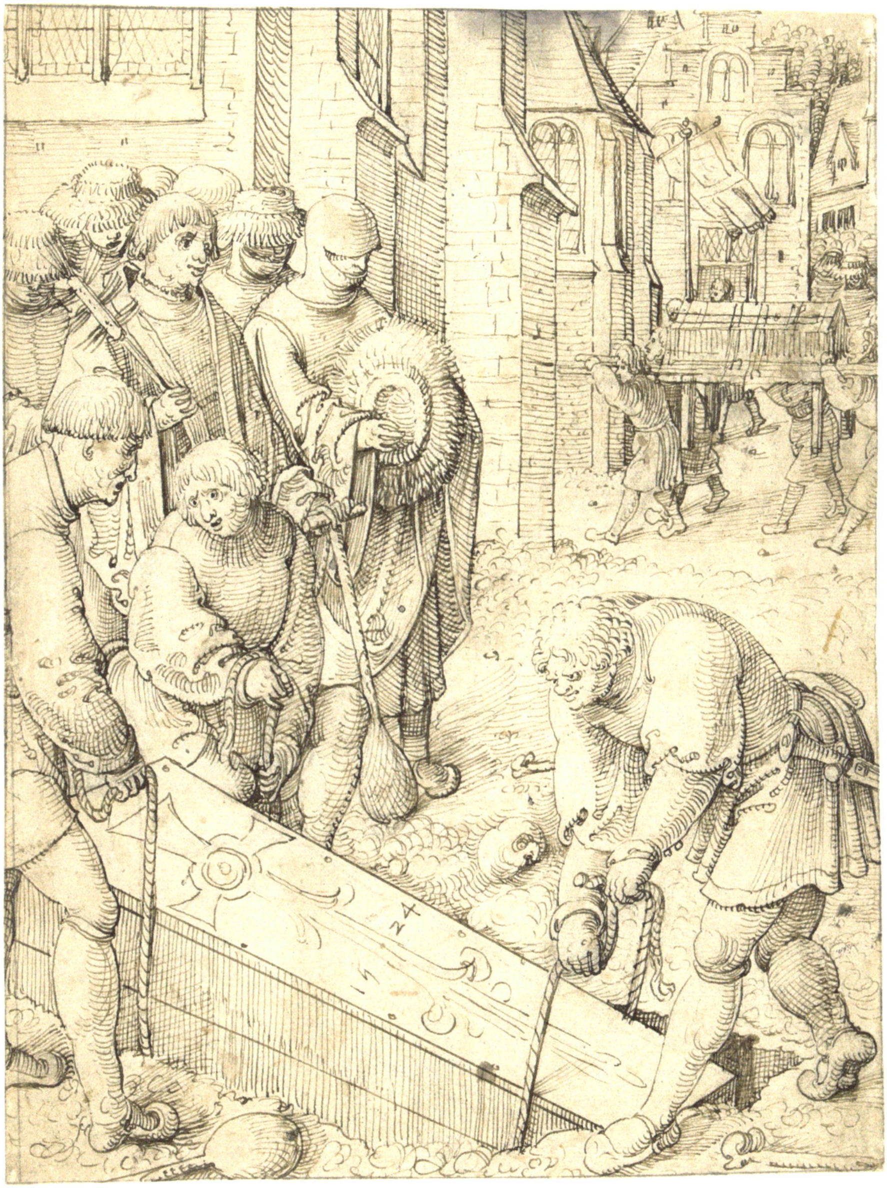

Fig. 18: 'Burying the death'. Note the two forms of coffin lids: a roof-shaped and a flat lid. Pen drawing dating from 1524 by Pieter Cornelisz. Kunst (circa 1484/1490-1560/1561). Collection Rijksmuseum Amsterdam (inv.nr. RP-T-1879-A-7; 247 x 191 mm).

funeral rites/rituals	church/interior	domestic waste
tombstones*	roof slates*	pottery*
iron coffin nails	roof tiles*	bone slaughter waste
iron coffin screws	roofing leads	dog bone
glass pane	bricks*	rotary millstones*
glass beads	mortar	clay tabacco pipes*
jet beads	coarse gravel (floor)	drinking glasses*
amber bead	stone tiles	glass bottles*
bone beads	ceramic tiles	spectacle glass*
bone crucifix	dried loam (wall)	gunflints
copper-alloy earrings	window glass*	lead bullets
leather puch	stained glass*	lead weights
copper-alloy bell	window leads*	lead cloth seal
copper-alloy tag ends	molten glass	lead spindle whorl
copper-alloy fingerrings	molten lead	shell mixing well*
copper-alloy necklace*	bronze puring scrap (bells)	copper-alloy balance
silver ornament	stone font*	copper-alloy spark arrestor
glass button	stone ornaments*	copper-alloy thimbles
bone buttons	stove tiles*	copper-alloy fish hook
copper-alloy needles	fire pot*	copper-alloy ear spoon
copper-alloy pins	copper alloy book furnishings	bone toothpick
copper alloy buckles	bronze candle-holder*	bone knife handle
bronze fastener	bronze chandeliers*	
bronze devotion medal	bronze stylus	
silk cord*	coal	
silk wire*		
linen shrouds*		
pipeclay figurine*		
terracotta figurine*		
coins		
lead tokens		

*Table 2: Classification of main categories of small objects, * = fragment(s).*

All human remains, both in primary as in secondary burials, were recorded in descriptive terms by two physical antropologists.[37] The total amount of separate human bones counts 7709 in primary burials and 2831 in secondairy burials (excluding phalanges and fragments of vertebrae). All primary burials were investigated in detail.[38] For each individual the completeness of the skeleton, nature of preservation, age of death, sex, body heigth, dental status, shape of the

37 Baetsen & Weterings-Korthorst 2013 (with osteological comparisons with other sites in the Netherlands and in England). With one field worker involved an average of four days was spent to excavate and sample one complete skeleton.

38 For comparisions per period the undated burials are not included in this paper but in Baetsen & Weterings-Korthorst 2013.

nr.	sex	age	dating	location	objects
3527	male	22-23	?	?	2 jet beads
3551	man	40-46	1700-1800	hands	1 copper coin (1710 AD)
0561	man	50-59	1700-1800	right lower leg	1 copper coin (1607-1609 AD)
4156	female	45	1650-1850	?	1 bone bead
1215	adult	60-69	1650-1850	right hand	1 lead token (1450-1550 AD)
1277	female	20-29	1650-1850	frontal bone	green stain (floral wreath)
1667	female	20-29	1650-1850	frontal bone	green stain (floral wreath)
3131	female	8	1650-1850	?	4 jet beads
2162	female	47	1650-1800	?	1 glass bead
2909	male	>20	1650-1800	?	26 bone beads
1912	female	56	1650-1800	?	1 jet bead
4170	man	60	1650-1800	?	1 bone bead
2181	man	0,75	1600-1800	?	1 glass bead
1834	man	10-12	1600-1650	neck and in right hand	53 bone beads, 1 amber bead, 1 jet bead and a leather pouch with 5 copper coins (1557-1579), with 1 bell and 1 tag end
3287	female	16-18	1500-1700	neck	1 copper crucifix with silk cord
2195	female	20-29	1500-1700	neck and chest	155 glass beads
3478	man	22-23	1500-1700	?	1 glass bead
0844	male	60-69	1500-1700	skull	2 copper earrings
3455	male	40-49	1500-1650	hands on pelvis	21 bone beads and 1 bone crucifix
2243	male	22	1500-1650	?	1 bone bead
3421	man	67	1500-1650	?	1 bone bead
3531	female	9-10	1436-1626*	frontal bone	green stain (floral wreath)
3181	male	18-20	1400-1600	right hand	double hooked copper fastener
3799	male	50-59	1400-1500	hands on pelvis	22 bone beads
1278	adult	>20	1400-1500	right hand	1 lead token (1450-1550 AD)
4068	male	40-49	1350-1500	hands on pelvis	12 bone beads
4384	male	9-11	1275-1325	chest	1 silver pendant (coin 1192-1423 AD with silk cord)

*Table 3: De variation and location of gravegoods (excluding artefacts associated with a shroud: copper-alloy pins, needles, bone and metal buttons and nests); * = range of calibrated radiocarbon date, ? = location unknown (sieved from the grave filling).*

skull, anatomical variants and pathological conditions were recorded. No sampling was done. After all the excavated area in itself is a sample of the whole graveyard. With an estimated total of 55,000 death during the period of use of the graveyard the number of excavated primary burials is only 1.4%, which would make further selection less responsible. In comparable cases elsewhere there is however too often selection, which is not scientifically sound. Sampling has become assimilated into archaeological jargon with the meaning that it is too expensive to include everything in the final report. For instance, at the graveyard of St. Plechelmus in Oldenzaal, excavated in 2011-2013, so far only 200 (7.3%) out of the 2750

Period	1200-1350	1350-1500	1500-1650	1650-1850
number of individuals	80	129	109	252
average per year	0.53	0.86	0.73	1.26
male (adult)	54%	56%	57%	58%
female (adult)	46%	43%	40%	41%
no sex determination (adult)	0%	1%	3%	2%
number of adults	71	106	74	210
number of non-adults (<20 years)	7	20	32	46
number without age determination	2	3	3	6
average age adult women		54.8	41.3	51.2
average age adult men		50.7	54.1	49.6
average height adult women	161 cm	160 cm	160 cm	161 cm
average height adult men	173 cm	172 cm	173 cm	171 cm

Table 4: General characteristics of 570 datable individuals per period.

excavated skeletons were examined in detail.[39] At the graveyard of St. Martin's in Tegelen in 2007 and 2010 almost 500 burials from 1867-1909 were excavated but only 155 (31.0%) were examined.[40] Surely this is a worrying development.

In the case of Eindhoven further analysis was done with all datable skeletons so as to ensure a view of similarities and differences over time (Table 4).

All periods have less females than males. This is not unusual, also elsewhere this is often the case.[41] The average height of the body is an important criterion for measuring general living conditions and thus for the social-economic situation of a population. For both females as males the average body height does not show many differences through the periods, so judging on the skeletons the living conditions seems to have been more or less stable. The overall development of body length, with a temporal decrease during the late medieval period and a low point during the 17th and 18th centuries, followed by a sharp rise during the 20th century, is barely perceptible in Eindhoven.[42] Concerning age the number of none-adults is low and the number of individuals aged 0-4 years is even severely underrepresented. This seems to indicate that most none-adults were buried elsewhere in the graveyard on a special part for children.

Health and disease

In Tables 5 and 6 the results of the investigation into health and disease are summarized. Compared to other excavated cemetery populations in the Netherlands and in England the number of individuals with bone fractures is low.

39 Altena, Kootker & Panhuysen 2016, 211.
40 Houkes & Burnier 2013.
41 Baetsen & Weterings-Korthorst 2013, 163-164.
42 Baetsen & Weterings-Korthorst 2013, 169-171.

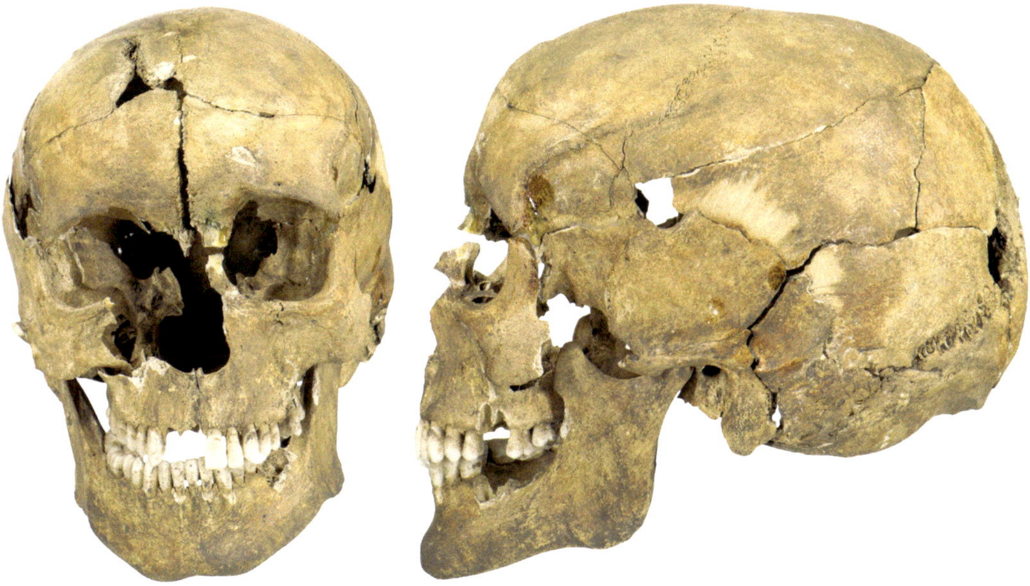

Fig. 19: Skull of a 22 years old man dating 1650-1850 with a drastic injury caused by a sharp weapon whereby the frontal bone was split, and in both sides of the occiput holes caused by a close shot from a firearm. The hole in the temporal bone is a post-mortem damage.

In the period 1650-1850 there is a notheworthy high percentage of individuals with a degenerative disc disease and osteoarthritis. Striking are four post-medieval individuals with scurvy which usually occurs among individuals who made long sea voyages or those with famine. Compared to other excavated graveyards the townsmen of Eindhoven had worse teeth and the tooth loss was above-average high, the same is true for the number of individuals with infected teeth.[43]

For only one individual the cause of death is entirely clear. It is a 22 years old male dating 1650-1850 with a dramatic injury in the skull caused by a sharp weapon such as a sword or an axe, whereby the frontal bone was spit. Furthermore, on both sides of his occiput there are holes clearly caused by a close-proximity shot from a firearm (Fig. 19). Possibly this is the historically known individual who was executed in 1693 with a sword.[44]

For all suitable primairy burials (N=410) soil samples were taken from the pelvis to investigate the possible presence of eggs of whipworm (*Trichuris trichiura*), an intestinal parasite which usually lives in the intestines of fox and dog.[45] The presence or absence of intestinal parasites can give information on former eating habits such as the consumption of unwashed plant food contaminated with urine of fox or dog of through unwashed hands. Most individuals infected with whipworm date from the middle ages: 18.9% (1200-1350) and 21.5% (1350-1500). During the post-medieval periods this infection was considerably lesser: 6.9% (1500-1650) and 12.4% (1650-1850).

43 Baetsen & Weterings-Korthorst 2013, 179.
44 Melssen 2009.
45 Lambregtse 2013.

period	1200-1350	1350-1500	1500-1650	1650-1850
number of individuals	82	134	141	260
traumata	5 (6%)	17 (13%)	11 (9%)	58 (22%)
periostitis	5 (6%)	18 (13%)	11 (9%)	26 (10%)
palatinitis	0	0	2 (1%)	0
osteomyelitis	0	0	0	1 (<1%)
tuberculosis	0	0	0	1 (<1%)
syphilis	0	0	0	2 (1%)
palatinitis	0	0	0	5 (2%)
echinococciasis	0	0	0	1 (<1%)
anemia	3 (4%)	1 (1%)	3 (2%)	5 (2%)
scarvy	0	0	3 (2%)	1 (<1%)
rachitics	0	2 (1%)	1 (1%)	2 (1%)
osteoporosis	0	1 (1%)	1 (1%)	3 (1%)
degenerative decline	11 (13%)	48 (36%)	71 (50%)	191 (73%)
rheumatoid arthritis	0	0	1 (1%)	0
scoliosis/kyphosis/lordosis	0	3 (2%)	7 (5%)	18 (7%)
DISH	2 (2%)	5 (4%)	4 (3%)v	27 (10%)
entesopathy	7 (9%)	26 (19%)	30 (21%)	48 (18%)
bipartietal osteodystrofis	0	0	0	1 (<1%)
button osteoma	2 (2%)	1 (1%)	6 (4%)	5 (2%)
endocranial depression	5 (6%)	12 (9%)	15 (11%)	34 (13%)
atrophy	0	1 (1%)	0	0
osteoarthritis	0	1 (1%)	0	0

Table 5: Modifications of bones as a result of diseases per period (absolute and relative numbers of individuals).

Before 1650 the infection mostly occurs in males while infection in non-adults is low in each period (maximum 1.4%). This seems to indicate that during the middle ages in Eindhoven hygienic conditions were considerably worse than during the post-medieval periods. So far there is hardy any research available on the subject elsewhere that could make comparisions with other excavated graveyards possible.

On the place of the liver in the skeletons of three individuals a calcified cyst was found which was caused by infection by tapeworm of fox or dog, probably via their faeces. The individuals are an adult female and an adult male from the period 1350-1500 and an adult male from the period 1650-1850.

DNA and isotope analysis

The 2005-2006 excavation in Eindhoven was the first Dutch project where DNA samples were structurally collectedand in a forensic way. All samples were taken from the molars which provide the biggest chance for finding DNA (Fig. 20).[46] This was possible for 381 (50.4%) out of the 754 excavated individuals in primairy

46 Hollund 2013; Hollund, Arts, Jans & Kars 2015.

period	1200-1350	1350-1500	1500-1650	1650-1850
loss of teeth during life	17.9	20.6	31.9	31.3
alveolar athrofy	71.0	82.5	86.3	78.4
caries	75	91	70	75
fistulae	9.7	28.1	60.8	35.1
abscesses	55.2	25.8	33.3	74.8
periodontitis	6.5	19.3	31,4	33.3
calculus	74.2	73.7	82.4	64.0
enamel hypoplasia	22.6	31.6	37.3	43.2

Table 6: The state of teeth per period (percentages of the number of individuals).

Fig. 20: All DNA-samples were taken forensically from molars.

burials; the remaining part was too incomplete or had no teeth left. The quality of teeth in only three skeletons appeared to be insufficient for DNA analysis. The research questions for DNA concern sex determination, geographic origin of individuals, kinship relations and ten medical themes (protection against hiv-virus, lactose-intolerance, diabetes type II, obesity, gluten intolerance, cystic fibrosis, hemochromatosis, natural protection against infection, longevity and artrosis). So far not all results of the DNA analysis are available.[47] Sex determination was possible for 88% of the individuals including 72% of the non-adults. With traditional

47 Altena, Smeding & De Knijff 2013.

physical-antropological methods that was only possble for 66%. A number of skeletons (12%) which were estimated to be male turned out to be female and 5% of the estmated females were actually male. DNA analysis also showed that the genetic group composition during the middle ages (1200-1500) was significantly different than the current population of Eindhoven. Four individuals have genetic characteristics which possibly originate from Asia or Africa.

Twenty individuals (five for each period) were examined for the composition of light carbon and nitrogen isotopes.[48] Samples taken from the femur and from the teeth. This exploratory study showed that diet indicates a coherent group during all four periods with barely any differences in food consumption during youth and at a later age. The diet was based mainly on cereals, milk, cheese, eggs and meat, probably with freshwater fish and freshwater poultry meat. One individual had a strict vegetarian diet. It is remarkable that females in the sample consumed more meat than males.

A remark on post excavation ethics

Mortuary archaeology in Eindhoven is most attractive for the public. It would seem that society today is facinated by the sight of the remains of the dead. To the public, the most appealing type of archaeological research seems to be excavations involving clearly visible human remains. This is also true for exhibitions of human remains (Fig. 21).[49] 'Archaeology tries to make the dry bones live, and it is hard to think ourselves into the situation of past people without feeling towards them some of the interpersonal attitudes that characterise our relationship with the living'.[50] Archaeologists have thus only a supporting role in society where in the interaction between the living and the dead, the dead have a starring role. Ethical taboos that archaeologists consider may still exists do seem to belong to the past. In Eindhoven only once it was commented (by the local Pensioners' Party) that the dead should be left were they were buried.

In the Netherlands it is legally proscibed that archaeological finds should be stored in an archaeological depot so that they are available for further (future) research. What is particularly remarkable is that for archaeologically excavated human remains exceptions are made.[51] In Haarlem the skeletal remains of at least 130 individuals (15th century) were excavated in 2012. In 2014 they were reburied with funerary rites in a wooden box, and the site marked with a specially made gravestone.[52] Similar funerary rituals also took place in Tegelen, Emmen and Gouda. In Tegelen almost 500 individuals were excavated in 2007 and 2010, only 155 of them were examined, and in 2010 all skeletons were reburied, albeit after a complete catholic funeral mass. In Emmen in 2014-2015 300 individuals were excavated, all were reburied in 2016.[53] In Gouda in 2015 in the chancel of St. John's several post-

48 Sonders 2013.
49 Not only in Eindhoven: see for instance Sayer 2010, 107.
50 Scarre 2006, 183.
51 Also see Waters-Rist, Schats & Hoogland 2018, 14-16.
52 Van Zalinge & Van der Linde 2015, 123-124.
53 Cf. Arts 2017, 244, also see Waters-Rist, Schats & Hoogland 2018, 15-16.

Fig. 21: Children experiencing human remains on display at the Eindhoven Heritage Centre in 2016.

medieval vaults and charnel pits were found and a report was made of a selection of the human remains and then reburied in 2016 in a 'special' vault.[54]

Therefore, at least in the Netherlands, among archaeologists there are still ethical taboos in handling human remains. This is a form of extreme conservatism which contrasts the widespread European attitude towards human remains as archaeological finds.[55] Even though last years in Dutch archaeology a comprehensive burocracy was introduced, specific recommendations or ethical codes for dealing with human remains are still lacking.[56]

The above examples of the way in which archaeological finds are treated, and there are others, are cause for great concern. In this way archaeologists are denied any chance for supplementary research in the future.[57] In Eindhoven all the bones have been stored in the municipal archaeological depot and remain accesible for any future research.[58] Eindhoven benefits from supplementary studies as they generate data to enrich the research goals of the original excavation; an increase in our body of knowledge of the past inhabitants of the town.

Final remarks

For archaeologists the building of a church on an already existing late medieval graveyard could cause the problem for which graves already existed before the church was built, and which dead were buried in the church. To make distinctions herein is

54 Groenendijk 2017.

55 Swain 2016, 181.

56 Waters-Rist, Schats & Hoogland 2018, 11.

57 See also Anthony 2016, 28.

58 E.g. Hollund 2013; Hollund, Arts, Jans & Kars 2015; Lepage 2018; Wouda 2017.

easy when grave pits are truncated by foundations of the church, but when this is not the case this can be hazardous. In the case of St. Catharine's in Eindhoven the grave of an about 9-11 years old boy excavated during the trial excavation in 2002, which was found between the foundations of the choir, was believed to be buried in the chancel. Together with the exotic grave good of a Venetian coin with a silk thread the location in the choir gave rise to the assumption that he was the child of a local elite. However, during the main excavation it appeared that the child's grave (dating circa 1300) was older than the chancel (dating after 1350), thus that this was a burial on the graveyard.

In recent years the archaeological research field of late medieval and post medieval death has been increasingly enriched with new descriptions, insights and interpretations. We now have the opportunity to develop this theme in a first synthesis on the Low Countries.

Bibliography

Altena, E., L.M. Kootker & R.G.A.M. Panhuysen, 2016: Populatieonderzoek. In G.L. Williams (ed.), *Memento Mori. Een archeologische opgraving rondom de St. Plechelmuskerk, Oldenzaal* (ADC Monografie 21). Amersfoort, 211-302.

Altena, E., R. Smeding & P. de Knijff, 2013: Het DNA-onderzoek: de eerste resultaten. In N. Arts (ed.), *Een knekelveld maakt geschiedenis. Het archeologisch onderzoek van het koor en het grafveld van de middeleeuwse Catharinakerk in Eindhoven, circa 1200-1850.* Utrecht, 213-227.

Anthony, S., 2016: Questions Raised in Excavating the Recent Dead. In H. Williams & M. Giles (eds.) *Archaeologists and the Dead. Mortuary Archaeology in Contemporary Society*. Oxford, 21-38.

Arts, N., 2002: *Marcus van Eindhoven. Een archeologische biografie van een middeleeuws kind.* Utrecht.

Arts, N., 2003: *Marcus van Eindhoven. An archaeological biography of a medieval child.* Utrecht.

Arts, N. (ed.), 2013: *Een knekelveld maakt geschiedenis. Het archeologisch onderzoek van het koor en het grafveld van de middeleeuwse Catharinakerk in Eindhoven, circa 1200-1850.* Utrecht.

Arts, N., 2017: Mortuary archaeology and variation in death culture in eastern North Brabant (The Netherlands), c. 900-1900 AD. In C. Bis-Worch & C. Theune (eds.), *Religion, Cults & Rituals in the Medieval Rural Environment* (Ruralia XI). Leiden, 241-251.

Arts, N. & J. Nollen, 2006: *Een bed van botten. Het archeologisch onderzoek van de middeleeuwse Cathatinakerk in Eindhoven in beeld/A bed of bones. The archaeological investigation of the medieval Church of St. Catherine – a story in pictures.* 's-Hertogenbosch.

Arts, N. & J. Nollen, 2013: Dateren met koolstof: C14-dateringen van menselijk botmateriaal. In N. Arts (ed.), *Een knekelveld maakt geschiedenis. Het archeologisch onderzoek van het koor en het grafveld van de middeleeuwse Catharinakerk in Eindhoven, circa 1200-1850.* Utrecht, 78-81.

Arts, N., & B. van den Broek, 2013: Archeologische vondsten uit het kerkterrein. In N. Arts (ed.), *Een knekelveld maakt geschiedenis. Het archeologisch onderzoek van het koor en het grafveld van de middeleeuwse Catharinakerk in Eindhoven, circa 1200-1850.* Utrecht, 82-105.

Baetsen, S. & L. Weterings-Korthorst, 2013: De menselijke overblijfselen. In N. Arts (ed.), *Een knekelveld maakt geschiedenis. Het archeologisch onderzoek van het koor en het grafveld van de middeleeuwse Catharinakerk in Eindhoven, circa 1200-1850.* Utrecht, 151-212.

Bamberger, G., 2001: Totenkronen von ca. 1750 bis 1850 im Großherzogtum Hessen. In W. Stolle, N. Fröhling, M. Jacoby & W. Strolle (eds.), *Der Tod. Zur Geschichte des Umgangs mit Sterben und Trauer.* Lorsch, 99-115.

Bassett, S., C. Dyer & R. Holt, 1992: Introduction. In S. Bassett (ed.), *Death in Towns. Urban Responses to the Dying and the Dead, 100-1600.* London, 1-7.

Bitter, P., 2002: *Graven en begraven. Archeologie en geschiedenis van de Grote Kerk van Alkmaar.* Hilversum.

Blockmans, W.P., G. Pieters, W. Prevenier & R.W.M. van Schaik, 1980: Tussen crisis en welvaart: sociale veranderingen 1300-1500. In D.P. Blok, A. Verhulst, H.P.H. Jansen, R.C. van Caenegem, A.G. Weiler & W. Prevenier (eds.), *Algemene Geschiedenis der Nederlandsen. Deel 4. Middeleeuwen.* Haarlem, 42-86.

Cuvelier, J., 1912: *Les Dénombrements de Foyers en Brabant (XIVe – XVIe Siècle).* Brussels.

Dezutter, W.P., 1975: Dodenmunt, penningkeerse en absolutiebrief. In W. van Nespen (ed.), *Miscellanea prof. em. Dr. K.C. Peeters. Door Vrienden en Collega's hem aangeboden ter gelegenheid van zijn emiraat.* Antwerp, 193-206.

Doppler, H.W., 2008. Fundmünzen. In H.R. Sennhauser, *Ausgrabungen in Stadtkirche ind Dreikönigskapelle Baden 1967/1968. Kirchen und Siedlungsgeschichte von der Frühzeit bis ins späte Mittelalter.* Zürich, 198-205.

Esser, K., 2013: Dierlijk botmateriaal. In N. Arts (ed.), *Een knekelveld maakt geschiedenis. Het archeologisch onderzoek van het koor en het grafveld van de middeleeuwse Catharinakerk in Eindhoven, circa 1200-1850.* Utrecht, 243-249.

Fahrenfort, J.J. & C. van de Graft, 1947: *Dodenbezorging en cultuur. II. De dodenbezorging bij de volken van Europa, inzonderheid in Nederland.* Amsterdam.

Gilchrist, R., 2008: Magic for the Dead? The Archaeology of Magic in Later Medieval Burials. *Medieval Archaeology* 52, 119-159.

Gilchrist, R., 2012: *Medieval Life. Archaeology and the Life Course.* Woodbridge.

Groenendijk, M., 2017: Begraven, opgegraven en herbegraven. Begravingen in het hoogkoor van de Goudse Sint-Janskerk. *Archeologie in Nederland* 1, 10-17.

Hirsch, R., 1921: *Doodenritueel in de Nederlanden vóór 1700.* Amsterdam.

Hollund, H.I., 2013: *Diagenetic screening of bone samples: tools to aid taphonomic and archaeometric investigations* (Geological and Bioarchaeological Studies Volume 15). Amsterdam.

Hollund, H.I., N. Arts, M.M.E. Jans & H. Kars, 2015: Are Teeth Better? Histological Characterization of Diagenesis in Archeologischal Bone-Yooth Pairs and a Discussion of the Consequences for Archaeometric Sample Selection and Analyses. *International Journal of Osteoarchaeology* 25, 901-911.

Houkes, M.C.E. & C.Y. Burnier, 2013: *Tegelen-Wilhelminaplein: leven en dood in de schaduw van de Martinuskerk. Archeologisch onderzoek naar de jongste fase (1867-1909) van het oude kerkhof van Tegelen* (Archeologisch Diensten Centrum rapport 1775). Amersfoort.

Johns, C. & J. Wallinga, 2013: Dateren met licht: OSL-dateringen van bakstenen. In N. Arts (ed.), *Een knekelveld maakt geschiedenis. Het archeologisch onderzoek van het koor en het grafveld van de middeleeuwse Catharinakerk in Eindhoven, circa 1200-1850.* Utrecht, 76-77.

Lambregtse, M., 2013: Darmparasieten en verkalkte lichaamsholten. In N. Arts (ed.), *Een knekelveld maakt geschiedenis. Het archeologisch onderzoek van het koor en het grafveld van de middeleeuwse Catharinakerk in Eindhoven, circa 1200-1850.* Utrecht, 236-242.

Lepage, H., 2018: *Activity and entheseal changes of the population of Eindhoven, buried at the Catharina church between 1500 and 1850.* MA thesis, Faculty of Archaeology University of Leiden. Leiden.

Melssen, J., 1979: *Het register van de cijnzen, die de heer van Cranendonk in Eindhoven ontving in de jaren 1590 tot 1640 en de schattingskohieren van de gegoedheid van de inwoners van Eindhoven in 1665 en 1687.* Eindhoven.

Melssen, J., 2009: *De 'kerk van Sinte Katalijn, maget ende martelaeresse, tot Eindhoven', het daarbij gelegen kerkhof en de begraafcultuur ter plaatse tot 1860.* Unpublished manuscript, Regional Historical Centre Eindhoven.

Melssen, J., 2013: De geschiedenis van de Catharinakerk: een kort overzicht. In N. Arts (ed.), *Een knekelveld maakt geschiedenis. Het archeologisch onderzoek van het koor en het grafveld van de middeleeuwse Catharinakerk in Eindhoven, circa 1200-1850.* Utrecht, 27-32.

Nollen, J., 2013a: Het archeologisch onderzoek van 2005 en 2006. In N. Arts (ed.), *Een knekelveld maakt geschiedenis. Het archeologisch onderzoek van het koor en het grafveld van de middeleeuwse Catharinakerk in Eindhoven, circa 1200-1850.* Utrecht, 38-49.

Nollen, J., 2013b: Bakstenen funderingen en andere strukturen. In N. Arts (ed.), *Een knekelveld maakt geschiedenis. Het archeologisch onderzoek van het koor en het grafveld van de middeleeuwse Catharinakerk in Eindhoven, circa 1200-1850.* Utrecht, 50-75.

Nollen, J., 2013c: Het grafritueel. In N. Arts (ed.), *Een knekelveld maakt geschiedenis. Het archeologisch onderzoek van het koor en het grafveld van de middeleeuwse Catharinakerk in Eindhoven, circa 1200-1850.* Utrecht, 117-150.

Nooijen, C., 2016: De metaalvondsten. In G.L. Williams (ed.), *Memento Mori. Een archeologische opgraving rondom de St. Plechelmuskerk, Oldenzaal* (Archeologisch Diensten Centrum Monografie 21). Amersfoort, 132-149.

Pelsdonk, J., 2003: *Pennincxkens van Loode. Een onderzoek naar in Nederland gevonden muntachtige voorwerpen uit de middeleeuwen en de 16e eeuw, aangevuld met een overzicht van de moderne penningen*. Goudswaard.

Pelsdonk, J., 2013: Begraven munten en penningen. Over grafgiften en vreemd geld. In N. Arts (ed.), *Een knekelveld maakt geschiedenis. Het archeologisch onderzoek van het koor en het grafveld van de middeleeuwse Catharinakerk in Eindhoven, circa 1200-1850.* Utrecht, 106-116.

Sayer, D., 2010: *Ethics and Burial Archaeology*. London.

Scarre, G., 2006: Can archaeology harm the dead? In C. Scarre & G. Scarre (eds.), *The ethics of archaeology. Philosophical perspectives on archaeological practice.* Cambridge, 181-198.

Sonders, M., 2013: Onderzoek van stabiele isotopen in menselijke overblijfselen. In N. Arts (ed.), *Een knekelveld maakt geschiedenis. Het archeologisch onderzoek van het koor en het grafveld van de middeleeuwse Catharinakerk in Eindhoven, circa 1200-1850.* Utrecht, 228-235.

Swain, H., 2016: Museum Practice and the Display of Human Remains. In H. Williams & M. Giles (eds.) *Archaeologists and the Dead. Mortuary Archaeology in Contemporary Society*. Oxford, 169-183.

Theuws, F., 2018: Rural cemeteries, cult places and community identities in the Central Middle Ages in the Kempen region (southern Netherlands). In R. van Oosten, R. Schats, K. Fast, N. Arts & H.M.P. Bouwmeester (eds.), *The Urban Graveyard. Archaeological Perspectives* (Urban Graveyard Proceedings 2). Leiden, 27-49.

Van Bulck, G., 2017: Religieuze medailles en andere devotionalia uit de archeologische site Sint-Romboutskerkhof in Mechelen. *Opgetekend Verleden (Uitgave van de Mechelse Vereniging voor Stadsarcheologie)* 7, 6-61.

Van de Vijver, K., F. Kinnaer & S. Depuydt, 2018: St. Rombout's cemetery in Mechelen, Belgium (10th – 18th century A.D.). In R.M.R. van Oosten, R. Schats, K. Fast, N. Arts & H.M.P. Bouwmeester (eds.), *The Urban Graveyard. Archaeological Perspectives* (Urban Graveyard Proceedings 2). Leiden, 239-285.

Van der Hammen, J. & A. Sassen, 1894: Telling der huizen en haardsteden in de stad en de meierij van 's-Hertogenbosch, gedaan in het jaar 1526. *Handelingen van het Provinciaal Genootschap van Kunsten en Wetenschappen in Noord-Brabant* 1891-1893, 221-263.

Van Oosten, R. & R. Schats, 2018: Preface. In R. van Oosten, R. Schats, K. Fast, N. Arts & H.M.P. Bouwmeester (eds.), *The Urban Graveyard. Archaeological Perspectives* (Urban Graveyard Proceedings 2). Leiden, 7-8.

Van Spelde, F.J. & M.L.P. Hoogland, 2018: A rural view of early modern mortuary practices. Context and material culture of the 18th- and 19th-century cemetery of Middenbeemster, the Netherlands. In R. van Oosten, R. Schats, K. Fast, N. Arts & H.M.P. Bouwmeester (eds.), *The Urban Graveyard. Archaeological Perspectives* (Urban Graveyard Proceedings 2). Leiden, 307-335.

Van Zalinge, A. & C. van der Linde, 2015: *Tot op het bot. Skeletten van middeleeuwse Haarlemmers op de Botermarkt & het Begijnhof*. Haarlem.

Waters-Rist, A.L., R. Schats & M.L.P. Hoogland, 2018: Ethical issues in human osteoarchaeology. Recommendations for best practice in the Netherlands. In R. van Oosten, R, Schats, K. Fast, N. Arts & H.M.P. Bouwmeester (eds.), *The Urban Graveyard. Archaeological Perspectives* (Urban Graveyard Proceedings 2). Leiden, 9-25.

Williams, G.L., 2016: Grafritueel. In G.L. Williams (ed.), *Memento Mori. Een archeologische opgraving rondom de St. Plechelmuskerk, Oldenzaal* (Archeologisch Diensten Centrum Monografie 21). Amersfoort, 171-200.

Wouda, R., 2017: *Health in Early Modern Eindhoven. A study of non-specific indicators of stress on subadult skeletons from St. Catharine's church in Eindhoven.* MA thesis, Faculty of Archaeology University of Leiden. Leiden.

The monastic cemetery of the Broederenkerk in Zutphen

For monks only?

Steffen Baetsen & Michel Groothedde

Introduction

During the Middle Ages, the Broederenkerk was part of a Dominican monastery complex that was founded in 1293 by Countess Margaretha van Dampierre on the territory of a former court of the counts of Gelre and Zutphen (Fig. 1). This court was established in the second half of the 12th century. Recent research has shown that the dormitory of the monastery dates to the time of the committal court and was constructed *c.* 1250 to serve as an auditorium.[1] Even more interesting is the observation that the Dominican church also contains evidence of earlier stages of construction dating from before the foundation of the monastery.[2] The interior of the church measures 44 x 20 meters, contains three aisles and probably also served as a knights' hall (Fig. 2). But it was never completed. The Count of Gelre, Reinald I (1271-1323), started the ambitious project, much like his brother-in-law Floris V of Holland in the Hague *c.* 1284-1288. The hall Floris finished in 1295 became famous as the Ridderzaal and is still used today for constitutional ceremonies. Construction of its counterpart in Zutphen was halted when Reinald lost the battle of Woeringen in 1288, was imprisoned, and had to be bailed out by his father-in-law, the Flemish earl Guido van Dampierre. As compensation, Guido received property in the county of Gelre and Zutphen for the duration of ten years. Unfortunately, Reinald went bankrupt and construction of the church was put on hold for five years until his wife Margaretha donated the property to the Dominican friars. They also took over the other buildings and turned the existing hall into a dormitory. The construction of the knights' hall was resumed but with a different architectonical concept: it became a three-aisled basilica, the monastery's church. The records of the tollbooth at Lobith in 1306 and 1307 show

1 Haans 2018.
2 Groothedde 2018.

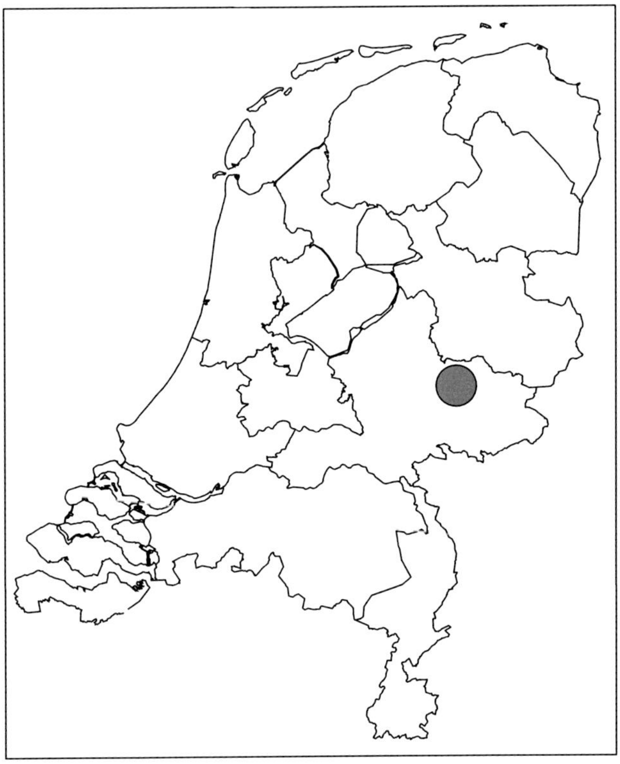

Fig. 1: Map of Zutphen.

that in this period the building activities were intensified: passing through were two ships loaded with stone material (trachyte and tuff) used to construct pillars and the arcs of the vaults: '*fratres de Sutphania de lapidibus constructam ecclesiam*' ('friars from Zutphen with stone material for the construction of the church').[3] From this we know that the church existed at the beginning of the 14th century, and it is assumed that burials began to take place at the same time. *Circa* 1400, the choir was added. This construction must have disturbed several graves, considering the amount of loose human bone present in archaeological trench pits along the foundation of the choir.

Any archival records of the monastery about burials or burial customs are scarce. The monastery, however, was at odds over burial rights with the Chapter of St. Walburgis, Zutphen's main church. In general, mendicant orders like the Dominicans and Franciscans were popular among the inhabitants of a town because of their devotion to poverty and modesty. Because the Dominican order was open to lay brothers and sisters, citizens, in return for receiving ecclesiastic sacraments, gifted the order with goods and money. One of the benefits the lay brothers and sisters apparently received was a right to be buried in the monastery graveyard. Consequently, this meant a loss of income for the other parish churches in Zutphen, particularly the Chapter of St. Walburgis. In 1390, the Chapter involved the dean of St. Maarten's Chapter in Emmerik, who, on behalf of St. Walburgis, excommunicated all the lay brothers and sisters in the Dominican

3 Alberts 1986.

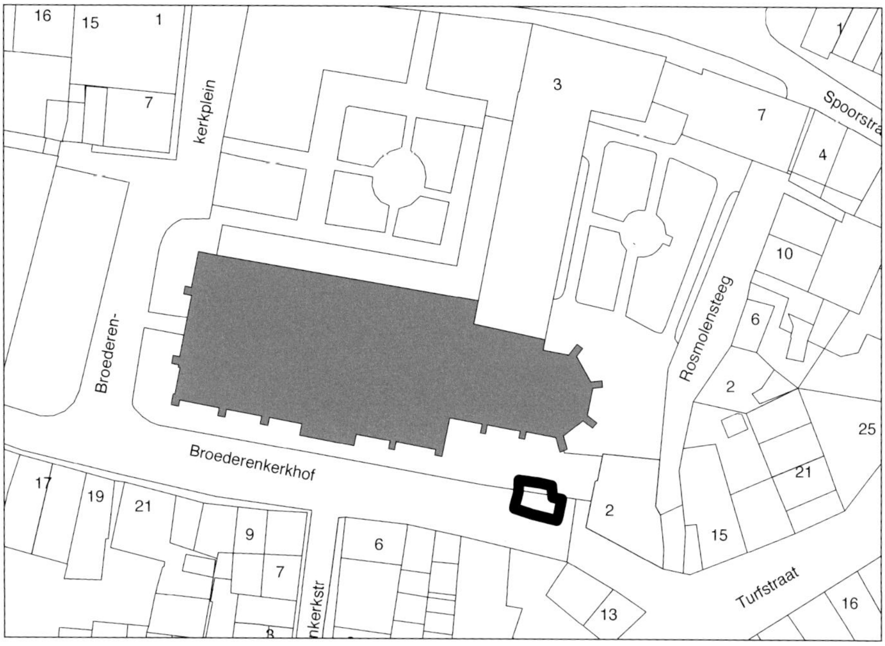

Fig. 2: Location of the Broederenkerk in Zutphen.

order.[4] At least 250 family names were implicated, including the town's elite. But the quarrel between the two institutions did not stop here. In the mid-15th century, the Chapter of St. Walburgis, supported by the Duke of Gelre, called in the pope's assistance. A monastery of observant Franciscans was founded just outside the town in 1455 to keep a watchful eye on the Dominicans, but it is doubtful that this measure worked. The Dominican monastery remained a rich institution with substantial income and was able to construct capacious buildings including a new library and refectory in 1487.

The Broederenkerk fell into disuse for decades after the Reformation. In Zutphen Protestantism was established in 1591 after the town was conquered by Prince Maurits of Nassau. The town's population decreased considerably as a result of the Eighty Years' War and occupation by the Spanish troops between 1572 and 1591. As a result, not every church was needed. But in the first half of the 17th century, when the town's population increased, several churches were restored by Protestants. In 1686 a Walloon community was founded in Zutphen, and the Broederenkerk was assigned to them as its church. It was specifically intended for Walloon inhabitants of Zutphen, natives of France or the French speaking southern parts of the Netherlands, who had fled north during inquisitions after the abrogation of the Edict of Nantes in 1685. This independent Walloon community existed in Zutphen until 1821 when it was disbanded and incorporated into the local Reformed church. Since 1983 the church has been used as the public library.

4 Hermans 1993.

The graveyard

The excavation in 2005/2006 of a small part of the cemetery of the Broederenkerk is the subject of this chapter. But this excavation is not the only archaeological activity involving the cemetery. In 1982 a sarcophagus containing a skeleton was found in the aisle of the courtyard of the church.[5] In the 1977 excavation, no burials were found in the northern part of the courtyard.[6] More recently in 2007, the cemetery's southern wall was documented, its southwest corner determined, and the western boundary located.[7] Finally in 2012, a test pit right behind the choir confirmed that the graveyard did not extend that far.[8] With these findings, the graveyard's location and size could be determined. It consisted of the interior of the church and the area southwest of the church. These later excavations determined that the 2005/2006 excavation and burials used in this study originated from the cemetery's southeast corner.

The oldest burials in the graveyard date from the first decade of the 14th century when construction of the church was finished and the building was consecrated. This is confirmed by datable archaeological finds related to some burials, for example, pottery, and their stratigraphic position beneath a 14th-century wall and floor. Below the oldest burials, traces of habitation and layers of embankment dating from the 13th century were found. Establishing a date for the most recent burials was more complex. Ceramic finds related to fillings of the burials can be dated from the 13th to 17th century. However, some of them undoubtedly ended up there by accident, a common problem in graveyards because layers of soils were thoroughly mixed over the centuries. However, in 1829 a general law was passed forbidding burials near churches situated in population centres with more than 1,000 people. This marks a date after which it was no longer possible to be interred in the cemetery near the church.

An interesting feature is that the oldest burials were preserved the best. Also, the spatial layout of the oldest burials was more organised than that of the more recent, post-medieval burials. The medieval graves were arranged in a chessboard pattern. Sometimes an individual had been subsequently placed in a burial pit, disturbing older burials in the same pit.[9] In one instance, there were five persons in one grave pit, suggesting a possible family plot. Another interesting phenomenon is that the burials were clustered in big rectangular ditches two meters wide. It seems that the burial location was cleaned from older soil and garbage before the burials took place, meaning that the older, contaminated ground was replaced with clean sand, probably already sanctified by the church and possibly brought in from another location. In total, five of these ditches were identified, some of them dissecting each other. Also remarkable were the wooden facings along the sides of them. Around 1400 a small brick building 2m x 2m was erected on top of the burial ditches. Its function is unclear, it could have been a charnel house or a depository for tools, like shovels.

---

5 Documented by P. Bitter. Physical anthropological data of the skeleton are unknown.
6 Groothedde 2001.
7 Groothedde & Fermin 2007.
8 Fermin & Kastelein 2012.
9 In Dutch *graf kavel*.

Fig. 3: A primary burial from the Broederenkerkhof.

The post-excavation report presented the project's excavations, dates, context, and other results.[10] The authors recommended all excavated human skeletal remains be studied according to physical anthropological standards in order to help answer some research questions: Was there a significant difference in the use of the cemetery during the reform period (1600-1830) and the time it was used by the friars of the monastery? To what extent were the skeletons preserved and how complete were they? What were their physical anthropological characteristics?[11]

In all, 34 features were classified as belonging to primary burials in which it was obvious to which individual the feature originally belonged (Fig. 3). Eventually a total of fourteen levels were excavated, eight of which contained primary burials (Fig. 4).

It has been suggested that burying the dead in a traditional Christian orientation only served a symbolic purpose for the bereaved because of the grave disruption. When constructing new graves, for instance, older burials were often disturbed, bones randomly removed, discarded, or moved to an ossuary,[12] which would surely complicate a physical resurrection.[13]

Based on stratigraphic and contextual characteristics, the burials can be divided into two periods. The most recent belong to the Reformation period post-1600 (N=17) and the older ones to 1300-1600 and associated with the Dominican monastery. Due to burials appearing underneath the 14th-century fundaments, the latter group can be separated into two periods: pre-1400 (N=9) and 1400-1600 (N=8).

10 Fermin & Groothedde 2006, 8-24.

11 Fermin & Groothedde 2006, 7.

12 Fermin & Kastelein 2012, 23-24.

13 Fermin & Groothedde 2006,14, 17.

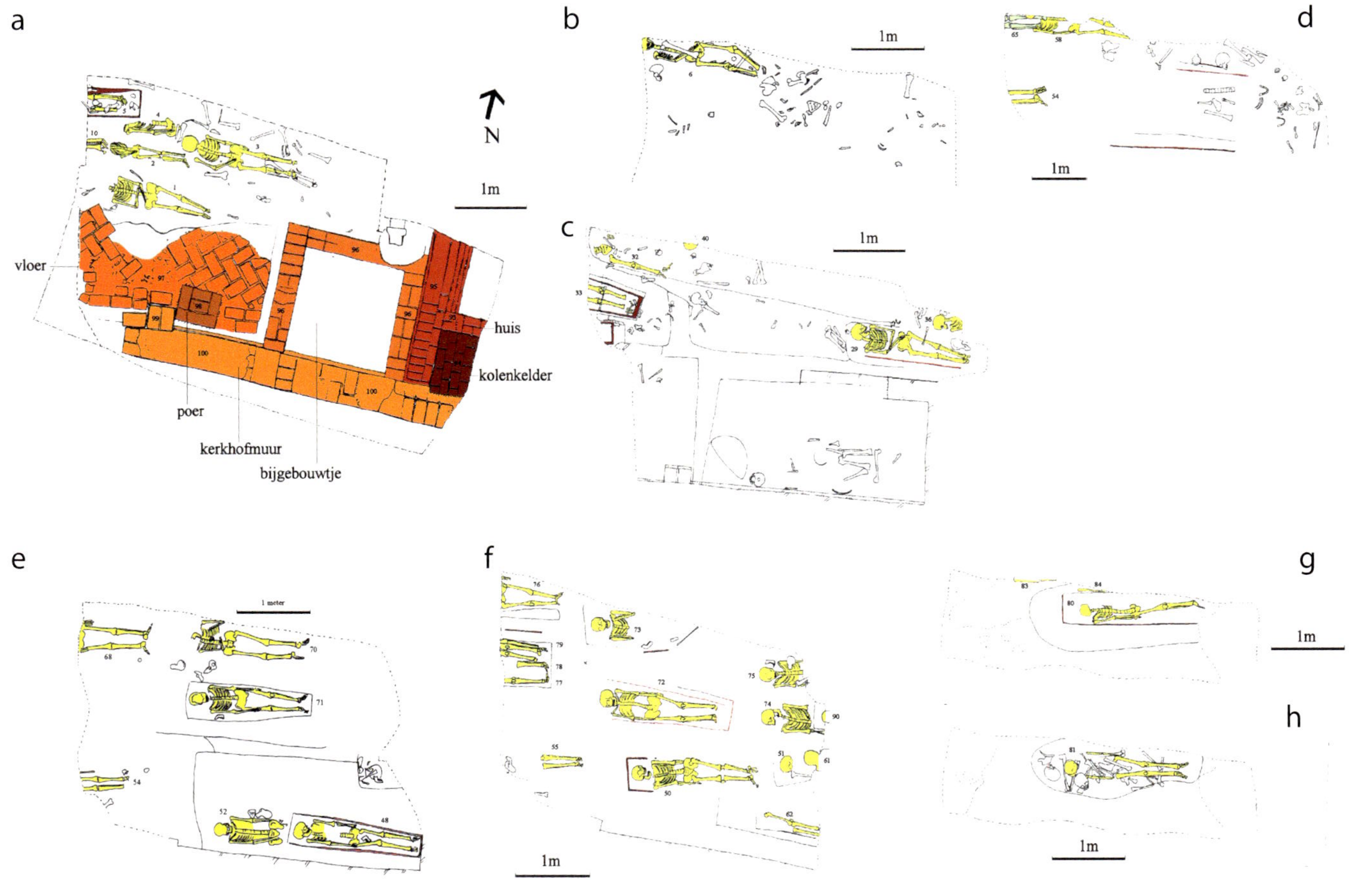

Fig. 4: Burials from the Broerenkerk
a) Excavation level 1, including feature numbers
b) Excavation levels 3-4, including feature numbers
c) Excavation levels 5-6, including feature numbers
d) Excavation levels 7-8, including feature numbers
e) Excavation level 9, including feature numbers
f) Excavation level 10, including feature numbers
g) Excavation level 11, including feature numbers
h) Excavation levels 12-13, including feature numbers

Methodology

The methods used in this project are a combination of the ones recommended by *Barge's Anthropologica*, Amsterdam Academic Medical Centre, and Leiden University's Laboratory for Human Osteoarchaeology, and are widely used.[14] Findings should include a discussion of preservation, completeness, body position, body orientation, gender, age at death, dental status, stature, pathology, and anomalies. Various projects have proven that detailing the variation in physical features is useful, for example, to compare rural and urban populations.[15] All the relevant results are stored in an Access database originally developed for physical anthropological purposes during a research project at the Church of St. Catharine in Eindhoven, the Netherlands.[16]

Physical anthropological analysis

Introduction

A total of 34 individuals underwent physical anthropological analysis. The completeness and preservation of the skeletons are shown in Table 1 and the Appendix. Multiple aspects influence the preservation of skeletons: the time since burial, the type of soil in which the burial took place, animal activity, and construction both past and present. The completeness and preservation of the skeletons varied among individuals as can be seen in Fig. 5. More than half (59%) of the skeletons were well-preserved. The bones were dense and hard, with no or little damaged bone material. Surprisingly, most of them (78%) originated in the earliest period (1300-1400). Possibly soil disturbances and fluctuations in the groundwater level affected the older burials, which were protected by the more recent ones above them, which were more exposed.

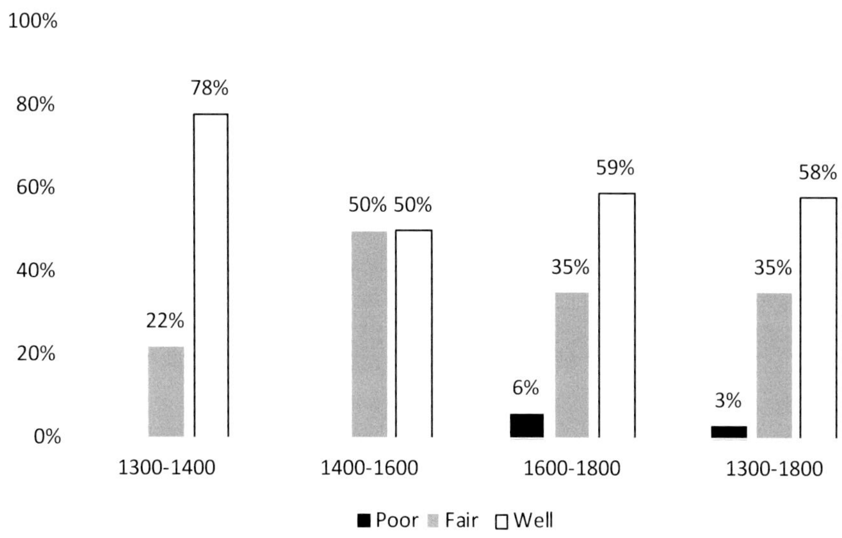

Fig. 5: Bone preservation by time period.

14 Maat, Van den Merwe & Hoff 2012; Water-Rist *et al.* 2016.
15 Brothwell 1994, 129; Baetsen 2008, 111-134; Schats 2017.
16 Baetsen & Weterings-Korthorst 2013.

	1300-1400	1400-1600	1600-1800	1300-1800
mostly complete	22%		18%	15%
incomplete with cranium & pelvis	22%	12%	6%	12%
incomplete with pelvis	0%	12%	34%	20%
incomplete with cranium	11%	38%	6%	15%
incomplete	11%	12%	18%	15%
mainly complete	22%	25%	18%	20%
cranium/mandibula	11%			3%

Table 1: Skeletal completeness by time period.

Almost half of the skeletons were mainly incomplete (20%) or incomplete with pelvis (20%). Out of the 34 individuals, only five (15%) had skeletal remains that were mostly complete. Again, most of the five (22%) were buried in the earliest period (1300-1400). Another interesting result was that a third of the skeletons from 1400-1600 were incomplete but with the cranium partially intact, and in the following period (1600-1800), a third were incomplete but with pelvic fragments. This could not be explained.

Demography of the Broederenkerk: estimation of sex and age

The estimation of sex was carried out by judging characteristic features of the pelvis and cranium. In all, 18 out of 31 adult individuals were examined in this way (see Appendix).

In some cases, additional metrical values helped if pelvic or cranial traits were not available or were indistinct (see Appendix).

The vertical diameters of proximal endings of humeri and femurs were used for the metrical determination of sex. Also, the maximum antero-posterior diameters of the femoral and tibial midshafts were measured. Using the dividing values calculated for this population and other references, the sex of another 12 individuals, in addition to the aforementioned 18 individuals, could be determined.[17]

In total there were 13 males (42%), 17 females (55%), and the sex of one adult (3%) could not be determined. Generally, the male-female ratio should not vary much from a one-to-one ratio.[18] While there were slightly more females in this grouping, the overall differences were small. Studies of other locations also show ratios varying between 40 and 60% (Table 2). In these studies, sometimes there were slightly more females, in other cases more men, but always the ratio was within the normal, natural proportions of that particular population at that time.[19]

Although the small size of our sample could have influenced our results, when we look at the ratios by period, large differences can be seen (Fig. 6). In the earliest period (1300-1400), 66% were women. In 1400-1600, this percentage

17 Clevis & Constandse-Westermann 1992, 70-72; Rijpma & Maat 2005, 6-7; Berk 2007, 35, Appendix 5; Baetsen 2008, 123; Jonge & Baetsen 2013, 218, 276.

18 Waldron 1994, 23; Chamberlain 2006, 97.

19 Maat, Mastwijk & Jonker 2002, 9.

Location	Source	Time Period	Male	Female	Indifferent
Susteren, Salvatorplein	Baetsen 1998, 9	800-1100	29%	64%	7%
Elst, Grote Kerk	Baetsen 2008, 122-123	1135-1525	53%	47%	
Deventer, Grote Kerkhof	Pijpelink 2008	1200-1650	82%	18%	
Oldenzaal, St. Plechelmusbasiliek	Kwakman 2010, 68-70	1200-1828	46%	54%	
Hellevoetsluis, Cisterciënzerabdij	Smits 1999	1250-1300	64%	36%	
Eindhoven, Catharinakerk	Baetsen & Weterings-Korthorst 2013, 162-164	1225-1350	54%	46%	
Delft, Oude en Nieuwe Gasthuis	Onisto, Maat & Bult 1998, 10, 26	1265-*c.* 1433	59%	37%	4%
Breda, Beijerd-Vlaszak	De Jonge & Baetsen 2013, 218-220	1294-1637	60%	40%	
Breda, Begijnenhof	Rijpma & Maat 2005, 26	1296-1535	8%	75%	17%
Delft, Oude en Nieuwe Gasthuis	Onisto, Maat & Bult 1998, 10, 27	*c.* 1433-1652	47%	53%	
Eindhoven, Catharinakerk	Baetsen & Weterings-Korthorst 2013, 162-164	1500-1650	57%	40%	3%
Elst, Grote Kerk	Baetsen 2008, 122-123	1525-1850	56%	44%	
Eindhoven, Catharinakerk	Baetsen & Weterings-Korthorst 2013, 162-164	1650-1850	58%	41%	2%
Alkmaar, Grote Kerk	Baetsen 2001, 27-29	1716-1830	45%	54%	1%
Zutphen, Nieuwstadskerk	Berk 2007, 34-35	1740-1826	50%	50%	
Zwolle, Broederenkerkhof (group A)	Clevis & Constandse-Westermann 1992, 70-71	1819-1828	43%	57%	
's-Hertogenbosch, Sint Janskerkhof	Maat, Mastwijk & Jonker 2002, 9-10	1830-1858	52%	48%	

Table 2: Sex ratio at other cemeteries.

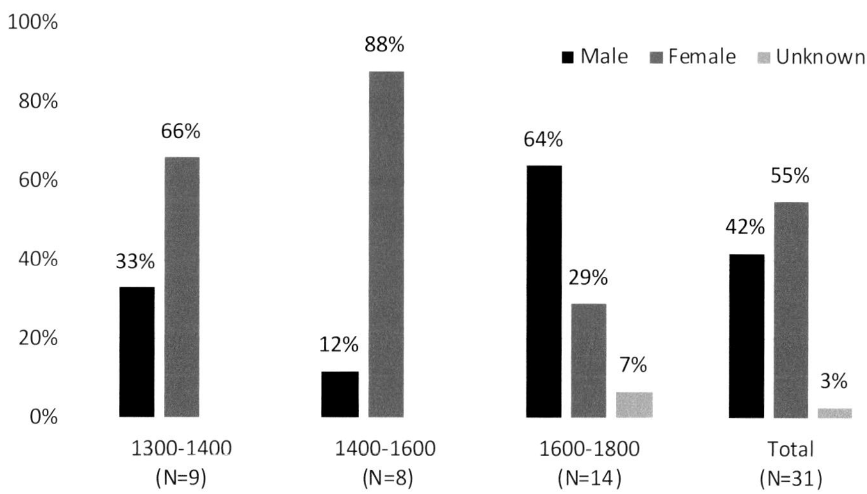

Fig. 6: Sex ratio by time period.

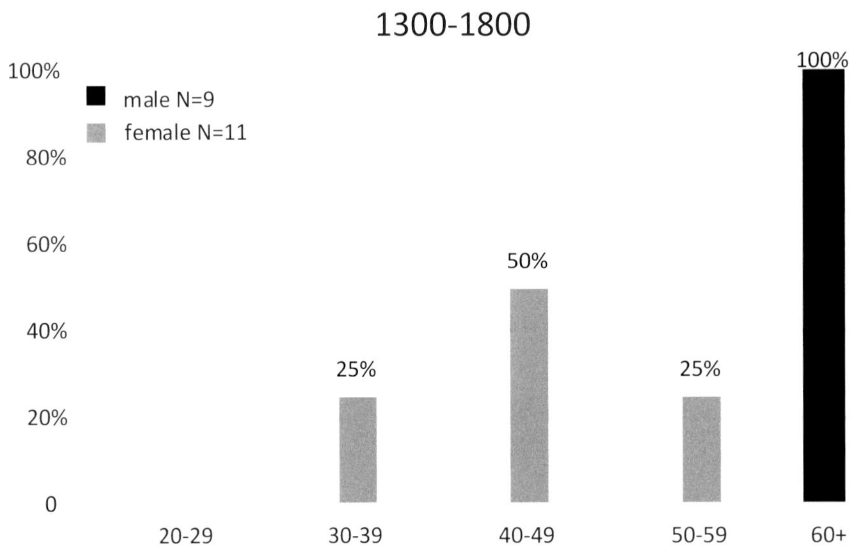

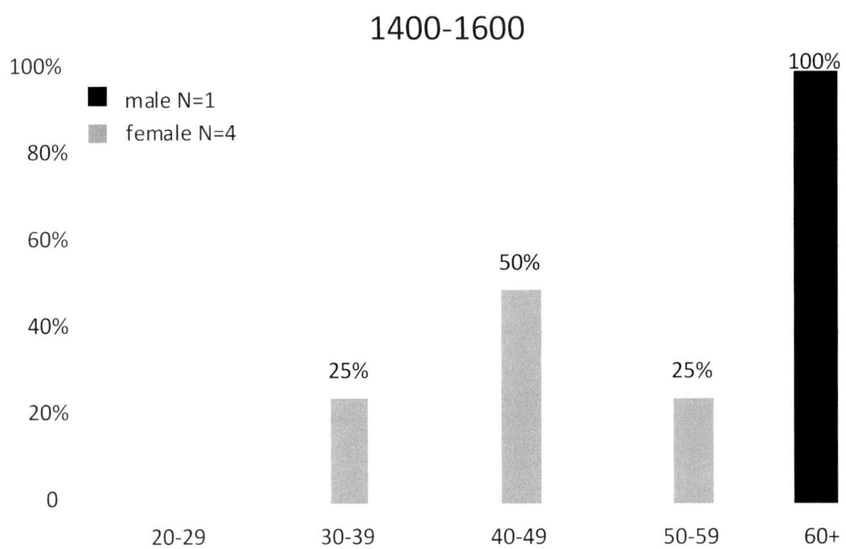

Fig. 7: (continued on opposite page) Age intervals by sex.
a) 1300-1800. Mean: 48.8; Mean male: 52.7; Mean female :45.5.
b) 1300-1400. Mean: 46.8; Mean male: 48.8; Mean female :46.8.
c) 1400-1600. Mean: 48.1; Mean male: 62; Mean female :44.6.
d) 1600-1800. Mean: 50.9; Mean male: 53.1; Mean female: 44.3.

increased to 88%. In the latest period (1600-1800), the ratio changed drastically when almost two thirds (64%) of the skeletons seem to be male. Relatively small differences in the ratio can be caused by such things as where in the cemetery the excavation took place, preservation of skeletons, and completeness of the bone material. A larger difference in the ratio could suggest a specific context of the burials, Breda and Susteren being cases in point where the majority of people buried were women (Table 2). In Breda the cemetery was used to bury beguines;

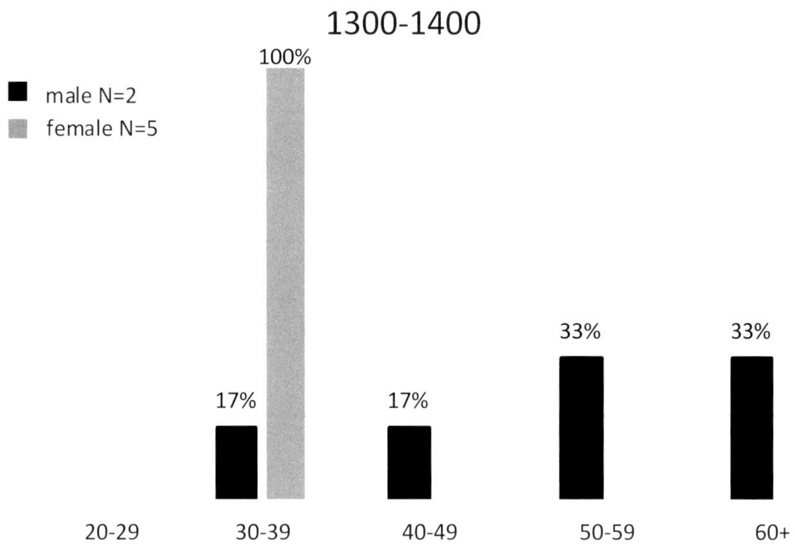

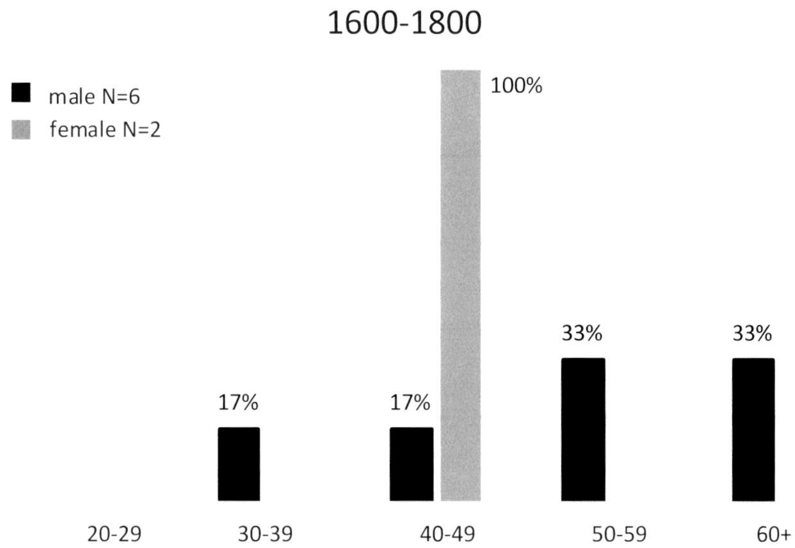

Fig. 7: (continued).

the few males buried appear to be confessors and workmen.[20] The cemetery in Susteren was reserved for the inhabitants of the nearby monastery, which mainly housed nuns.[21] Therefore, it is not surprising that a high number of females were buried in those cemeteries. The high percentage of males in 14th-century Delft can be explained as the result of the violent siege by the Duke of Holland in 1359 and the Hock and Cods wars.[22] It has been suggested that in early medieval Maastricht, different cemeteries had a complementary character, meaning that

20 Rijpma & Maat 2005, 7.
21 Baetsen 1998, 1-3.
22 Onisto, Maat & Bult 1998.

the men (or women) of a community could be buried at another cemetery (perhaps unknown to archaeologists) other than the one of the community itself.[23] However, it is not clear if there was a specific area reserved for males. In the late-medieval Dominican monastery in Zutphen, three-quarters of the area excavated consisted of female burials (N=13) and just one quarter were male burials (N=4). This high female-to-male ratio in the cemetery of the friars can be explained from historical sources. During this period, from approximately 1300 to 1600, it was possible for men and women who had become lay brothers or sisters, and their children, to be buried in the monastery's cemetery for a fee.[24] Considering the presence of the many women buried at the monastery, it seems that many opted for this.

Skeletal age at death

Only three individuals were non-adults, that is, under 20 years old. This results in a non-adult/adult ratio of 9:91%. Among the 31 adults, the specific age group of 10 could not be determined; there were just enough age characteristics available to determine that they were adults.

The three non-adults were all interred between 1600 and 1800. Two of them died at about age eight and one at about age sixteen. No foetuses, infants, or young children were buried in the cemetery, at least not in the excavated area. In a random sample of deceased in an average medieval population, one would expect this young and vulnerable group to be present at a high rate considering the general high incidence of infant deaths in the late medieval period.[25] Because the cemetery in Zutphen was part of a monastery until 1600, it is likely that infants and young children were buried elsewhere, perhaps in the parish church. For example, at the St. Jan cemetery in 's-Hertogenbosch, a cluster of child burials was discovered, comprising 30% of the total burials.[26] This is more in line with what would be expected given the 25-50% rate of child mortality in pre-industrial societies.[27] At Tilburg, for instance, at the beginning of the 19th century, the non-adult mortality rate was 50%, based on written, historical sources.[28] For the same time period at Spitalfields in London, mortality rates were between 45% and 58% according to historical records.[29] However, a strong under-representation of non-adults in most archaeological samples of burials in graveyards, not only from medieval times, has been noted in several publications.[30]

Of the 31 adults in the group, 20 could be classified by sex and age group (Fig. 7). The mean age at death for all adults in the period between 1300 and 1800 was 48.8 years with an average of 52.7 for men (N=9) and 45.5 for women

23 Panhuysen 2005, 270-271.
24 Fermin & Groothedde 2006, 13-14; Fermin & Kastelein 2012, 13-14.
25 Brothwell 1994; Chamberlain 2006, 64-92.
26 Maat, Mastwijk & Jonker 2002, 6, 10-11.
27 Waldron 1994, 18.
28 Heyden 1995, 71-72; Berk 2007, 24-25.
29 Molleson & Cox 1993, 208-209.
30 Clevis & Constandse-Westermann 1992, 73; Molleson & Cox 1993, 209; Baetsen 2001, 29-30; Berk 2007, 37; Baetsen 2008, 132; Baetsen & Weterings-Korthorst 2013, 164-169.

Location	Source	Time Period	Mean overall	Mean male	Mean female	N
Elst, Grote Kerk	Baetsen 2008, 123-124, 132-133	694-1135	50	56	43	9
Elst, Grote Kerk	Baetsen 2008, 123-124, 132-133	1135-1525	58	60	55	22
Oldenzaal, St. Plechelmusbasiliek	Kwakman 2010, 32-37	1200-1828	54.8	53.9	56.1	29
Delft, Oude en Nieuwe Gasthuis	Onisto, Maat & Bulten 1998, 26	1265-*c.* 1433	45	43	47	41
Dordrecht, Minderbroederklooster	Maat, Mastwijk & Sarfatij 1996, 41	1275-1572	44.1	45	43.3	199
Breda, Beijerd-Vlaszak	De Jonge & Baetsen 2013, 220-225	1294-1637	40.1	40.9	40	246
Breda, Begijnenhof	Rijpma & Maat 2005, 7-8, 26	1296-1535	43.2	43.1	43.0	89
Eindhoven, Catharinakerk	Baetsen & Weterings-Korthorst 2013, 164-169	1350-1500	51.9	50.7	54.8	13
Delft, Oude en Nieuwe Gasthuis	Onisto, Maat & Bulten 1998, 27	*c.* 1433-1652	46	43	49	41
Gorinchem, Minderbroederklooster	Maat & Mastwijk 2000, 144	1455-1527	52.1	53.3	50.6	21
Eindhoven, Catharinakerk	Baetsen & Weterings-Korthorst 2013, 164-169	1500-1650	50.1	54.1	41.3	25
Elst, Grote Kerk	Baetsen 2008, 123-124, 132-133	1525-1850	43	47	38	121
Eindhoven, Catharinakerk	Baetsen & Weterings-Korthorst 2013, 164-169	1650-1850	50.6	49.6	51.2	51
London, Christ Church Spitalfields	Molleson & Cox 1993, 208-209	1700-1850	-	60.5	60.8	166
Alkmaar, Grote Kerk	Baetsen 2001, 29-33	1716-1830	-	60	55	188
Zwolle, Broerenkerk (group A)	Clevis & Constandse-Westermann 1992, 74	1819-1828	50	-	-	69
Zutphen, Nieuwstadskerk	Berk 2007, 36-40	1740-1826	47.7	46.2	48.7	25
's-Hertogenbosch, Sint Janskerkhof	Maat, Mastwijk & Jonker 2002, 10, Table 3	1830-1858	42.2	43.4	41.4	161

Table 3: Mean adult skeletal age at death by location and time period.

(N=11). None of the adults were between the ages of 20 and 30 when they died, and no woman reached an age older than 60.

Age groups were also separated by time period (Fig. 7). The average age at death between the different time periods varied from 47 (1300-1400) to 51 (1600-1800). In the period between 1300 and 1400, the mean age at death was the same for men and women (47). Remarkably, in the subsequent time periods, the mean skeletal age at death for men increased by six years to 53 (1400-1600) and 16 years to 62 (1600-1800), while the average for females remained around 44 years.

Considering the different age intervals, most women died between 40 and 49, while the men were more evenly distributed over the different age categories. The extreme high rate of 100% in some categories was caused by the low number of individuals present in the study: one man in the period 1400-1600 and two women in the next period.

The overall mean skeletal age at death for the period 1300-1800 was 48.8 years at the Zutphen cemetery. This is within the ranges found at other cemeteries (Table 3).

Compared with the inhabitants of Zutphen buried in the Nieuwstadskerk in the 18th and early 19th centuries, men buried at the Broederenkerkhof seemed to be better off than women. This is in contrast to the general higher life expectancy of women. Other studies shown in Table 6 suggest that a mean age of about 60 years was possible for males in, for example, rural, medieval Elst and prosperous urban, post-medieval Alkmaar and Spitalfields. Yet the mean skeletal age at death of a group, or even the comparison between groups, appears to be deceptive and should be contested.[31]

Stature

During fieldwork it became obvious that the majority of the skeletons were not completely articulated. Much post-depositional activity, including bioturbation, is responsible for disarticulation of joints. Therefore, measuring stature in situ was unreliable and at times impossible because most of the skeletons were missing feet or skull.

For 24 adult individuals, it was possible to calculate their mean stature based on long bone length during the physical anthropological analysis (see Appendix) The results, by time period and sex, are shown in Table 4.

Overall, the average stature of the 14 women was 162.3 cm. The mean stature for the 10 men was 175.2 cm according to the Trotter method and 172.0 cm according to Breitinger. A difference of 10 to 13 cm between men and women is within the expected range.[32] An interesting observation is that the stature of men increased over the course of time while that of women decreased. The average stature of women decreased from 164.2 cm in 1300-1400, to 161.5 cm in 1400-1600, to 159.6 cm in 1600-1800. For males the average stature increased from 168.8 cm in 1300-1400, to 176.7 cm in 1600-1800 according to the Trotter method. In the earlier time period, the difference between men and women was only four cm, but in the most recent one it reached a remarkable 17 cm. Multiple studies consider stature as one of the more reliable indicators of general health and therefore socioeconomic and hygienic circumstances.[33] The trends in stature change would imply that life worsened for women and improved for men in Zutphen between 1300 and 1800.

The mean statures of men and women in Zutphen were also compared to the averages at other graveyards (Table 5). A clear pattern or significant trend is difficult to identify in these values. For women the averages varied from

---

31 Often averages are not calculated in the same way or even described. Some studies use the averages of the different age categories rather than the age calculated by person. In addition, sometimes the average age is not designated by gender, which makes a comparison more difficult. Most important, extreme ages in populations can range tremendously while the average ages appear to be more or less the same. Therefore, the calculation of mean skeletal age at death is of variable importance for comparison of demographic characteristics.

32 Oppers 1966; Wieringen 1986.

33 Oppers 1966; Maat 1984; Wieringen 1986; Frederiks *et al.* 2000; De Beer 2001.

Period		Stature A[1]	Stature B[2]	Femoral length
1300-1800	Male mean	175.2 (10)	172.0 (10)	46.6 (5)
	Female mean	162.3 (14)		43.1 (7)
1300-1400	Male mean	168.8 (2)	168.1 (2)	46.9 (1)
	Female mean	164.2 (6)		42.0 (1)
1400-1600	Male mean			
	Female mean	161.5 (5)		43.8 (3)
1600-1800	Male mean	176.7 (8)	172.9 (8)	46.6 (4)
	Female mean	159.6 (3)		42.9 (3)

Table 4: Mean stature and femoral length (cm) by time period and sex. Total number of individuals given in brackets.
[1] Trotter & Gleser 1958; Trotter 1970;
[2] Breitinger 1937.

Site	Source	Time Period	Male A[1]	Male B[2]	Female[3]
Maastricht, Bosschstraat	Panhuysen 2005, 238	600-725	170.5	169.1	160.5
Elst, Grote Kerk	Baetsen 2008, 123, 125	694-1135		171.5	161.1
Maastricht, Sint Servaaskerk	Panhuysen 2005, 253	*c.* 700-950	177.1	174.2	161.5
Susteren, Abdijklooster	Baetsen 1998	800-1100	174.4	172.5	162.9
Maastricht, Stiftskapel Sint Servaas	Janssen & Maat 1998, 14-15, 28-29	1070-1521	177.6	173.9	
Elst, Grote Kerk	Baetsen 2008, 123, 125	1135-1525		173.8	165.0
Oldenzaal, St. Plechelmusbasiliek	Kwakman 2010, 40-41	1200-1828	170.7	170.0	160.8
Elst, Grote Kerk	Baetsen 2008, 123, 125	1525-1850	175.5	173.1	162.4
Eindhoven, Catharinakerk	Baetsen & Weterings-Korthorst 2013, 169-173	1225-1350	173.87	172.3	160.9
Delft, Oude en Nieuwe Gasthuis	Onisto, Maat & Bult 1998, 10-11, 26	1265-*c.* 1433	171.8	170.5	164.4
Dordrecht, Minderbroederklooster	Maat & Mastwijk 1998, 15-16, 41	1275-1572	172.5	170.6	160.8
Breda, Beijerd-Vlaszak	De Jonge & Baetsen 2013, 225-229	1294-1637	170.4	169.4	160.4
Breda, Begijnenhof	Rijpma & Maat 2005, 8, 26	1296-1535	165.2		159.9
Eindhoven, Catharinakerk	Baetsen & Weterings-Korthorst 2013, 169-173	1350-1500	172.8	171.3	160.7
Delft, Oude en Nieuwe Gasthuis	Onisto, Maat & Bult 1998, 10-11, 27	*c.* 1433-1652	170.8	168.9	162.2
Eindhoven, Catharinakerk	Baetsen & Weterings-Korthorst 2013, 169-173	1500-1650	174.4	171.9	159.9
Eindhoven, Catharinakerk	Baetsen & Weterings-Korthorst 2013, 169-173	1650-1850	172.6	170.4	160.9
Alkmaar, Grote Kerk	Baetsen 2001, 35-38	1716-1830	170.6	170.0	159.9
Zutphen, Nieuwstadskerk	Berk 2007, 40-42	1740-1826	173.2		161.4
Zwolle, Broerenkerk (group A)	Clevis & Constandse-Westermann 1992, 78-81	1819-1828	172.9		164.1
's-Hertogenbosch, Sint Janskerkhof	Maat, Mastwijk & Jonker 2002, 11-13, Table 3	1830-1858		169.6	160.5

Table 5: Mean stature (cm) by cemetery and time period.[1] Trotter 1970; [2] Breitinger 1937; [3] Trotter & Gleser 1958.

Project/Site	Source	Date	Male	Female
Maastricht, Bosschstraat	Panhuysen 2005, 164-165	600-725	45.9	42.9
Elst, Grote Kerk	Baetsen 2008, 123	694-1135	46.3	43.8
Maastricht, Sint Servaaskerk	Panhuysen 2005, 164-165	*c.* 700-950	48.9	42.4
Elst, Grote Kerk	Baetsen 2008, 123	1135-1525	48.1	44.5
Oldenzaal, St. Plechelmusbasiliek	Kwakman 2010, 42, 78-79	1200-1828	46.3	43.2
Elst, Grote Kerk	Baetsen 2008, 123	1525-1850	48.2	43.6
Eindhoven, Catharinakerk	Baetsen & Korthorst 2013, 169-173	1225-1350	47.2	45.0
Delft, Oude en Nieuwe Gasthuis	Onisto, Maat & Bult 1998, 11, 26	1265-*c.* 1433	46.0	44.2
Dordrecht, Minderbroederklooster	Maat & Mastwijk 1998, 41	1275-1572	46.2	42.6
Breda, Beijerd-Vlaszak	De Jonge & Baetsen 2013, 228-229	1294-1637	45.7	43.3
Eindhoven, Catharinakerk	Baetsen & Korthorst 2013, 169-173	1350-1500	46.7	43.2
Delft, Oude en Nieuwe Gasthuis	Onisto, Maat & Bult 1998, 10-11, 27	*c.* 1433-1652	45.5	43.3
Eindhoven, Catharinakerk	Baetsen & Korthorst 2013, 169-173	1500-1650	47.3	41.2
Eindhoven, Catharinakerk	Baetsen & Korthorst 2013, 169-173	1650-1850	46.9	43.3
's-Hertogenbosch, Sint Janskerkhof	Maat, Mastwijk & Jonker 2002, 11-13, Table 3	1830-1858	45.7	42.8

Table 6: Mean maximal femoral length (cm) by sex and location.

approximately 160 to 165 cm. It seems, therefore, that the women in Zutphen were better off than their contemporaries between 1300-1400 but reached a comparable, common mean stature level between 1600-1800. A reverse development is seen for men. Compared to their male contemporaries, women's socioeconomic circumstances in Zutphen appear to have improved in 1600-1800. But, as with mean ages, any comparison of different studies should be done with caution. The changes in mean stature of both men and women could have been influenced by the low number of individuals in this study.

Given that the stature of an individual is calculated using the length of the different long bones available, errors can occur. Therefore, comparisons of the mean maximal femoral length may be more representative.[34] For individuals from Zutphen, these lengths were measured and are presented by sex and time period in Table 6 and the Appendix. The mean maximal femoral length for men was 46.6 cm and for women, 43.1 cm. With results of 46.9 and 46.6 cm, there is hardly any difference between men of different time periods. But again, only a few individuals were part of the sample, one in 1300-1400 and none in the following time period. Although sample size is an issue, the femoral lengths of the men appear to be shorter than those measured in other studies (Table 6).

The same can be said for the female mean maximal femoral length, although in 1400-1600 the mean length was a little greater. However, this average is based on only three individuals, therefore, its value may not be representative. In all, mean femoral maximum length displays a less extreme difference in development compared with mean stature for males and females in the various time periods.

34 Maat, Mastwijk & Jonker 2002, 12.

	1300-1800	1300-1400	1400-1600	1600-1800
Erupted	82.8%	93.1%	96.1%	47.9%
Inspected	80.2%	87.9%	74.8%	69%
Antemortem loss	7.9%	3.4%	11.4%	13%
Postmortem loss	11,9%	8.7%	13.8%	17.4%
Tooth decay/cariës	10.2%	7.6%	10.9%	18.8%
Abscess	58.3%	40%	100%	33.3%
Alveolar resorption	83.3%	100%	75%	66.7%
Tartar (calculus)	66.7%	80%	50%	66.7%
Periodontal disease	8.3%	-	25%	-

Table 7: Dental eruptions in percentages by period.

Dental status

The dental status could be inspected for twelve adult individuals (see Appendix). There were a total of 318 dental eruptions, which is 83% of what would be expected.[35] From all the erupted elements, 255 (80%) could be analysed. In addition, 25 elements were lost antemortem (8%) and 38 (13%) postmortem. No additional elements were noted, but with three individuals, a total of five elements appeared to be missing congenitally.

It is interesting to note that in 1600-1800 less than 70% of all erupted teeth could be inspected as a result of higher percentages for ante- and postmortem tooth loss. Compared to the antemortem tooth loss rates at other cemeteries, the 8% in Zutphen is low (Table 8).

High percentages were found in Alkmaar, Eindhoven, and Zutphen (Nieuwstadskerk).[36] An explanation for this is the presence of many individuals who passed away at a relatively old age (60+) in those collections. A high antemortem tooth loss rate is very common in the older age categories, as was confirmed by the extensive dental study of individuals from the Broerenkerk in Zwolle.[37]

The presence of tooth decay, or cariës, seems high, affecting 10 (83%) out of 12 individuals. If calculated by dental elements, however, only 26 (10%) teeth out of 255 were decayed. This is slightly lower, but similar, to the rates calculated for other cemeteries (Table 9).

Considered by period, a relatively high percentage of tooth decay (18,8%) was found for Zutphen in 1600-1800. Caution is in order because only three individuals represented this 200-year time period. Another distorting effect to consider is the impossibility of determining decay in teeth lost ante- or postmortem.[38] However, the overall cariës rates in Alkmaar and Zutphen were distinctly lower than in Eindhoven and 's-Hertogenbosch. The study in Eindhoven suggests a fatal combination of poor hygienic standards and a more starchy diet as an explanation for higher tooth decay percentages in these southern cities in the Netherlands.[39]

35 12 individuals x 32 dental elements = 384 elements.
36 Baetsen 2001, 40-41; Baetsen & Weterings-Korthorst 2013, 172-175; Berk 2007, 43-47.
37 Over 44% in the group of 65+. Clevis & Constandse-Westermann 1992, 131-133.
38 Clevis & Constandse-Westermann 1992, 107-108.
39 Baetsen & Weterings-Korthorst 2013, 173.

Site	Source	Time Period	AM Loss
Maastricht, Stiftskapel Sint Servaaskerk	Janssen & Maat 1998, 15, Table 7	1070-1521	6.4%
Deventer, Grote Kerkhof	Pijpelink 2008	1200-1650	7.5%
Oldenzaal, St. Plechelmusbasiliek	Kwakman 2010, 42-46	1200-1828	7.9%
Eindhoven, Catharinakerk	Baetsen & Weterings-Korthorst 2013, 174	1225-1350	17.9%
Delft, Oude en Nieuwe Gasthuis	Onisto, Maat & Bulten 1998, 11, Table 9	1265-*c.* 1433	13.4%
Dordrecht, Minderbroederklooster	Maat, Mastwijk & Sarfatij 1996, 23-24, Table 11	1275-1572	8.1%
Breda, Beijerd-Vlaszak	De Jonge & Baetsen 2013, 231-232	1294-1637	12.2%
Breda, Begijnenhof	Rijpma & Maat 2005, 7-8, 26	1296-1535	15.5%
Eindhoven, Catharinakerk	Baetsen & Weterings-Korthorst 2013, 174	1350-1500	20.6%
Delft, Oude en Nieuwe Gasthuis	Onisto, Maat & Bulten 1998, 11, Table 9	*c.* 1433-1652	16.4%
Eindhoven, Catharinakerk	Baetsen & Weterings-Korthorst 2013, 174	1500-1650	31.9%
Eindhoven, Catharinakerk	Baetsen & Weterings-Korthorst 2013, 174	1650-1850	31.3%
Alkmaar, Grote Kerk	Baetsen 2001, 40-43	1716-1830	44.2%
Zutphen, Nieuwstadskerk	Berk 2007, 43-47	1740-1826	29%
's-Hertogenbosch, Sint Janskerkhof	Maat, Mastwijk & Jonker 2002, 13-14, Table 5	1830-1858	12.8%

Table 8: Overall percentages of antemortem tooth loss by cemetery and time period.

Location	Source	Time Period	Tooth Decay
Maastricht, Stiftskapel Sint Servaas	Janssen & Maat 1998, 15, Table 7	1070-1521	17%
Deventer, Grote Kerkhof	Pijpelink 2008	1200-1650	5%
Oldenzaal, St. Plechelmusbasiliek	Kwakman 2010, 42-46	1200-1828	12.8%
Eindhoven, Catharinakerk	Baetsen & Weterings-Korthorst 2013, 172-178	1225-1350	16%
Delft, Oude en Nieuwe Gasthuis	Onisto, Maat & Bulten 1998, 11, Table 9	1265-*c.* 1433	7.6%
Dordrecht, Minderbroederklooster	Maat, Mastwijk & Sarfatij 1996, 23-24, Table 11	1275-1572	11.8%
Breda, Beijerd-Vlaszak	De Jonge & Baetsen 2013, 233-234	1294-1637	11.4%
Breda, Begijnenhof	Rijpma & Maat 2005, 7-8, 26	1296-1535	10.4%
Eindhoven, Catharinakerk	Baetsen & Weterings-Korthorst 2013, 172-178	1350-1500	20%
Delft, Oude en Nieuwe Gasthuis	Onisto, Maat & Bulten 1998, 11, Table 9	*c.* 1433-1652	12.3%
Eindhoven, Catharinakerk	Baetsen & Weterings-Korthorst 2013, 172-178	1500-1650	24%
Eindhoven, Catharinakerk	Baetsen & Weterings-Korthorst 2013, 172-178	1650-1850	21%
Alkmaar, Grote Kerk	Baetsen 2001, 44-45	1716-1830	12.2%
Zutphen, Nieuwstadskerk	Berk 2007, 43-47	1740-1826	14%
's-Hertogenbosch, Sint Janskerkhof	Maat, Mastwijk & Jonker 2002, 13-14, Table 5	1830-1858	20.7%

Table 9: Overall percentages of tooth decay by cemetery and time period.

Pathology

Several diseases were present among the individuals from Zutphen (see Appendix). Health and sex-related diseases were not linked to specific healthier time periods. The sample size, however, was very small in each period. Especially in the earliest two time periods, there were only a few individuals whose skeletons were complete enough to be studied in this respect. For this reason, a direct pathological comparison between the different time periods is not appropriate.

The various pathological conditions were classified in five main categories and are presented in Table 10.These categories are based on probable causes and often used in physical anthropological studies.[40] In addition, the table includes pathological conditions that were specifically looked for but for which evidence was absent in this collection.

Trauma

In Zutphen, healed fractures were seen in three men and one woman: ribs (2), vertebral arc (1), and metacarpal of the left little finger (1). In the last case, the women 37-49 years old, a skull fracture was also present; a rectangular-shaped opening about 2 cm wide running along the sagittal suture of the right parietal bone is visible. There appears to be no evidence of healing of the bone and the roof of the skull is fully perforated. Therefore, this wound was most likely the result of a blow from a pointed object resulting in instant death.[41] This is a remarkable find because generally these violent trauma wounds are seen in men.[42]

Compared to other populations, the fracture locations and rates are similar. In the early Middle Ages the thorax, clavicle, and wrist were most commonly fractured.[43] In the 18th and 19th centuries, in Zutphen, nearby Zwolle, Elst, and locations more distant, the fibula, tibia, and vertebral bodies also displayed healed trauma.[44]

A 36-45-year-old woman, buried between 1300 and 1400, showed a loose arc at the fifth lumbar vertebra. This condition is known as spondylolysis, a stress fracture of the pars interarticularis, the thin portion of the vertebra that connects the upper and lower facet joints. This is generally caused by repeated strenuous activity or movement, but environmental factors and genetics can also contribute to this condition.[45] Rates commonly vary between 1 and 10% and in rare cases can be as high as 30-50%.[46]

An interesting find is that four out of 31 adult individuals showed bone changes defined as osteochondritis dissecans. Today this trauma is more often found in young adult males, particularly in the knee joint.[47] The lesion is characterised by a round or oval shaped depression in the joint surface in which the underlying

---

40 Maat, Van den Merwe & Hoff 2012.

41 Fermin & Groothedde 2006, 16.

42 Panhuysen 2005, 183-186; Baetsen 2014, 313-315.

43 Baetsen 1998, 11-12; Panhuysen 2005, 178-181; Groen & Ridder 2007, 44.

44 See, for example, Clevis & Constandse-Westermann 1992, 88-89; Molleson & Cox 1993, 82-83; Baetsen 2001, 51; Brickley *et al.* 2006, 119-122; Bellen & Vandenbruaene 2006, 224-230; Berk 2007, 52-54; Baetsen 2008, 126.

45 Waldron 2009, 151.

46 Roberts & Manchester 2005, 106-107.

47 Roberts & Manchester 2005, 121, Aufderheide & Rodríguez-Martin 1998, 81; Ortner 2003, 351-352.

Category	N individuals*	Percentage
Traumata		
Skull	1 (12)	8.3%
Fractures (healed)	4 (31)	12.9%
Vertebral (third lumbar facet)	1 (10)	10%
Rib	2 (12)	16.7%
Finger (fifth left metacarpal)	1 (9)	11.1%
Spondylolysis (fifth lumbar)	1 (12)	8.3%
Osteochondritis dissecans	4 (31)	12.9
Infections		
Osteomyelitis	0 (31)	
Periostitis (hematogenic/traumatically)	4 (31)	12.9%
Gout	1 (31)	3.2%
Deficiencies		
Rickets (tibia/fibula)	0 (15)	
Cribra orbitalia	0 (13)	
Anaemia (sternal)	0 (8)	
Degenerative		
Vertebral disc	9 (13)	69.2%
Cervical vertebra	3 (9)	33.3%
Thoracic vertebra 1-6	3 (13)	23.1%
Thoracic vertebra 7-12	4 (13)	30.8%
Lumbar vertebra	4 (11)	36.4%
Facet joint vertebra	2 (13)	15.4%
Peripheral joint degeneration overall	7 (31)	22.6%
Dens apex	1 (9)	11.1%
Skull/lower jaw	1 (8)	12.5%
Wrist	1 (9)	11.1%
Hip	2 (16)	12.5%
Knee	2 (15)	13.3%
Feet	1 (9)	11.1%
Miscellaneous		
DISH	0 (13)	
Multiple enthesopathies	7 (31)	22.6%
Scoliosis	0 (13)	
Tumours	0 (31)	
Endocranial depressions	1 (12)	8.3%

Table 10: Pathological bone changes by categories of probable cause.
**Total number of bones exhibiting trauma in brackets.*

spongy bone has become visible. Generally it is caused by the separation of a small bone fragment (osteonecrosis) in the joint as a result of local loss or diminished supply of blood, which is most likely the result of repeated trauma or stress, but genetics can contribute to this as well.[48] Among the individuals buried at

48 Aufderheide & Rodríguez-Martín 1998, 81; Ortner 2003, 351-352; Roberts & Manchester 2005, 121; Mann & Hunt 2005, 158-159; Waldron 2009, 153.

the Broederenkerkhof, the condition was present in both males and females and appeared twice in knee joints, once in an ankle, and once in a foot.

Infections

Another pathological category is bone damage due to infections. It is important, however, to realize that most infections mainly affect soft tissue and only in advanced stages cause bone damage.[49] Two non-specific changes, periostitis and osteomyelitis, are distinctive. Osteomyelitis affects the bone marrow and is often accompanied by periostitis. In the latter, the bone reacts to an infection or irritation by trauma of the periosteum that envelopes the bone.[50] Sometimes these changes indicate diseases such as tuberculosis or syphilis, but often a definitive cause is difficult to ascertain.[51] In osteomyelitis, bacteria enters the medullary cavity through infection or trauma.[52] If the infection is prolonged, bone tissue will respond to the infection by creating irregular new bone, and characteristic openings in the bone are formed to drain pus,[53] which can lead to skin ulcers.[54] In Zutphen, however, no deformations could be linked to osteomyelitis. Bone reaction caused by periostitis was present in one non-adult and four (13%) adults, two men and two women. Their ages varied from 20+ to 50-70 years. All affected individuals were dated 1600-1800, which suggests that infection rates were higher in the post-medieval period, possibly because of worsened hygienic circumstances. The skeletal parts affected were all lower limb bones. Femora and fibulae were affected twice, and in three cases the tibia was involved. Often periostitis is found on tibia and fibula because they are situated just below the skin and therefore more susceptible to irritation and trauma.[55]

The percentage of individuals with periostitis in Zutphen was slightly higher than commonly found. In studies of cemeteries in Breda, Eindhoven, Alkmaar, Delft, and Dordrecht, rates of periostitis were well below 10%.[56] Surprisingly, no periostitis was found in Elst and 's-Hertogenbosch, but high percentages (21-29%) were present in Oldenzaal and Zutphen (Nieuwstadskerk).[57] While there can be differences in how the pathological condition is recorded, an explanation for these varying percentages can be attributed to differences in living circumstances or the socioeconomic status of the populations under study.[58]

A 54-59-year-old man buried in the period 1600-1800 demonstrated bone damage in several joints that was caused by gout. Affected joints were the shoulder, carpal, and phalanges. Multiple characteristic, defective round openings were identified in the left and right tarsal, and metatarsal bones but had been formed asymmetrically. This

49 Waldron 2009, 84.
50 Ortner 2003, 208.
51 Brothwell 1981, 128-129.
52 Roberts & Manchester 2005, 168-169; Aufderheide & Rodríguez-Martín 1998, 172.
53 Roberts & Manchester 2005, 168-172; Ortner 2003, 199; Waldron 2009, 84-85.
54 Aufderheide & Rodríguez-Martín 1998, 172.
55 Aufderheide & Rodríguez-Martín, 1998, 179.
56 De Jonge & Baetsen 2013; Baetsen & Weterings-Korthorst 2013; Baetsen 2001, 54-55; Onisto, Maat & Bult 1998, 40-41; Maat, Mastwijk & Sarfatij 1998, 16.
57 Baetsen 2008, 133; Janssen & Maat 1998, 16, 31; Kwakman 2010, 91-93; Berk 2007, 55.
58 Clevis & Constandse-Westermann 1992, 89.

condition is usually the result of metabolic problems (uric acid) which lead to painful ulcers in joints especially of hands, wrists, ankles, and feet.[59] Inflammation and damage of joint cartilage and bone tissue can be some of the consequences. Males are thought to be more susceptible than females, particularly if they are 50+ years.[60] Although the disease has a long history and is not uncommon, its characteristic bone damage is not often seen in archaeological human skeletal remains. This may be due to the relatively low presence or even absence of individuals 50+ years old in some samples. More likely, however, is that very often the small bones of the wrists, hands, ankles, and feet, where the bone deformations can be seen, are missing from skeletons.

Deficiencies

Remarkably, no bone damage in Zutphen was noticed that could be attributed to deficiency diseases like rickets and anaemia. These diseases are often the result of an insufficient or an unbalanced diet depending on, for example, the use of only basic agriculture technology, limited knowledge of food processing, and scarce fertile land and natural resources. Political, economic, and social structures of a population also influence the prevalence of these diseases.[61]

Deficiency diseases are regularly reported in physical anthropological studies.[62] However, anaemia was not found among the rural populations of Elst and no bending of long bones, indicating rickets, was present in Zutphen (Nieuwstadskerk).[63] It is possible that individuals showing evidence of deficiency diseases were absent in the sample coincidentally, but it seems that the individuals buried at the Broederenkerk in Zutphen did not lack adequate vitamins.

Degenerative bone changes

Degenerative bone changes are known as arthropathies, a classification of joint diseases, which is used to describe degeneration of joint structures, which generally starts in the soft tissue of the joint. In archaeology, this becomes visible when bone is affected by such degeneration. The criteria used to describe these reactions are derived from several widely used publications.[64] Depending on appearance and location, the changes are divided into three categories: degeneration of the vertebral disc, degeneration of the vertebral facet joints, and peripheral joint degeneration. The latter are both referred to as osteoarthritis.[65] The changes involved are, for example, bony outgrowths known as osteophytes, pitting, and eburnation.

The prevalence of degenerative bone changes are presented in table 10 and the Appendix. For 13 out of the 31 adult individuals, sufficient bone material of the spine was present to record if degenerative changes were present. Overall, nine

---

59 Roberts & Manchester 2005, 157, 161-163; Waldron 2009, 67-70.

60 Aufderheide & Rodríguez-Martín 1998, 108; Roberts & Manchester 2005, 161-163; Waldron 2009, 67-70.

61 Molleson & Cox 1993, 37; Berk 2007, 17-27.

62 See, for example, De Jonge & Baetsen 2013; Baetsen & Weterings-Korthorst 2013; Onisto, Maat & Bult 1998; Maat, Mastwijk & Sarfatij 1998, 42; Maat, Mastwijk & Jonker 2002, 15-16, Table 6; Berk 2007.

63 Baetsen 2008, 128; Kwakman 2010, 54; Berk 2007, 56-57.

64 Rogers & Waldron 1995; Maat, Mastwijk & Van der Velde 1995, 289-298; Waldron 2009, 24-70.

65 Rogers & Waldron 1995, 20-45.

(69%) individuals showed degenerative vertebral disc disease, two (15%) showed degeneration of vertebral facet joints, and seven (23%) of peripheral joints. Both men and women were affected, and the joint diseases were present in all three time periods. To investigate the prevalence of degenerative changes in more detail, the specific joints and parts of the spine were studied separately. The spine was divided into four sections: cervical (neck), lumbar, upper thoracic (TH1-6), and lower thoracic (TH7-12). As a result of this division, rates changed: degenerative disc disease in the lumbar vertebrae scored the highest (36%) and upper thoracic somewhat lower (23%). Degeneration in the vertebral facet joints was not noticed in the lumbar vertebral arcs. Among the peripheral joints, the rates did not vary a lot. The highest percentage of degenerative bone changes was present in the knee joint (13%). No changes were noticed in the shoulder and elbow joints.

Studies of degenerative bone changes can generate details about activities and physical stress in groups of people from the past.[66] Stress can be due to work pressure, tension, or physical load on the joints. The presence of high percentages of degenerative changes implies higher physical stress for the group involved. However, connecting degenerative changes and physical stress to particular activities is not possible. In London, for example, the contribution of work-specific activities performed by weavers in the development of degenerative changes in the spine, shoulder, and hand joints could not be proven.[67] Climate, body weight, diet, disease, and genetics are also influential factors.[68] Age is an important causal factor as well; in people younger than 40, degenerative changes are noted much less often than in people over 40, and with advancing age, the risk increases.[69] In most cases the individual will suffer pain and stiffness and in later stages, their mobility will be decreased.[70]

The percentages of degenerative bone changes in individuals buried at the Broederenkerkhof in Zutphen differ from rates at other cemeteries, but the number of individuals studied may have influenced the results. The overall rate for degenerative vertebral disc disease in Zutphen (69%) appears to be high, but percentages of about 60% were found in Dordrecht, 's-Hertogenbosch, Alkmaar, and Zutphen (Nieuwstadskerk) as well.[71] In Eindhoven the rates went up to as high as 88%.[72] If we look at the location on the spine of the affected bone, it is noticeable that at other cemeteries the lower thoracic vertebrae were more affected than in the individuals from Zutphen.[73] Unfortunately, it was not always obvious if percentages were calculated based on present and inspected locations or on overall individuals, which makes it difficult to compare prevalence between sites.[74] Notably in Zutphen, no individuals

66 Larsen 1997, 162.
67 Molleson & Cox 1993, 73-75.
68 Larsen 1997, 162-163; Waldron 2009, 28.
69 Larsen 1997, 163; Waldron 2009, 28-31.
70 Molleson & Cox 1993, 73.
71 Maat, Mastwijk & Sarfatij 1998, 45; Maat, Mastwijk & Jonker 2002, Table 7; Baetsen 2001, 61-63; Berk 2007, 88-89.
72 Baetsen & Weterings-Korthorst 2013, 190.
73 Baetsen & Weterings-Korthorst 2013, 188-192; De Jonge & Baetsen 2013, 247-251; Berk 2007, 88-89.
74 Waldron 1995, 383-389; Baetsen, Bitter & Bruintjes 1996, 628-630; Waldron 2009, 34-39.

had degeneration in the shoulder or elbow. The knee joint had a relatively higher rate, as did the hip.[75] Combining the higher rates in the lumbar vertebrae, knee, and hip joints, it appears that higher stress on the weight-bearing joints existed in Zutphen. What activity or situation caused this higher risk can unfortunately not be determined because the individuals represent an extended time period of 500 years.

Enthesopathies and DISH

Enthesopathies are the result of ossified connective soft tissue in tendons, ligaments, and cartilage.[76] They appear on the edge of the ilium (iliac whiskering), posterior aspect of the heel bone where the Achilles tendon is attached (calcaneal spurring), front side of the kneecap (patellar tufting), and the elbow end of the ulna (olecranon tufting). Enthesopathies present at several of these locations represent the initial stage of diffuse idiopathic skeletal hyperostosis (DISH).[77] A true case of DISH may only be classified if thoracic vertebrae have been fused (ankylosis) by an ossified band of connective tissue on the right front side in combination with multiple enthesopathies.[78] However, none of the individuals buried at the Broederenkerkhof showed the characteristic bony ankylosing thoracic vertebrae. But multiple enthesopathies were present on seven persons (see Table 10 and the Appendix). In six cases the heel bone (calcanear spurring) was affected. Furthermore, enthesopathies were visible on the front of the kneecap and the edge of the backside of the thigh bone (linea aspera) on three individuals. The demographic features of the group with multiple enthesopathies (five males and two females) were not remarkable. The men are all over 45 years, and all individuals, except one woman, were dated to the most recent time period (1600-1800). In several studies, a correlation has been drawn between these typical bone changes and monasteries and a high status lifestyle, both linked to an ample diet.[79] Males particularly above 40 years are more likely to get the disease.[80] Although true DISH seems absent at the Broederenkerkhof, the percentage of individuals with multiple enthesopathies was relatively high (23%). In 's-Hertogenbosch, for example, the rate was lower (11%) and can be explained by poor diet; according to historical records, the relevant population was of low status.[81] In Oldenzaal (10%) and Zutphen Nieuwstadskerk (11%), as well, relatively low percentages were calculated.[82] In contrast, the canons from the chapel of St. Servaaskerk in Maastricht who had a high status lifestyle, had a 100% incident rate of DISH.[83] If DISH is linked to monastic life, this was not apparent in the group from the Broederenkerkhof in Zutphen. It is possible, however, that the friars were not among the individuals excavated, or at least not many of them, a highly probable suggestion because of the presence of the high number of females in the time period until 1600.

---

75 Waldron 1995, 385-389; Baetsen, Bitter & Bruintjes 1996, 628-630.
76 Maat, Mastwijk & Van der Velde 1995: 289-298; Janssen & Maat 1998: 17; Waldron 2009: 72-77.
77 Janssen & Maat 1998, 17, 32-33; Baetsen 2001, 60-61; Maat, Van den Merwe & Hoff 2012, 17-18.
78 Rogers & Waldron 2001, 362-363; Waldron 2009, 77.
79 Janssen & Maat 1998, 17; Waldron 2009, 75-76.
80 Waldron 2009, 74.
81 Maat, Mastwijk & Jonker 2002, 17.
82 Kwakman 2010, 95; Berk 2007, 57.
83 Janssen & Maat 1998, 17.

Conclusion

In summary it can be said that the cemetery belonging to the Dominican monastery in Zutphen contained a remarkable surplus of women in the period 1300-1600. Perhaps the women were more attracted to the better conditions, financial perhaps, the Broederenkerkhof offered compared to those of other religious institutions, for example, the Chapter of St. Walburgis. Another remarkable demographic find is the increase in mean age at death and stature for men buried in the period 1300-1800, indicating improved economic and/or environmental conditions for males in Zutphen. However, an important question remains: How representative are the numbers and percentages when only 34 people represent 500 years of burials in the cemetery? Still, this study shows that it is far from only monks who were buried in the Broederenkerkhof in Zutphen.

Bibliography

Alberts, W.J., 1986: *Het Rijnverkeer bij Lobith Anno 1306. De tolrekening van Lobith over het jaar 1306-1307 betreffende invoer en uitvoer van handelsgoederen*, Zutphen.

Aufderheide A.C. & C. Rodríguez-Martín, 1998: *The Cambridge Encyclopedia of Human Paleopathology*, Cambridge University Press.

Baetsen, S., 1998: *Het menselijk skeletmateriaal van het Salvatorplein te Susteren*, Amersfoort: Rijksdienst voor het Oudheidkundig Bodemonderzoek.

Baetsen, S., 2001: *Graven in de Grote Kerk. Het fysisch-antropologisch onderzoek van de graven in de St. Laurenskerk van Alkmaar*, Alkmaar (Rapporten over de Alkmaarse Monumentenzorg en Archeologie; nr. 8).

Baetsen, S., 2006: *Fysisch antropologisch onderzoek Julianaplein, Wijk aan Zee, gemeente Beverwijk*, Amsterdam: Archeologisch Centrum Vrij Universiteit (Zuidnederlandse Archeologische Notities 62).

Baetsen, S., 2008: 'Het fysisch antropologisch onderzoek van de menselijke skeletresten', in: A.M.J. Derks, J. van Kerckhove & P.G. Hoff, *Nieuw archeologisch onderzoek rond de grote kerk van Elst,* Amsterdam: Archeologisch Centrum Vrij Universiteit (Zuidnederlandse Archeologische Rapporten 31), 117-134.

Baetsen, S., 2014: Het menselijk botmateriaal in J. van Renswoude & D. Habermehl (red), *Archeologische opgravingen te Tiel-Dominicuskwartier, onderzoek naar een vroeg-middeleeuwse ringwalburg, een motte versterking, Ottoonse nederzettingsresten, een versterkt huis en laat- en postmiddeleeuwse resten in de oude binnenstad*, Amsterdam: VUhbs Archeologie (Zuidnederlandse Archeologische Rapporten 56), 301-318.

Baetsen, S. & L. Weterings-Korthorst, 2013: 'De menselijke overblijfselen', in N. Arts (ed.), *Een knekelveld maakt geschiedenis, het archeologisch onderzoek van het koor en het grafveld van de middeleeuwse Catharinakerk in Eindhoven, circa 1200-1850*, Utrecht: Matrijs, 151-212.

Baetsen, S., P. Bitter & Tj. D. Bruintjes, 1996: 'Hip and knee Osteoarthritis in an eighteenth century urban population', *International Journal of Osteoarchaeology 1996,* 7: 628-630. https://doi-org.ezproxy.leidenuniv.nl:2443/10.1002/(SICI)1099-1212(199711/12)7:6<628::AID-OA391>3.0.CO;2-R

Bellens, T. & M. Vandenbruaene, 2006: *Het allerheiligenklooster van de Antwerpse Augustijnen (prov. Antwerpen), archeologische en fysisch-antropologische gegevens*, Brussel (Relicta 2) 197-234.

Berk, B.W.M., 2007: *Hongerende Heren? Onderzoek naar 18e en begin 19e -eeuwse begravingen uit de Nieuwstadskerk te Zutphen*, Unpublished Masterthesis Vrije Universiteit Amsterdam.

Breitinger, E.,1937: 'Zur berechnung der Körperhöhe aus den langen Gliedermassenknochen', *Anthropologischer Anzeiger* 14, 249-274.

Brickley, M., S. Buteux, J. Adams & R. Cherrington, 2006: *St. Martin's Uncovered: Investigations in the churchyard of St. Martin's-in-the-Bull Ring*, Birmingham: Oxbow Books: Oxford, 90-151.

Brothwell, D.R., 1981[3]: *Digging up Bones. The excavation, treatment and study of human skeletal remains,* London: British Museum (Natural History).

Brothwell, D.R., 1994: On the possibility of urban-rural contrasts in human population palaeobiology, in: A.R. Hall & H.K. Kenward (eds.), *Urban-rural connexions. Perspectives from environmental archaeology*, Oxford (Symposia of the Association for Environmental Archaeology no. 12/Oxbow Monograph 47), 129-136.

Centraal College van Deskundigen Archeologie 2010: *Kwaliteitsnorm Nederlandse Archeologie 3.2; landbodems,* Stichting Infrastructuur Kwaliteitsborging Bodembeheer, Gouda.

Chamberlain, A., 2006: *Demography in archaeology*, Cambridge (Cambridge manuals in archaeology).

Clevis, H. & T. Constandse-Westerman (eds.), 1992: *De doden vertellen; Opgraving in de Broerenkerk te Zwolle 1987-88*, Kampen, Stichting Archeologie IJssel/Vechtstreek.

De Beer, H. de, 2001: *Nutrition, health and labour in the Netherlands during the nineteenth centrury. A contribution to anthropometric history*, Thesis, Utrecht.

De Jonge, L. & S. Baetsen, 2013: 'Fysische antropologie van de begraven individuen', in: J. Hendriks, H. de Kievith & E. Peters (eds.): *'Tot behoef van de siecken ende armen, Archeologisch onderzoek naar het Bredase Gasthuis, 1958-2006*, Breda: Bureau Cultureel Erfgoed (Erfgoed Rapport Breda 95), 199-276.

Fermin, B. & M. Groothedde, 2006: *Het Diftarproject in Zutphen, 25 verhalen uit de binnenstad*, Zutphen (Zutphense Archeologische Publicaties 23).

Fermin, B. & D. Kastelein, 2012: *Graven langs het kerkhof, archeologisch proefputtenonderzoek achter het koor van de Broederenkerk in Zutphen*, Zutphen (Zutphense Archeologische Publicatie 73).

Frederiks, A.M., S. Van Buuren, R.J.F. Burgmeijer, J.F. Meulmeester, R.J. Beuker, E. Roede, M.J. Verloove-Vanhorick & J-M Wit, 2000: 'Continuing positive secular growth changes in the Netherlands 1955-1997', *Pediatric Research 47,* 316-323.

Groen, W.J. & T. De Ridder, 2007: *Gat in de Markt 01.101, het menselijke botmateriaal uit de periode 1000-1050,* Vlaardingen (VLAK-verslag 15.3).

Groothedde, M., 2001: *Opgraving Broederenkerkplein 1977*, Zutphen (Intern rapport gemeente Zutphen, dossier Broederenkerkplein 1977).

Groothedde, M., 2018: 'A Zutphen Great Hall ...... Which Never Materialized?', in: M. Kars, R. van Oosten, Marcus A. Roxburgh (eds.), *Rural riches & Royal rags? Studies on medieval and modern archaeology, presented to Frans Theuws,* Zwolle/ Amsterdam: SPA-Uitgevers/Dutch Society of Medieval Archaeology, 206-213.

Groothedde, M. & H.A.C. Fermin, 2007: *Verdwenen huizen, tufstenen torens en houten straten rond de Apenstert*, Zutphen (Zutphense Archeologische Publicaties 27).

Haans, F.A.C., 2018: *Bouwhistorisch onderzoek voormalig dormitorium & refter, Broederenklooster, Zutphen*, Zutphen: Monumenten Advies Bureau.

Hermans, R., 1993: 'De predikheren te Zutphen (1288-1591). Brief in het archief van de predikheren dd. 27 augustus 1390', *Tijdschrift voor de historie van Zutphen en omgeving 1993,* 47-50.

Heyden, C.G.W.P. van der, 1995: *Het heeft niet willen groeien, zuigelingen- en kindersterfte in Tilburg 1820-1930, omvang, oorzaken en maatschappelijke context*, Tilburg.

Janssen, H.A.M. & G.J.R. Maat, 1998: *Kanunniken begraven in de stiftskapel van de Sint Servaas te Maastricht 1070 – 1521 na Chr., een paleopathologisch onderzoek*, Leiden (Barge's Anthropologica nr. 5).

Kwakman, S., 2010: *De proefsleuven rond het St. Plechelmusbasiliek te Oldenzaal, demografie, pathologie en representativiteit*, Unpublished Masterthesis Vrije Universiteit Amsterdam.

Larsen, C.S., 1997: *Bioarchaeology, Interpreting behaviour from the human skeleton*, Cambridge (Cambridge Studies in biological anthropology 21).

Maat, G.J.R., 1984: 'A search for secular growth changes in The Netherlands preceding 1850', in: J. Borms, R. Hauspie, A. Sand, C. Susanne & M. Hebbelinck (eds.): *Human Growth and Development*, New York, 185-191

Maat, G.J.R. & R.W. Mastwijk, 2000: Avulsion Injuries of Vertebral Endplates, *International Journal of Osteoarchaeology 10*, New York.

Maat, G.J.R., R.W. Mastwijk & E.A. van der Velde, 1997: 'On the reliability of non-metrical morphological sex determination of the skull compared with that of the pelvis in the low countries', *International Journal of Osteoarchaeology 7,* 575-580. https://doi.org/10.1002/(SICI)1099-1212(199711/12)7:6<575::AID-OA308>3.0.CO;2-4

Maat, G.J.R., R.W. Mastwijk & H. Sarfatij, 1998: *Een fysisch antropologisch onderzoek van begravenen bij het Minderbroeder-Klooster te Dordrecht 1275-1572 AD*, Amersfoort (Rapportage Archeologische Monumentenzorg 67).

Maat, G.J.R., R.W. Mastwijk & M.A. Jonker, 2002: *Citizens buried in the 'Sint Jans' Cathedral of 's-Hertogenbosch in the Netherlands,* Leiden (Barge's Anthropologica 8).

Maat, G.J.R., A.E. van den Merwe & Th. Hoff, 2012[7]: *Manual for the Physical Anthropological Report*, Barge's Anthropologica/Academic Medical Centre, Amsterdam (Barge's Anthropologica 6).

MacLaughlin, S.M. & M.F. Bruce, 1985: A simple univariate technique for determining sex from fragmentary femora and tibiae: It's application to a Scottish short cist population, *American Journal of Physical Anthropology 67,* 413-417. https://doi.org/10.1002/ajpa.1330670413

Mann, R.W. & D.R. Hunt, 2005[2]: *Photographic regional atlas of bone disease. A guide to pathologic and normal variation in the human skeleton (rev. edition),* Springfield.

Molleson. T. & M. Cox, 1993: *The Spitalfields project, volume 2: the anthropology, the middling sort,* York (Council for British Archaeology Research Report 86).

Oppers, V.M., 1966; The secular trend in growth and maturation in the Netherlands, *Tijdschrift voor Geneeskunde 44,* 539-548.

Ortner, D.J., 2003: *Identification of pathological conditions in human skeletal remains*, London.
Onisto, N., G.J.R. Maat & E.J. Bult, 1998: *Human remains from the infirmary "Oude en Nieuwe Gasthuis" of the city of Delft in the Netherlands 1265-1652 AD*, Leiden (Barge's Anthropologica 2).
Panhuysen, R.G.A.M., 2005: *Demography and Health in early medieval Maastricht. Prospographical observations on two cemeteries*, PhD thesis University of Maastricht.
Pijpelink, A., 2008: *Het Grote Kerkhof in Deventer, Onderzoek naar de menselijke resten gevonden tijdens de opgraving op het Grote Kerkhof in Deventer*, Masterthesis University of Leiden, Leiden.
Rijpma, F.E. & G.J.R. Maat, 2005: *A physical anthropological research of the beguines of Breda 1267 to 1530 AD,* Leiden (Barge's Anthropologica 11).
Roberts, Ch. & K. Manchester, 2005[3]: *The archaeology of disease*, New York
Rogers, J. & T. Waldron, 1995: *A field guide to joint disease in archaeology*, Chichester.
Rogers, J. & T. Waldron, 2001: 'DISH and the Monastic way of life', *International Journal of Osteoarchaeology 11,* 357-365. https://doi.org/10.1002/oa.574
Stirland, A.J., 2005: *The men of the Mary Rose, raising the dead.* Gloucestershire.
Schats, R., 2016: *Life in transition, an osteoarchaeological perspective of the consequences of medieval socioeconomic developments in Holland and Zeeland (ad 1000-1600),* PhD thesis Leiden University.
Smits, E., 1999: Het onderzoek van het menselijk skeletmateriaal in: A. Carmiggelt, T.A. Goossens, A.J. Guiran & E. Smits, *Een 13e-eeuwse begraafplaats te Hellevoetsluis bij de uithof Oosthoek van de Vlaamse Cisterciënzerabdij Ter Doest*, Rotterdam (BOORrapporten 47), 76-90.
Trotter, M. & G.C. Gleser, 1958: 'A re-evaluation of estimation of stature based on measurements of stature taken during life and of long bones after death', *American Journal of Physical Anthropology* 16, 79-123.
Van Wieringen, J.C., 1986: 'Secular growth changes', in: F. Falkner & J.M. Tanner (eds.): *Human Growth III,* New York, 307-331.
Waters-Rist, A.L., R. Schats, J. Palmer, E. de Kok & M.L.P. Hoogland (eds.), 2016: *Manual for the laboratory assignment MSc, Methods used in the skeletal recording form*, Laboratory for Human Osteoarchaeology, Leiden University.
Waldron, H.A., 1994: *Counting the dead. The epidemiology of skeletal populations*, Chichester.
Waldron, T., 1995: 'Changes in the distribution of osteoarthritis over historical time', *International Journal of Osteoarchaeology* vol. 5, issue 4, 385-389.
Waldron, T., 2009: *Palaeopathology*, Cambridge (Cambridge Manuals in Archaeology).
Workshop of European Anthropologists, 1980: Recommendations for age and sex diagnosis of skeletons, *Journal of Human Evolution* 9, 517-549.

Appendix: Data Zutphen Broederenkerk

Feature	Completeness	Preservation	Period
1	Incomplete with pelvis	Good	1600-1800
2	Incomplete with pelvis	Good	1600-1800
3	Mostly complete	Good	1600-1800
4	Incomplete with pelvis	Good	1600-1800
5	Incomplete	Fair	1600-1800
6	Incomplete with cranium and pelvis	Good	1600-1800
10	Mainly incomplete	Fair	1600-1800
29	Mostly complete	Good	1600-1800
32	Incomplete	Fair	1600-1800
33	Incomplete	Good	1600-1800
36	Incomplete with cranium	Fair	1600-1800
48	Mostly complete	Fair	1300-1400
50	Mostly complete	Good	1300-1400
52	Incomplete with cranium and pelvis	Good	1300-1400
54	Mainly incomplete	Good	1300-1400
55	Mainly incomplete	Good	1300-1400
58	Incomplete with pelvis	Fair	1600-1800
61	Only cranium and mandibula	Good	1300-1400
62	Incomplete	Good	1300-1400
64	Mainly incomplete	Bad	1600-1800
65	Mainly incomplete	Good	1600-1800
68	Incomplete with pelvis	Good	1600-1800
70	Incomplete with pelvis	Fair	1600-1800
71	Mostly complete	Unknown	1600-1800
72	Incomplete with cranium and pelvis	Good	1400-1600
73	Incomplete with cranium	Good	1400-1600
74	Incomplete with cranium	Good	1400-1600
75	Incomplete with cranium	Fair	1400-1600
76	Incomplete with pelvis	Fair	1400-1600
77	Mainly incomplete	Fair	1400-1600
78	Mainly incomplete	Good	1400-1600
79	Incomplete	Fair	1400-1600
80	Incomplete with cranium and pelvis	Good	1300-1400
81	Incomplete with cranium	Fair	1300-1400

Table A: Characteristics of burials.

Feature	Pelvis	Weight	Cranium	Weight	Sex
3	-0.47	19	-1.08	12	Female
4	1.74	19			Male
6	1.68	19			Male
29	1.47	19	0.75	24	Male
48	0.08	12	-1.62	21	Female
50	-0.86	14	-0.75	24	Female
52	-0.93	14	-0.50	24	Female
58	0.70	10			Male
61			1.42	24	Male
68	1.62	13			Male
70	-0.50	14			Female
72			-0.83	24	Female
73			-0.44	18	Female?
74			0.96	23	Male
75			-1.33	24	Female
76	-0.13	8			Female??
80	1.71	14			Male
81			-1.10	20	Female

Table B: Determination of sex by feature.

Feature	Sex morphological	APD Fem L	APD Fem R	Mean	APD Tib L	APD Tib R	Mean	MPD Fem Ep L	MPD Fem Ep R	Mean	MPD Hum Ep L	MPD Hum Ep R	Mean	Sex metrical
3	Female	25.30	25.00	25.15	28.60	29.30	28.95	44.40	44.60	44.50	42.10	41.90	42.00	
4	Male											52.50		
5		24.40	25.20	24.80	27.10	27.70	27.40							Female
6	Male	31.80	33.50	32.65	29.10	29.90	29.50	50.30	50.10	50.20	45.00			
10					37.60									Male
29	Male	29.60	29.10	29.35	30.40	29.50	29.95	48.10	49.00	48.55	48.20	46.60	47.40	
32			24.10			27.60			41.80					Female
33			30.90		31.80	31.40	31.60							Male
48	Female	24.10	24.10	24.10	24.60	23.40	24.00							
50	Female	25.40	26.40	25.90	25.00	25.10	25.05	41.70	42.10	41.90	38.90	39.70	39.30	
52	Female										42.60	44.10	43.35	
54		31.00	30.90	30.95	34.90	35.00	34.95							Male
55					27.20	27.90	27.45							Female
58	Male		26.10			28.10			41.30			41.10		
62		26.50			29.60	29.90	29.75	45.40						Female?
64					30.40									Male
65					36.90	37.10	37.00							Male
68	Male	29.50	29.80	29.65	33.40	33.90	33.65	49.00	48.40	48.70				
70	Female	25.90	25.60	25.75	28.40	28.20	28.30	46.10	46.80	46.45		43.40		
72	Female	28.10	27.90	28.00	28.30	27.50	27.90	45.10	45.00	45.05	45.80	46.30	46.05	
73	Female?										39.40			Female

Table C (continued on next page): Metrical determination (mm) of sex by feature.
L = Left; R = Right APD = Antererior-Posterior Diameter (maximum); MPD = Maximum Proximal Diameter (vertical)
Ep = Epifysis; Fem = Femur; Tib = Tinia; Hum = Humerus

Feature	Sex morphological	APD Fem L	APD Fem R	Mean	APD Tib L	APD Tib R	Mean	MPD Fem Ep L	MPD Fem Ep R	Mean	MPD Hum Ep L	MPD Hum Ep R	Mean	Sex metrical
74	Male										44.90	45.60	45.25	
75	Female										41.90	41.80	41.85	
76	Female??	28.00	25.90	26.95	29.90	29.60	29.75	43.60	45.70	44.65				Female?
77			26.60		28.10									Female?
78			24.60		25.30	25.10	25.20		38.10					Female
79		24.00	24.40	24.20	25.60			40.80	40.40	40.60				Female
80	Male		30.50			35.10			47.10			49.80		
81	Female	23.40	23.80	23.60	26.10	25.70	25.90							
	Mean Female	25.74	25.53	25.64	27.27	26.97	27.12	44.18	44.84	44.51	41.76	42.87	42.51	
	Mean Male	30.30	29.97	30.55	30.97	31.30	31.03	49.13	48.65	49.15	46.03	47.12	46.33	

Table C (continued).

Feature	Minimal	Maximum	Average	Interval	Time period
1	15	17	16	1	1600-1800
2	7	10	8.5	0	1600-1800
3	37	49	43	4	1600-1800
4	35	40	37.5	3	1600-1800
5	20			Adult	1600-1800
6	54	59	57	5	1600-1800
10	20			Adult	1600-1800
29	45	52	48.5	4	1600-1800
32	20			Adult	1600-1800
33	50	70	60	6	1600-1800
36	6	8	7	0	1600-1800
48	48	60	54	5	1300-1400
50	36	45	40.5	4	1300-1400
52	40	49	44.5	4	1300-1400
54	20			Adult	1300-1400
55	20			Adult	1300-1400
58	55	66	60.5	6	1600-1800
61	50	60	55	5	1300-1400
62	40	60	50	5	1300-1400
64	20			Adult	1600-1800
65	20			Adult	1600-1800
68	50	60	55	5	1600-1800
70	42	49	45.5	4	1600-1800
71				Adult	1600-1800
72	35	39	37	3	1400-1600
73	43	65	54	5	1400-1600
74	55	69	62	6	1400-1600
75	40	45	42.5	4	1400-1600
76	20			Adult	1400-1600
77	20			Adult	1400-1600
78	20			Adult	1400-1600
79	35	55	45	4	1400-1600
80	35	42	38.5	3	1300-1400
81	40	50	45	4	1300-1400

*Table D: Skeletal age at death by feature**
**It was possible to determine the skeletal age at death for all 34 individuals.*

Feature	Period	Sex	Stature	Femoral length
			Trotter & Gleser 1958; Trotter 1970; Breitinger 1937.	Knussman 1998; Maat & Mastwijk 2004.
3	1600-1800	Female	160.7	43.5
4	1600-1800	Male	175.8/173.8	
6	1600-1800	Male	175.6/173.0	47.6
10	1600-1800	Male	184.9/176.3	
29	1600-1800	Male	170.8/169.2	46.7
32	1600-1800	Female	157.3	41.7
33	1600-1800	Male	179.6/174.3	
48	1300-1400	Female	165.4	
50	1300-1400	Female	158.1	42.0
52	1300-1400	Female	169.6	
54	1300-1400	Male	166.1/164.4	
55	1300-1400	Female	161.3	
58	1600-1800	Male	164.8/165.9	43.3
62	1300-1400	Female	166.1	45.4
65	1600-1800	Male	186.8/177.3	
68	1600-1800	Male	176.8/173.5	48.8
70	1600-1800	Female	160.8	43.4
72	1400-1600	Female	168.9	46.0
73	1400-1600	Female	160.6	
75	1400-1600	Female	159.4	
76	1400-1600	Female	158.0	42.6
78	1400-1600	Female	160.7	42.9
80	1300-1400	Male	171.6/171.9	46.9
81	1300-1400	Female	164.8	

Table E: Stature and femoral lenght (cm).

	1300-1800	1300-1400	1400-1600	1600-1800
N individuals	12	5	4	3
Ideally	384	160	128	96
Erupted	318	149	123	46
Non-erupted	2		2	
Inspected	255	131	92	22
Antemortem loss	25 (8)	5 (2)	14 (4)	6 (2)
Postmortem loss	38 (10)	13 (4)	17 (4)	8 (2)
Congenital absence	5 (3)	2 (2)	2 (1)	
Additional elements	-	-	-	-
Tooth decay/caries	26 (10)	10 (4)	10 (4)	6 (2)
Abscess	22 (7)	3 (2)	11 (4)	8 (1)
Alveolar resorption	-10	-5	-3	-2
Tartar (calculus)	-8	-4	-2	-2
Periodontitis	-1	-	-1	-
Clay pipe wear holes	-	-	-	-

*Table F: Dental characteristics by time period.**
**Number of individuals in brackets.*

Feature	Time Period	Sex	Age	Pathology
1	1600-1800		15-17	Periostitis
3	1600-1800	Female	37-49	Skull trauma, fracture carpalia, periostitis, osteochondritis dissecans, degenerative disc disease
4	1600-1800	Male	35-40	Rib fractures, degenerative disc disease
5	1600-1800	Female	20>	Osteochondritis dissecans
6	1600-1800	Male	54-59	Rib fractures, gout, degenerative disc disease, degenerative joint disease, multiple enthesophytes
10	1600-1800	Male	20>	Osteochondritis dissecans, periostitis
29	1600-1800	Male	45-52	Multiple enthesophytes
32	1600-1800	Female	20>	Periostitis, degenerative joint disease, multiple enthesophytes
33	1600-1800	Male	50-70	Periostitis, osteochondritis dissecans, degenerative joint disease, multiple enthesophytes
50	1300-1400	Female	36-45	Spondylolyse, degenerative disc disease, degeneration facet joints
52	1300-1400	Female	40-49	Degenerative disc disease
54	1300-1400	Male	20>	Degenerative joint disease
55	1300-1400	Female	20>	Multiple enthesophytes
58	1600-1800	Male	55-66	Multiple enthesophytes
68	1600-1800	Male	50-60	Multiple enthesophytes
70	1600-1800	Female	42-49	Degenerative disc disease, degenerative joint disease
72	1400-1600	Female	35-39	Endocranial depressions
73	1400-1600	Female	43-65	Degenerative disc disease, degenerative joint disease
74	1400-1600	Male	55-69	Degenerative disc disease, degeneration facet joints
75	1400-1600	Female	40-45	Degenerative disc disease
76	1400-1600	Female	20>	Degenerative joint disease
80	1300-1400	Male	35-42	Vertebral fracture, rhomboid fossa

Table G: Pathological bone changes by feature.

In sickness and in health

An archaeological and osteoarchaeological analysis of St. Gertrude's infirmary in Kampen (1382-*c.* 1611)

Rachel Schats & Michael Klomp

Introduction

In 2011 and in 2014, large-scale excavations were conducted at the Margaretha and Myosotis area, west of the city centre of Kampen, as a result of the planned construction of a new care home at the site. The excavations brought to light remains of a medieval infirmary that included a chapel (*gasthuiskapel*), cemetery as well as houses from the 14th century. This chapter will focus on the infirmary and 89 primary skeletal remains found in 2014 to learn more about medieval health care in Kampen. Specific questions will address who was cared for in the hospital and what kind of diseases were treated in this infirmary. To place the results in a broader context, comparisons will be made with other hospital collections from the Netherlands. This article will conclude with a discussion on whether hospital collections have a specific osteoarchaeological signature, that is, are hospital patients recognisable through demographic and palaeopathological characteristics?

St. Gertrude's infirmary complex

The infirmary was located on a large plot of land bordered by the Boven Nieuwstraat, Burgwal, Geerstraat, and the current Burgwalstraat, formerly known as Extersteeg (Fig. 1). In 1382, Johan van Hattem left money to St. Gertrude's infirmary in his will, which indicates that in 1382 the hospital must have been operational.[1] In this early period, the size of the complex was fairly small, most likely consisting of an infirmary hall (*ziekenzaal*) but not much else. A reference from 1405 indicates that eight beds on one side of the hall were reserved for the sick, while on the other side an unspecified number of beds were meant to be used by the poor and mendicants, generally referred to in historical sources as *arme ellendigen* (the miserable poor). In 1487, the alderman and the council of Kampen decided that the infirmary would

1 Jager 2015, 352; Van Santen 2017, 30.

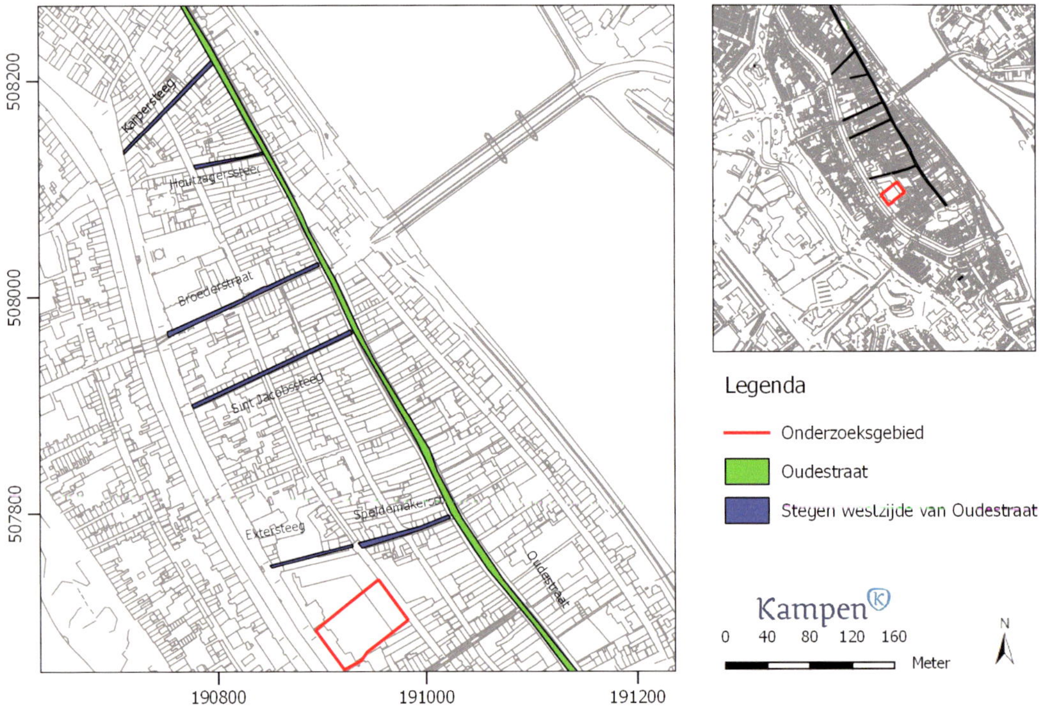

Fig. 1: Location of the research area (indicated in red) and adjoining streets (blue and green).

not be allowed to take in more than 40 people, which indicates that over the course of 80 years, the infirmary expanded dramatically. From this period onwards, there were also places on the infirmary grounds for the *proveniers*, individuals, both men and women, who paid a sum of money in order to receive board and care for the duration of their lives. Those individuals were most likely not housed in the main infirmary hall but were allowed to live in small houses adjacent to the main building. In addition to the sick, *arme ellendigen*, and *proveniers*, occasionally other types of people were admitted to the hospital. In the 16th century in relation to the Eighty Years' War, Prince Mauritz requested the hospital take in wounded soldiers. Important to note is that when the *proveniers* or other patients died in the hospital, their possessions and other assets became the property of the infirmary.[2]

The first indication of the presence of a chapel on the complex is from 1418. In that year, a new altar was installed in the northern part of the chapel.[3] Adjacent to the back of the chapel were two privy cellars which may have belonged to a later annex of St. Gertrude's infirmary. The annex appears to have been a free-standing building behind the chapel that had been incorporated into a garden wall. The cesspits and the nature and composition of the finds in them allow a tentative interpretation of these structures as the hospital's kitchen and privy.

2 Van Santen 2017, 31.
3 Klomp 2017, 95.

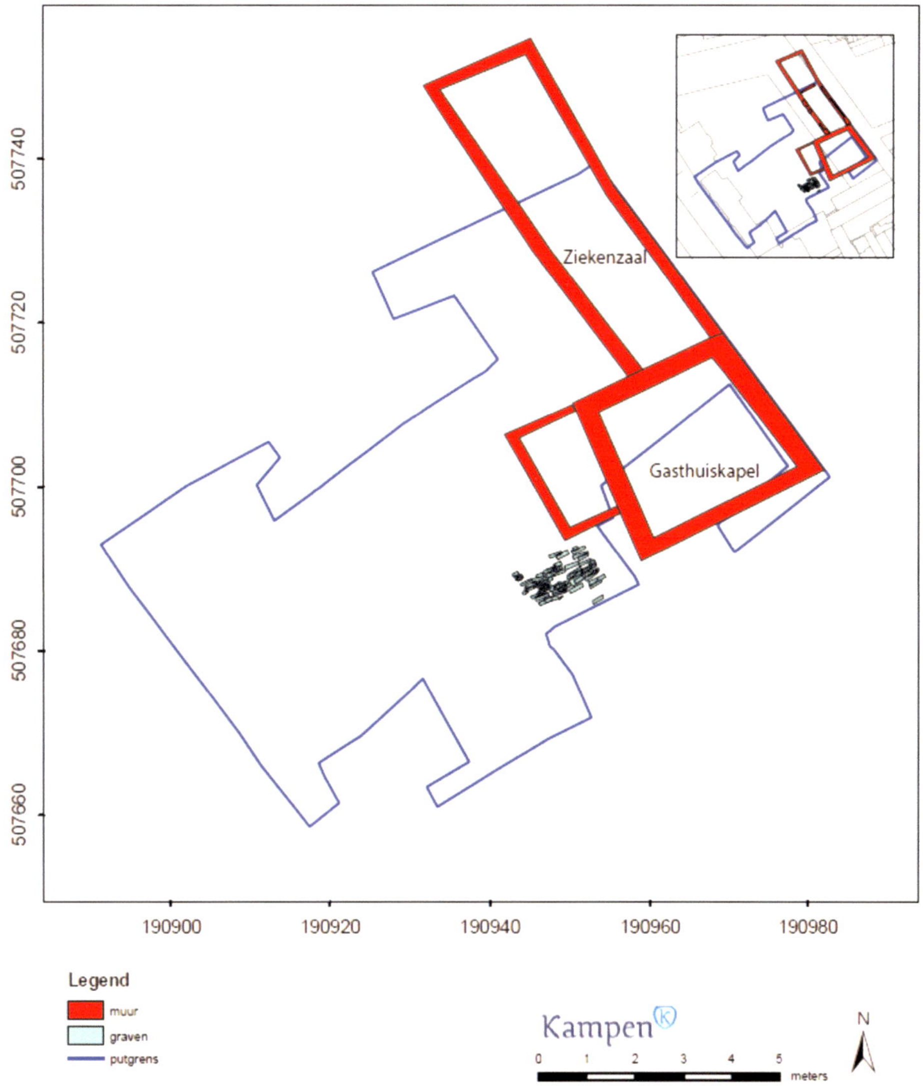

Fig. 2: Overview of excavated area (blue outline). Walls of the chapel and infirmary hall are indicated in red. Location of the burials is indicated in light blue.

St. Gertrude's infirmary existed as such until 1598, when it was amalgamated with other infirmaries in Kampen. However, the complex functioned up until 1611 when the chapel was destroyed. While the infirmary hall remained standing until 1897,[4] the associated cemetery became inactive after the destruction of the chapel. The cemetery will be discussed in more detail in the next section.

The archaeological excavations in 2011 and 2014 revealed traces of the infirmary hall, the chapel, and the cemetery (Fig. 2). The infirmary hall was located in the northeastern corner of the complex, parallel to the Boven Nieuwstraat. In 2011,

4 Jager 2015, 352.

the most northern part of the hall was excavated.[5] In 2014, the excavation began where it had ended in 2011, and the pit was extended towards the south, revealing a cross wall. Evidently, the infirmary hall had been divided into two rooms. It is possible that this more southern area of the infirmary hall dates to a later phase, which could be related to the expansion of the infirmary in the early 15th century.[6] In 2014, excavations also revealed the foundations of the chapel directly to the southwest of the infirmary hall, extending along the Boven Nieuwstraat.

St. Gertrude's cemetery

The cemetery lay to the south and southwest of the chapel. Part of this cemetery had already been destroyed in the construction of the kitchen of the care home in 1970. It is to be expected that the cemetery was much larger in medieval times than the area excavated in 2014. Yet a total of 89 primary inhumations and some secondary depositions were recovered from the cemetery. Burials most likely began around the time the infirmary was founded in the early 1380s and ceased in the beginning of the 17th century; unfortunately, a more detailed internal chronology is currently not available.

Coffins?

Based on the lack of wood associated with the burials, it is unlikely that coffins were regularly used for burial at the infirmary cemetery. Wood remains suggestive of a coffin were encountered with one burial, but this was an exception. Considering that wood was preserved very well at the site,[7] it is to be expected that if coffins were used, remnants of those would have been encountered more frequently during excavation. The bones, however, suggest that there was some initial protection from the soil. In most of the burials for which this is observable, flattening of the rib cage and pelvis was noted, a clear sign that initial decomposition of the soft tissues took place in an open space, that is, no soil around the body.[8] In addition, there were some displacement of bones outside of the volume of the body, indicating that upon decomposition there was space around the body. So if this space was not the interior of a coffin, it is likely that shrouds were used to cover the bodies upon interment.

Orientation and position

All individuals in the cemetery were buried in an extended supine position with their head to the southwest and feet to the northeast. This is a slight deviation from the norm: it is more common in Christian cemeteries to be buried with the head to the west and feet to the east, as on the Day of Judgement the deceased would then be facing east where Christ would be coming when they rose.

Interestingly, there is one individual who was found in a prone position (face down) (Fig. 3). It is possible that this was deliberate, but it could also have been an accidental occurrence. Or it is also possible that shortly after death the burial

5 Bouma & Korenberg 2014, 49-50.
6 Klomp 2017, 100.
7 Several remains of wooden houses and partial foundations were found at the site (Klomp 2017, 99).
8 Duday 2009, 32-38.

Fig. 3: Individual S4013V1008 buried in a prone position, evidenced by the visible posterior view of the legs and thorax.

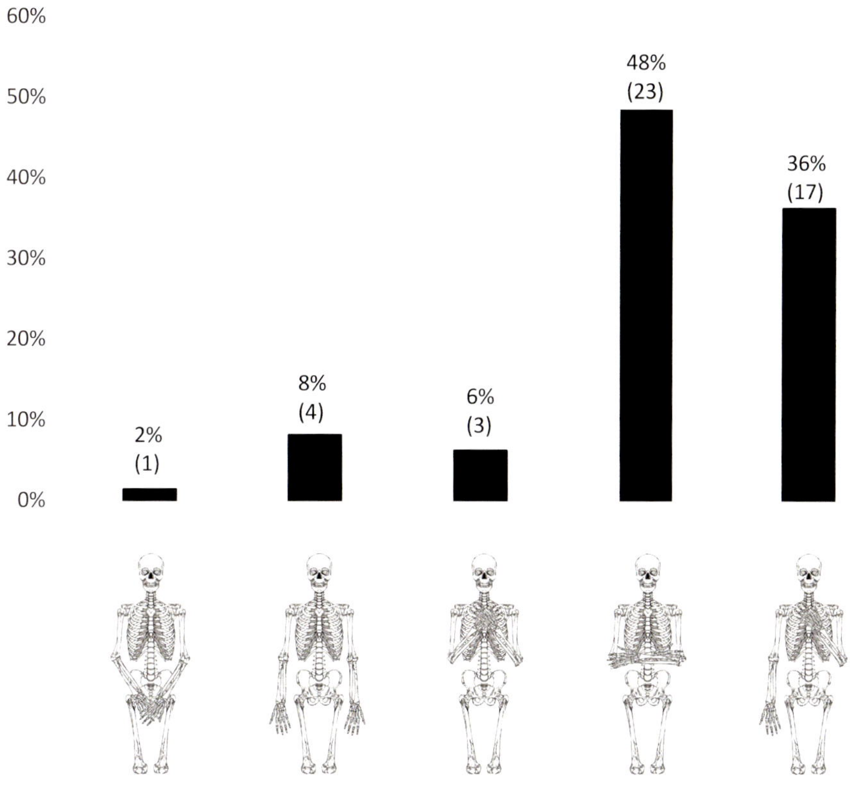

Fig. 4: Arm positions (N=48).

environment changed (i.e., a secondary void was created), resulting in the body rotating.[9] This individual was still oriented southwest-northeast.

9 See Duday's discussion on secondary voids in burial contexts (2009, 46-52). Generally, secondary voids are created by the decomposition of perishable materials within the grave context, such as head supports, clothing or even coffins.

The arm positions appear to have varied in the burials at this site, although both arms could only be observed for 48 individuals. The majority of individuals were buried with their arms and hands on the abdomen (48%), while a smaller portion of individuals had their arms extended alongside the body. There were some individuals with tightly or very tightly flexed lower arms, either positioned on the chest or even on the upper arm. Interestingly, for a large portion of individuals for who both arms could be observed, there were differences between the position of the right and left arm (36%) (Fig. 4). This variation in arm positions may be related to the absence of coffins, upon burial a body in a shroud is less constrained than a body in a coffin, potentially allowing for movement of arms. The legs were extended and positioned next to each other in all burials for which femora, tibiae and fibulae were observable.

St. Gertrude's skeletal population

All 89 primary burials were subjected to a physical anthropological analysis to study the demographic composition of the buried individuals as well as perform an assessment of the present pathological conditions, which is particularly interesting considering that this was an infirmary context. Below, an overview of sex and age-at-death estimations[10] will be presented and then special attention will be given to the evidence of disease in this collection. Comparison will be made with skeletal collections from other infirmary contexts, specifically those from Breda (1294-1637)[11] and Delft (1265-1652).[12]

Demographic composition

Sex could be estimated for 66 of the 78 adult individuals (85%) excavated at the infirmary site. In total, there were 42 men (64%) and 24 (36%) women in the collection. Clearly, there were more men buried in the cemetery. Interestingly, this appears to be common at other hospital sites as well. At the medieval infirmary in Breda, there were also substantially more men than women in the skeletal sample.[13] The same is true for the *Oude en Nieuwe Gasthuis* in Delft, although there the difference in numbers between the sexes was smaller (53% vs. 45%).[14] For the Breda collection, the researchers explained the large sex difference by the occurrence of several violent conflicts during the active period of the infirmary, which would have resulted in a high number of male casualties. Considering that Kampen was besieged during the Eighty Years' War like Breda, it is possible that this contributed to the male surplus in the Kampen collection as well. As indicated above, Prince Mauritz requested that several groups of wounded soldiers be taken in by the hospital, which fits with the osteoarchaeological findings.

---

10 Adult sex and age at death have been estimated using the methods outlined in the WEA 1980; Buikstra & Ubelaker 1994; Buckberry & Chamberlain 2002; Phenice 1969. For estimating age at death in non-adults the methods described by Schaefer *et al.* 2009 were employed.

11 De Jonge 2017; De Jonge & Baetsen 2013.

12 Onisto *et al.* 1998.

13 De Jonge 2017, 96-97.

14 Onisto *et al.* 1998, 10.

The age-at-death estimation of the 89 individuals showed that the majority were over 18 years when they died (Fig. 5). Only 11 of the 89 individuals (12.4%) were non-adults. Of these 11, all are above the age of four years at time of death. While this would be remarkable at regular cemetery excavations, though not uncommon, considering the general high mortality of children in the medieval period,[15] this is not extraordinary for an infirmary site. Sick children were generally cared for at home or brought to a foundling asylum.[16] This may explain the lack of infants under the age of three in the cemetery. However, it also has to be taken into account that previous disturbances at the site damaged graves, which could have resulted in the destruction of some of the non-adult graves. This lack of infants seems to have occurred at other infirmary cemetaries sites as well. At the Delft infirmary, only 5.8% of the individuals were under the age of ten when they died.[17] In Breda, there are some infants and young children buried (<5 years), but this group only represents 4.9% of the total burial population.[18]

Of the adults in the Kampen collection, we see that the majority of individuals died between the ages of 36 and 45 years (Fig. 5). However, when we separate the adults according to sex, a different pattern emerges (Fig. 6). Most of the men in the collection died between the ages of 26 and 35. It is possible that the large portion of younger men is related to the soldiers housed in the infirmary, although then a larger number of men in the youngest age category (19-25 years) could be expected as well. For the females, there is a radically different pattern: most of the females died between the ages of 19 and 25 years or between the

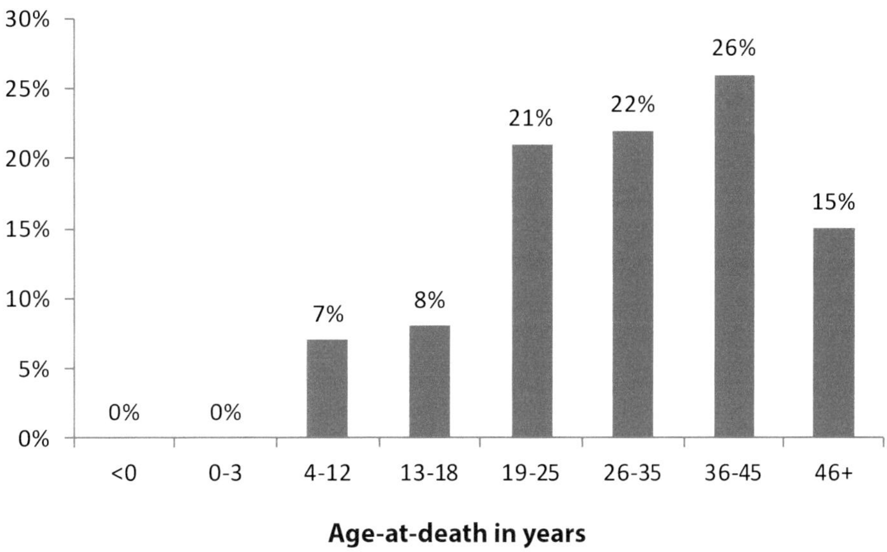

Fig. 5: Age-at-death distribution (N=89).

15 Lewis 2006, 22.
16 Onisto *et al.* 1998, 15.
17 Onisto *et al.* 1998, 36.
18 De Jonge 2017, 97-99.

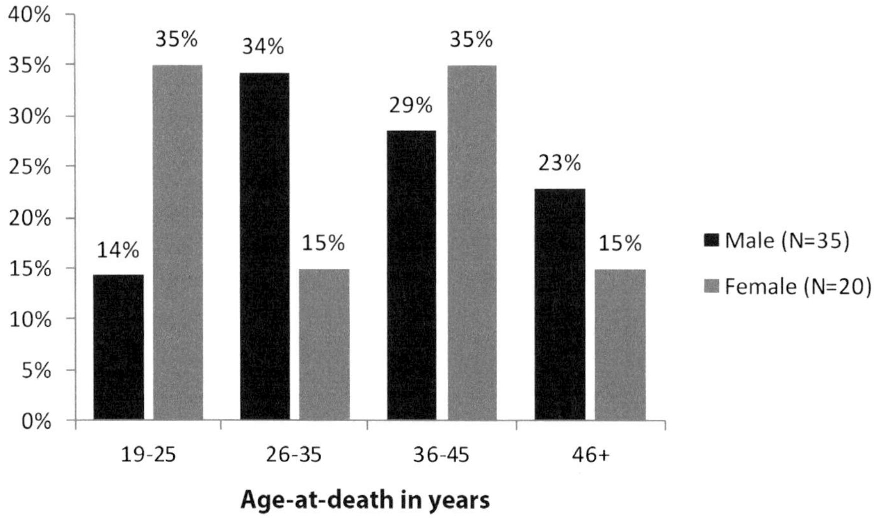

Fig. 6: Adult sex and age-at-death distribution (N=55).

ages of 36 and 45 years. A high number of females in the younger age category is generally explained by the risks associated with childbirth. Although this is a plausible explanation in regular parish cemeteries, it is not expected that women with childbirth complications would be admitted to the hospital. Therefore, it is more likely that there is a different explanation for the high percentage of females between 19 and 25 years in the Kampen skeletal collection. Although the presence of several maidservants[19] would increase the number of young women in the infirmary, it is unlikely that they would have all died young, and even if they had, it is unlikely they would be buried in the infirmary cemetery. As of yet, there is no satisfactory explanation for the high percentage of young females other than coincidence.

Health and disease

Considering that this is an infirmary population, the discussion on the type of pathological conditions is particularly interesting. In the following section, the frequency of diseases in relation to the context and in comparison with the other infirmary collections mentioned above will be discussed. The focus will be on a selection of the occurring diseases and afflictions; for a complete overview, please review the skeletal report.[20]

Infections

What stands out in this collection is the high percentage of individuals who showed signs of infection. Almost 40% of individuals demonstrated periosteal new bone (PNB) on their legs as a result of an inflammation of the periosteum. While this type of pathology can be caused by various factors, such as local trauma or

19 Van Santen 2017, 33.
20 Schats 2017a.

strenuous activity,[21] when new bone formation is noted bilaterally and on multiple bones within the same individual this generally points to a systemic infection. Since this was the case for most individuals with this type of pathology, it is possible to say that many of the individuals in the Kampen collection experienced a systemic infection. Unfortunately, due to the non-specific nature of this lesion, it is not possible to identify the infection. Although the large number of individuals with PNB is not out of the ordinary considering that this is a hospital collection, the percentage of affected individuals is very high in comparison with the Breda infirmary skeletons, where only 5.9% of individuals were affected.[22] It is unfortunately difficult to explain this large difference between the two infirmary collections. Potentially this could be an indication that different types of people were admitted in Kampen in comparison to Breda.

When PNB is found on the ribs, it can be attributed to a more specific cause: lung infection. Even though some scholars equate the presence of PNB on the ribs with tuberculosis, it is not possible to specifically identify the type of lung disease. Although this type of lesion is very common in individuals with tuberculosis, other chronic lung infections, such as bronchitis or pleuritis, cannot be excluded on the basis of this lesion alone.[23] In the Kampen collection, there were four individuals (6.2%) with PNB on the ribs. This type of lesion does not appear in the Breda and Delft collections, although the characteristic vertebral lesions definitively associated with tuberculosis were found in both other infirmary sites. The definitive skeletal lesions directly caused by tuberculosis were not found in Kampen, which is interesting considering the clear presence of the disease in other urban and hospital collections dating to similar time periods.[24] Yet, seeing as tuberculosis only results in skeletal lesions in 2% of infected individuals, it is possible that the disease was present but not expressed in the skeletal record.

The only specific infection that was identified in the Kampen collection was syphilis. Three individuals demonstrated the skeletal lesions associated with this sexually transmitted disease. Syphilis, caused by bacteria of the *Treponema pallidum* species, is a chronic and debilitating illness. The onset of the disease is manifested by minor skin lesions, usually around the genitalia, but can result in marked skeletal lesions in the third stage of the disease.[25] The affected Kampen individuals, two adults (male and female) and an adolescent (male), show lesions on the long bones and skull (Fig. 7). The ribs and vertebrae remain unaffected, as is characteristic for this disease.[26] It is possible that the individuals who were affected by bilateral marked PNB on their long bones, suffered from syphilis as well, although it is not possible to say this definitively.

---

21 Waldron 2009, 115-117.
22 De Jonge and Baetsen 2013, 241.
23 Waldron 2009, 117.
24 Clear cases of tuberculosis were also found in the medieval Franciscan cemetery in Alkmaar. See Schats 2016, 96-98.
25 Waldron 2009, 105-108.
26 Waldron 2009, 105-108.

The presence of syphilis at this site is notable considering the longstanding debate regarding the origin of the disease. One of the hypotheses is that Columbus brought the disease back to Europe in 1493,[27] so if these individuals predate the return of Columbus, this hypothesis would be called into question. Considering the fact that burial at Kampen took place from 1380 onwards, the three syphilitic individuals may potentially predate 1493. To study this, rib samples were sent to the Centre for Isotopic Research in Groningen for radiocarbon dating. Unfortunately, although there is a 68% chance that the individuals died before 1493, the ^{14}C dates of these individuals have a broad range and therefore do not rule out the possibility that the individuals died post-1493. Moreover, the stable nitrogen and carbon isotopes ($\delta^{15}N$ and $\delta^{13}C$) indicate that the individuals most likely consumed fish. As a result of the reservoir effect,[28] the individuals may be younger than the radiocarbon results suggest.[29]

Syphilis was also encountered in the infirmary in Breda. Two adults and two non-adults appear to have been affected by this infection. The two non-adults show the dental lesions associated with congenital syphilis, indicating that the infection was transferred from mother to child in utero. As with the Kampen patients, the syphilitic individuals from Breda were subjected to radiocarbon dating to determine whether they predated 1493. Unfortunately, yet again, the range for most of the dates was broad, making it impossible to definitely state that the individuals died before the return of Columbus to Europe. The dates for one of the non-adults suggest a pre-Columbian date, but the diagnosis of congenital syphilis for this individual is less certain.[30]

Trauma

Just like the high rates of infection, the high number of individuals with trauma is noteworthy. Of the 89 individuals studied, 28 demonstrated one or multiple fractures (31.5%). Most of the fractures had healed well and were located on the ribs, and are therefore unlikely to be the reason why these affected individuals ended up in the infirmary. Interestingly however, there were two elderly male individuals whose upper leg neck had been fractured (Fig. 8). Today this type of fracture is very common amongst the elderly and poses a major public health problem impacting survival rates and quality of life.[31] Although the present hip fractures had already healed when death occurred, it is likely that medical care would have been sought for a fracture like this and may therefore be the reason why they were in the infirmary. If they were cared for in the hospital for an extended period of time, this may explain the stage of healing. Five individuals showed a fracture in

27 Meyer *et al.* 2002, 41-42.

28 The term 'reservoir effect' refers to 'an offset ^{14}C between contemporaneous organisms that derive their carbon from the terrestrial environment and those organisms that live wholly or partly in the marine environment' (Ascough *et al.* 2005, 533). As a result of the limited ability of a body of water to take in atmospheric carbon, the marine environment is depleted of ^{14}C in comparison with the surrounding atmosphere. Therefore, organisms that contain large amounts of marine carbon or consume products with a large amount of marine carbon may appear older than they, in fact, are.

29 CIO 2015, 2017; Schats 2017b.

30 De Jonge & Baetsen 2013, 242-244.

31 Cooper *et al.* 1992, 285.

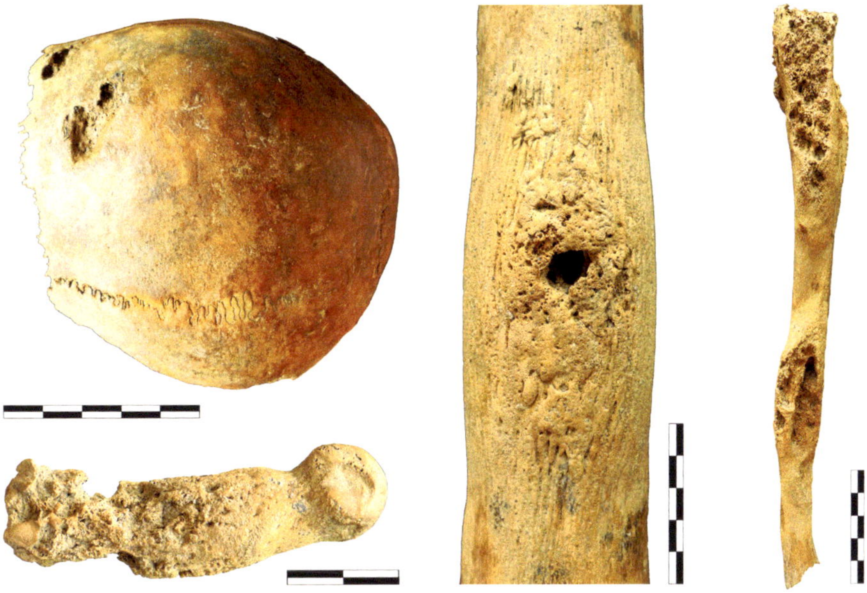

Fig. 7: Skeletal lesions associated with syphilis in an adult female (S4084V1086). Top left: Caries sicca on skull. Bottom left: destruction and new bone formation, 4th right metacarpal. Centre: Cloaca (drainage hole for pus) with new bone formation on left upper leg. Right: Posterior aspect left ulna showing destruction and new bone formation.

Fig. 8: Trauma. Left: Fractured right femoral neck, note the extensive new bone formation on the anterior aspect. Right: Incomplete spondylolysis in a lumbar vertebra.

their lumbar vertebrae where the neural arch is separated from the body, a type of fracture also referred to as spondylolysis (Fig. 8). While this is very unlikely to be the cause for their stay in the hospital, the prevalence of this fracture type is relatively high (8.3%). Considering that spondylolysis is related to strenuous physical work, it may speak to the type of people being admitted to the infirmary. In comparison to the Delft (11.8%) and Breda (10.8%) fracture prevalence,[32] the number of individuals in the Kampen collection with fractures is high.

32 De Jonge & Baetsen 2013, 240; Onisto *et al.* 1998, 40-41.

In addition to fractures, there were two individuals (3.0%) with a dislocated arm. In both individuals, the arm was not reset to its original position and as a result created a new joint surface on the anterior portion of the scapula (shoulder blade). One of the individuals, an elderly male, had also broken several ribs and his right ulna, potentially as a result of the same traumatic event. Dislocated joints were also found in four individuals in Breda (1.4%).[33]

Diffuse Idiopathic Skeletal Hyperostosis

In the Kampen collection, six individuals (10%) showed lesions associated with Diffuse Idiopathic Skeletal Hyperostosis (DISH). DISH is generally characterised as a metabolic bone disease and results in ossifications of connective tissue in the spine and in other places of the body. In the spine, it is visible as a candlewax-like bone formation on the right side of the vertebral column, connecting two or more vertebrae together (Fig. 9) It is hypothesised that the bone formation is limited to the right side since the aorta, the largest blood vessel in the human body, runs to the left of the vertebrae. The pulsating of this main artery results in constant movement of the tissue on the left side and thereby prevents ossification.[34] The extra-spinal lesions in the form of bony spurs are often located on the patella and calcaneus, but those can occur throughout the skeleton.

While it is known that DISH is more common in males and that the prevalence increases with age, the cause of this disease is not well understood. DISH however appears to be associated with a wealthier lifestyle since it seems to be linked to a high body mass and diabetes mellitus type 2.[35] In the archaeological record, this pattern is present as well, as DISH is particularly common in monastic populations. For example, 100% of the canons interred in the *Stiftskapel* in Maastricht demonstrated the classic skeletal lesions associated with DISH.[36] Considering that all the individuals were clergy who were likely to have led a more privileged life, this fits well with clinical observations. Even though the prevalence in the Kampen collection is not particularly high, it is interesting because you would not expect the *arme ellendigen* in the infirmary to have a wealthy lifestyle with an associated rich diet. It is, however, possible that the individuals with DISH in this skeletal population represent the *proveniers*. Considering that they had to pay to be cared for, it is possible that led a richer lifestyle before being admitted, which may have continued during their stay in the infirmary.

Discussion and conclusion

The excavation at the St. Gertrude complex revealed traces of the infirmary hall, chapel and cemetery. The historical data suggest that mainly the poor and passers-by were cared for in this infirmary, but that later, *proveniers* were also admitted. The skeletal data is in line with what is known historically. The prevalence of infection is high as are the cases of traumatic injuries, an observation which fits

---

33 De Jonge & Baetsen 2013, 240.
34 Waldron 2009, 73-77.
35 Van der Merwe *et al.* 2012, 203.
36 Janssen & Maat 1999, 15.

Fig. 9: DISH in thoracic vertebrae with clear ossification on the right side of the spine.

with the results from other infirmary datasets. The presence of DISH may suggest that the *proveniers* had a richer life style than the other residents in the infirmary. In comparison with regular skeletal collections (i.e., not infirmary assemblages), some interesting differences can be noted. Firstly, the demographic composition of this population is different than that of parish church cemeteries from the same time period. In comparison, for example, with the demographic composition of the medieval skeletal collections from Alkmaar[37] and Dordrecht,[38] it is clear that sex and age-at-death distribution in the Kampen collection are aberrant. In both Alkmaar and Dordrecht, the number of men versus women is much more equally distributed and also the age-at-death distribution is more regular. This is most likely the result of the fact that the Kampen skeletal collection is not a reflection of the general population. It reflects individuals who died in the infirmary and were buried in its cemetery. It is interesting, however, that there appear to be similarities between the Kampen collection and other infirmary populations.

With regards to pathological conditions, it is very difficult to comment on the differences and similarities, mainly because there are only a limited number of diseases that leave marks on the skeleton. Most fatal conditions do not leave skeletal lesions, therefore, individuals without lesions may be those in whom the disease progressed quickly.[39] All diseases and traumatic injuries that were found in the Kampen collection are also present in regular cemetery collections. The prevalence of infection appears to be high in the Kampen collection in comparison with other skeletal assemblages, but since this is not the case in other hospital collections, this cannot be regarded as an osteological signature of an infirmary collection. Therefore, the answer to the question posed in the introduction whether hospital patients are recognisable through demographic and palaeopathological characteristics, has to be no. While demographically there appears to be a pattern, it is clear that pathologically there is no such thing as an osteoarchaeological signature of an infirmary population.

---

37 Schats 2016, 91.

38 Maat *et al.* 1998, 17.

39 Also known as the osteological paradox. See Wood *et al.* 1992.

Bibliography

Ascough, P., G. Cook & A. Dugmore, 2005: 'Methodological approaches to determining the marine radiocarbon reservoir effect', *Progress in Physical Geography: Earth and Environment* 29, 532-547. https://doi.org/10.1191/0309133305pp461ra

Bouma, N. & G. Korenberg, 2014: 'Sporen en structuren', in: N Bouma (ed.), *Kampen Burgwal. Een archeologische opgraving*, Amersfoort (ADC Archeo Projecten, Rapport 3737), 44-70.

Buckberry, J.L. & A.T. Chamberlain, 2002: 'Age Estimation from the Auricular Surface of the Ilium: A Revised Method', *American Journal of Physical Anthropology* 119, 231-239. https://doi.org/10.1002/ajpa.10130

Buikstra, J.E. & D.H. Ubelaker, 1994: *Standards for Data Collection from Human Remains,* Fayetteville (Arkansas Archaeological Survey Research Series No. 44).

CIO (Centrum voor Isotopen Onderzoek), 2015: Report CIO-496/PWL by prof. J. van der Plicht, Groningen.

CIO (Centrum voor Isotopen Onderzoek), 2017: Report 2719-1103-17 by Dr. S. Palstra, Groningen.

Cooper, C., G. Campion, & L.J. Melton, 1992: 'Hip fractures in the elderly: A world-wide projection', *Osteoporosis International* 2, 285-289. https://doi.org/10.1007/BF01623184

De Jonge, L., 2017: 'De begraafplaats van het Gasthuis in Breda (ca. 1300-1650)', in: R.M.R van Oosten, R. Schats, N. Arts & H.M.P. Bouwmeester (eds.), *De Stad en de Dood. Archeologische Perspectieven,* Leiden, 85-106.

De Jonge, L. & S. Baetsen, 2013: 'Fysische Antropologie van de Begraven Individuen', in: J. Hendriks, H. de Kievith, en E. Peters (eds.), *'Tot Behoef van den Siecken ende Armen'. Archeologische Onderzoek naar het Bredase Gasthuis, 1958-2006,* Breda (Erfgoedrapport Breda 95).

Duday, H., 2009: *The archaeology of the dead: Lectures in Archaeothanatology*, A. Cipriani & J. Pearce, trans., Oxford.

Jager, A., 2015: *Middeleeuws Kampen: De Ruimtelijke en Economische Structuur van de Stad aan de hand van Archeologische, Bouwhistorische, Numismatische en Historische Bronnen*, Zwolle.

Janssen, H.A.M. & G.J.R. Maat, 1999: *Canons buried in the "Stiftskapel" of the Saint Servaas Basilica at Maastricht, 1070-1521 AD. A palaeopathological study*, Leiden (Barge's Anthropologica 5).

Klomp, M., 2017: 'Het Sint Geertruidengasthuis', in: M. Klomp (ed.), *Myosotis, in de schaduw van het Sint Geertruidengasthuis. Archeologisch onderzoek tussen Boven Nieuwstraat en Burgwal*, Zwolle, 95-102.

Lewis, M.E., 2006: *The Bioarchaeology of Children,* Cambridge.

Maat, G.J.R., R.W. Mastwijk & H. Sarfatij, 1998: *Een Fysisch Antropolologisch Onderzoek van Begravenen bij het Minderbroedersklooster te Dordrecht, circa 1275-1572 ADI,* Amersfoort (Rapportages Archeologische Monumentenzorg 67).

Meyer, C., C Jung, T. Kohl, A Poenicke, A. Poppe, and K.W. Alt, 2002: 'Syphilis 2001 – a Palaeopathological Reappraisal', *Homo* 53, 39-58. https://doi.org/10.1078/0018-442X-00037

Onisto, N., G.J.R. & E. Bult, 1998: *Human Remains from the Infirmary "Oude en Nieuwe Gasthuis" of the City of Delft in the Netherlands 1265-1652 AD*, Leiden (Barge's Anthropologica 2).

Phenice, T.W., 1969: 'A Newly Developed Visual Method of Sexing the Os Pubis', *American Journal of Physical Anthropology* 30, 297-301. https://doi.org/10.1002/ajpa.1330300214

Schaefer, M., S. Black, & L. Scheuer, 2009: *Juvenile Osteology: A Laboratory and Field Manual,* Massachusetts.

Schats, R., 2016: *Life in transition. An osteoarchaeological perspective of the consequences of medieval socioeconomic developments in Holland and Zeeland (AD 1000-1600)* (unpublished PhD thesis Leiden University), Leiden.

Schats, R., 2017a: 'Fysisch Antropologisch rapport Margaretha terrein Kampen', in: M. Klomp (ed.), *Myosotis, in de schaduw van het Sint Geertruidengasthuis. Archeologisch onderzoek tussen Boven Nieuwstraat en Burgwal*, Zwolle, 233-256.

Schats, R., 2017b: 'A Probable Case of Pre-Columbian Syphilis in The Netherlands', Poster presented at Annual Conference British Association for Biological Anthropology and Osteoarchaeology, Sheffield.

Van der Merwe, A.E., G.J.R. Maat & I. Watt, 2012: 'Diffuse Idiopathic Hyperostosis: Diagnosis in a Palaeopathological Context', *HOMO-Journal of Comparative Human Biology* 63, 202-215. https://doi.org/10.1016/j.jchb.2012.03.005

Van der Meyer, C., C Jung, T. Kohl, A. Poenicke, A. Poppe & K.W. Alt, 2002: 'Syphilis 2001 – a Palaeopathological Reappraisal', *Homo* 53, 39-58. https://doi.org/10.1078/0018-442X-00037

Van Santen, S., 2017: 'Op ziekenbezoek. Een kijkje in het dagelijks leven van het Sint Geertruidengasthuis', in: M. Klomp (ed.), *Myosotis, in de schaduw van het Sint Geertruidengasthuis. Archeologisch onderzoek tussen Boven Nieuwstraat en Burgwal*, Zwolle, 27-38.

Waldron, T., 2009: *Palaeopathology.* Cambridge Manuals in Archaeology, Cambridge.

Wood, J.W., G.R. Milner, H.C. Harpending & K.M. Weiss, 1992: 'The osteological paradox: Problems of inferring health from skeletal samples', *Current Anthropology* 33, 343-370. https://doi.org/10.1086/204084

Workshop for European Anthropologists (WEA), 1980: 'Recommendations for Age and Sex Diagnoses of the Skeletons'. *Journal of Human Evolution* 9, 517-549. https://doi.org/10.1016/0047-2484(80)90061-5

Diversity in death

Skeletal evidence of burial preferences in a late to post-medieval convent in Aalst (Belgium)

Jessica L.A Palmer

Introduction and historical context

The town of Aalst is located on the southwestern bank of the Dender River. Both archaeological finds and toponomy indicate continuous human presence in this area from prehistoric times to the present.[1] The earliest historical record of Aalst is a 9th-century reference to the Villa Alost, although this settlement probably had its roots in earlier Merovingian times.[2] Largely because of its favorable location on the bank of the river and as a crossing point for a land trade route between Bruges and Cologne,[3] Aalst grew into a thriving town. It obtained city rights in 1174, which granted the town autonomy.[4] Its general layout was established in the early 13th century with the construction of ramparts and moats, which are still visible in the current-day townscape.[5] As Aalst only outgrew these fortifications in the 19th century,[6] the town center forms a rich but complex archaeological palimpsest.

In post-medieval times, the economy of Aalst flourished because of specialized crafts, most notably the cloth industry[7] and its monopoly of the trade in hops.[8] Under Spanish rule (1555-1713) the town's economy is thought to have contracted, while under Austrian rule (1713-1792), the economy picked up again.[9] Historians estimate the population in 1395 to have been approximately 4,000, with a steady increase over time to 8,460 individuals in 1725.[10]

---

1 De Groote 2010, 252.
2 De Groote 2010, 253.
3 De Groote 2010, 255.
4 De Schryver 2001.
5 De Groote 2010, 258-259.
6 Callebaut 1983.
7 Courteaux & Martens 1973, 258.
8 Aerts 1999, 105.
9 De Schryver 2001.
10 De Brouwer 1968.

Fig. 1: Map of Aalst by Braun and Hogenberg (1588). a=Louis D'haeseleerstraat convent; b=Hopmarkt convent; c=St. Martin's Church.

In addition to the wealth of historical information, Aalst has seen increased archaeological research in recent decades. Excavations were first undertaken in 1982, yet the first large-scale excavation at the Hopmarkt occurred only in 2004/2005. Archaeological research in and around the historic town is steadily expanding, as the city is engaging in larger infrastructural works to accommodate its growing population and innovate the cityscape. The resultant increase of archaeological data about the town and its inhabitants provides an as yet untapped wealth of information for synthetic and comparative research.

The current article presents osteological data from one recent excavation in the Louis D'haeseleerstraat and compares it to data from two other burial locations within the city, the aforementioned Hopmarkt and St. Martin's Church (Fig. 1), to identify the socio-economic status of the individuals buried at the Louis D'haeseleerstraat site and provide insights into life and death in this vibrant town.

Archaeological and socio-historical context

Louis D'haeseleerstraat

This chapter focuses primarily on data from the 2016 excavations at Louis D'haeseleerstraat. This archaeological site encompasses part of the area where the convents of three consecutive Christian religious orders were located (Fig. 1). In *c.* 1450, Franciscan sisters started a convent, which, after destruction by the

Geuzen in the 16th century, was rebuilt in 1667 by the sisters of the Order of the Annunciation. A new church was built for the convent in the 18th century. In 1797 the French Republic closed the convent, and it was not rebuilt until 1836, this time by Teresian nuns. The current excavation took place in the garden of the earlier convent, and includes archaeological remains dated between 1450 and 1797.[11] The exact location of the buildings from the previous convent phases was unknown at the time of excavation and analysis.

Within the excavation area, there were three discernible zones where human remains were found, (Fig. 2). Most of the human skeletal material represented primary burials, with approximately 200 burials recovered. All burials had a northeast-southwest orientation, with the head in the southwest, and were organized in layers in a systemized pattern.[12] Aside from a few deviant burials, individuals were buried in a supine position with their arms either extended alongside the body or crossed over the torso.

It is as yet unclear which area of the pre-1797 these three burial zones were located in. In post-medieval Flanders, the most expensive burials usually took place inside the church, with the middle class being buried in the cloister garth, and a general cemetery where the lower classes were buried.[13] The burials in the Louis D'haeseleerstraat site are located in the convent garden of the 19th-century convent. Therefore, it can be hypothesized that this was either the cloister garth of the earlier convent or its general cemetery, as a church's location is the most static component of a convent and least likely to have changed during rebuilding in 1836.

Taking into account the orientation (all northeast-southwest) and distribution (no square area with a low-density middle ground) of the skeletons in zone 3, it is plausible that this was a general cemetery rather than a cemetery in the cloister garth/alley. Zone 2 was situated to the northwest of the current convent buildings, with a maximum of four layers of organized primary burials present. Approximately 55 individuals were identified during excavation. This zone has been disturbed more than zone 3, complicating assessment of the burial context. Based on the excavation plan, this area could be a continuation of the general cemetery, but a cloister or church at this location is not impossible. Both burial areas of zones 2 and 3 probably extended beyond the excavated area. Zone 1 was a small section at the very extremity of the excavated area, which suggests that this area was separate from the general cemetery, representing either church or cloister burials.

Hopmarkt and St. Martin's Church

The data from the Louis D'haeseleerstraat excavation are compared to two other burial contexts within the city of Aalst: the Carmelite friary located at the current Hopmarkt and St. Martin's Church.[14]

---

11 Bruggeman *et al.* in prep.

12 All burial context information based on excavation data provided by Dr. Natasja Reyns and Drs. Jordi Bruggeman of All-Archeo bvba.

13 De Groote *et al.* 2018, 220.

14 All data were gathered by the author unless otherwise specified.

The Carmelite friary (1497-1797)[15] was excavated in two phases. In the first phase (2004/2005), skeletons from the church, cloister alleys, and cloister garth were uncovered, and in the second phase (2011), burials in the cloister garden and alleys were excavated.[16]

If the Louis D'haeseleerstraat pre-1797 convent is hypothesized to contain mainly regular lay people, the Carmelite convent site primarily contained burials of upper-class individuals and clerics.[17] For the first phase of the Hopmarkt excavation, a dietary stable isotope study was done on all three burial zones, i.e., church, cloister alley, and cloister garth, for males and females.[18] Demographically, the first excavation phase of the Hopmarkt contained few subadults (29 subadults versus 209 adults). The hypothesis was put forward that most children were buried in the unexcavated general cemetery, as archival records attest to the majority of burials being that of children.[19] The second excavation phase, the other half of the cloister alleys, uncovered 95 skeletons (31 subadults and 64 adults) which were complete enough for a detailed osteological analysis.[20] Even when combined with the results of phase one, significantly fewer children were accounted for than the archival data attest to.

St. Martin's Church is the main church of Aalst, with a long, multi-phased history. However, the skeletal sample that was excavated in 1997/1998 was dated 1655-1782.[21] Unfortunately, no isotopic data are as yet available. Analysis of the 29 skeletons that were complete enough for osteological research revealed that of the 18 individuals buried in the church, only four were subadults.[22] However, of the 11 individuals excavated in the cemetery outside the church, only two were subadults. Preservation could be a key issue here. The 1997/1998 excavation covered an area that had been cross-cut by the construction of a wall, leading to many skeletons effectively losing their upper or lower half. It is not unlikely that some smaller child skeletons would have been completely obliterated by this construction and not recovered in the rescue excavation. Thus, this demographic sample is too small to be useful for comparison.

The St. Martin's Church excavation does provide one striking pathological find. In the group of burials located inside the church, a middle-aged woman was found with an advanced case of metastatic carcinoma, most likely the result of breast cancer.[23] This woman had extreme osteoclastic activity in her entire axial skeleton, including major bone resorption on the skull and along the spinal canal. The extent and severity of the lesions attest to her living with this pathology for quite some time.

15 De Maeyer *et al.* 2014.
16 De Groote *et al.* 2018, 224; De Maeyer *et al.* 2014, 108.
17 De Groote *et al.* 2011, 127, 130, 194.
18 Quintelier *et al.* 2014, 207.
19 De Groote *et al.* 2011, 127.
20 Palmer 2014, 2.
21 De Groote & Moens 1999, 56.
22 Palmer 2016, 3.
23 Palmer *et al.* 2017.

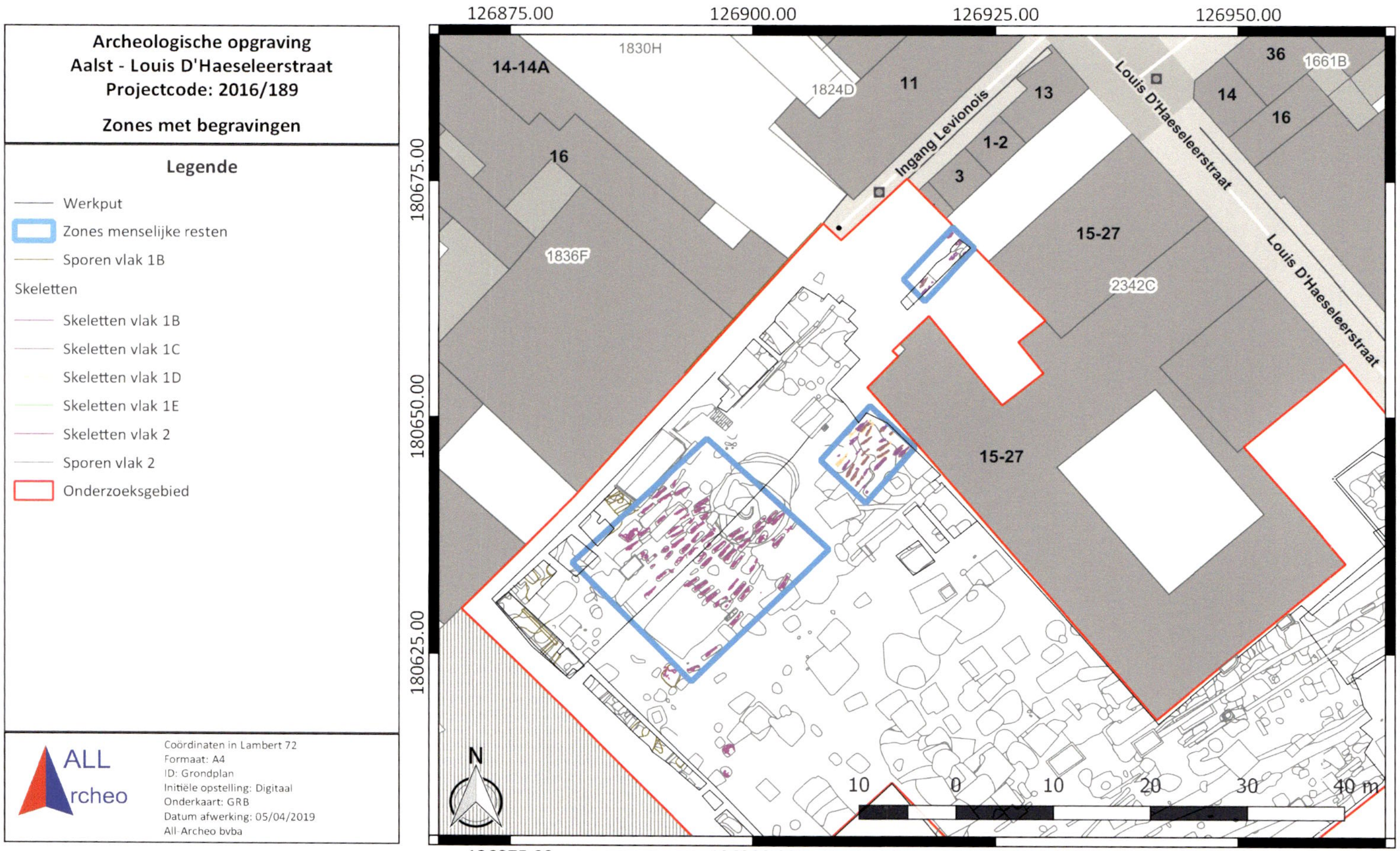

Fig.2: St. Martin's Church excavation area. The three zones where human remains were uncovered are outlined in blue.

Socio-economic context

Historical information on the lives and occupations of the poorer individuals buried in Aalst is limited. More data are available for the middle class. In Aalst, this middle class consisted in large part of specialized crafts- and tradesmen (the most important being blue- and blackdyers, tailors, bakers, and shopkeepers). These *ambachten* employed predominantly local people.[24] Historical sources also make a clear distinction between *poorters* (townspeople) and *niet-poorters* (foreigners). When niet-poorters moved to the town, they usually came from the immediate surrounding countryside.[25] From a physical anthropological perspective, this means that the middle-class component of the cemeteries consisted of a relatively small genetic group, as Aalst preferred to train and employ townspeople in the trades. Given the social distinction of niet-poorters and the generally limited migration radius, it is likely that the poorer and richer people buried in this town represent a similarly limited gene pool. As for the lives and occupations of the high-class individuals of Aalst, they were probably highly placed members of the crafts and trade guilds or high-ranking clericals.

Physical anthropological methods

The historical and archaeological context outlined above suggests that the Louis D'haeseleerstraat sample most likely consisted of the general population buried in the general cemetery and some high-ranking individuals, possibly clerics, buried in the cloister garth or church. To test this hypothesis, physical anthropological analyses were undertaken. Both general osteological data and dietary isotopes were studied. Of the approximately 200 individuals recovered, 164 were complete and preserved well enough for an assessment of sex, age-at-death, and pathology. Sex was estimated through traits on the pelvis, cranium, and mandible, following the Workshop for European Archaeologists guidelines,[26] the Phenice pubic traits,[27] and metrics.[28] Age was estimated using the morphology of the pubic symphysis,[29] auricular surface,[30] and sternal rib end,[31] as well as dental attrition,[32] cranial suture closure,[33] and the fusion state of late fusing epiphyses. Subadult age was estimated using Scheuer and Black and Schaefer *et al.*[34] Carbon and nitrogen stable isotope analysis was performed on a subsample of 50 adult individuals to research dietary differences potentially linked to socio-economic status.

---

24 De Schryver 2001.
25 De Schryver 2001.
26 Ferembach *et al.* 1980.
27 Phenice 1969.
28 McCormick *et al.* 1991; Stewart 1979; Steyn & Işcan 1999.
29 Suchey & Brooks 1990.
30 Buckberry & Chamberlain 2002.
31 Işcan *et al.* 1984.
32 Maat 2001.
33 Meindl & Lovejoy 1985.
34 Scheuer & Black 2000; Schaefer *et al.* 2009.

Results

Demography

Of the 164 individuals analyzed, 68 were subadults and 96 were adults (Fig. 3). The subadults were divided into three age categories. Infants (0-3), children (4-12), and adolescents (13-18). No individuals younger than 40 weeks in utero were identified. Children formed the largest group of subadults in the cemetery.

Adults were divided into four age categories: early young adult (19-25), late young adult (26-35), middle-aged adult (36-50), and old adult (50+). Exact age estimation was impossible for four adults, therefore an 18+ age estimation was given to them. In the adult group, middle-aged adults formed the largest segment of the demographic.

Of the 96 adults analyzed for sex, 53 individuals were female, 40 were male, and the sex of three individuals could not be reliably determined. When sorted by age, there were slightly more men in the early young adult category than women.

When we compare the Louis D'haeseleerstraat data to the Hopmarkt, the former site had a much larger relative number of subadults. Thus, these results support the hypothesis of De Groote *et al.* that children were buried in the general cemetery, or at least less often in the cloister garth and alleys of the convents in post-medieval Aalst.

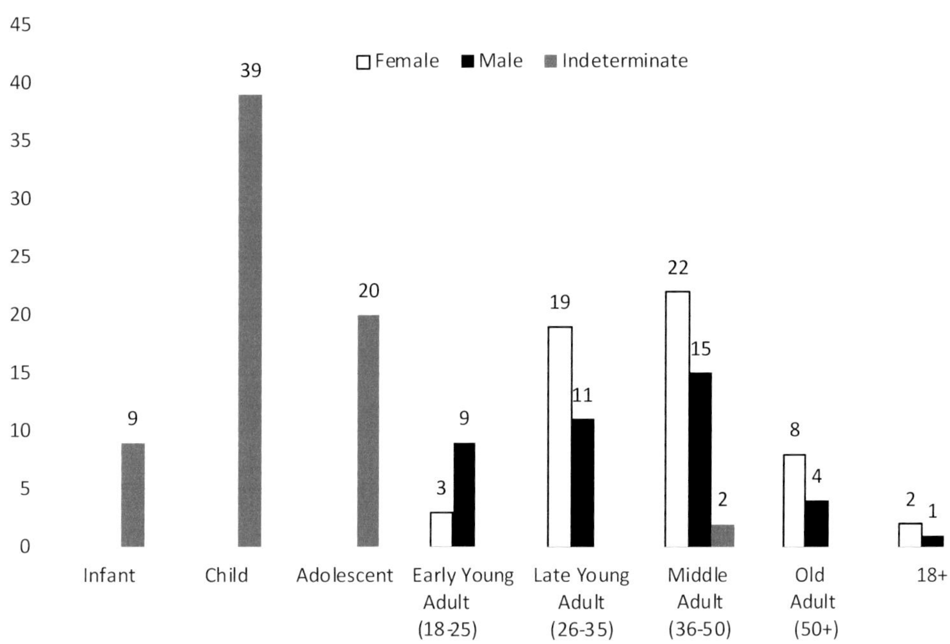

Fig. 3: Demographic distribution (n=164).

Pathology

Two individuals within the Louis D'haeseleerstraat population had pathological conditions which set them apart from the rest of the population. Their pathology will be discussed, for one individual to elucidate why she was included in the isotopic research and for the other, for comparison to a similar case from St. Martin's Church.[35]

The first individual, SK80, was a middle-aged woman with severe lesions to the right hand and knee (Fig. 4). The normal distal femoral and proximal tibial joint surfaces were entirely destroyed, with granular new bone and large pores. A new pseudo-joint had formed at the knee, with an associated new pseudo-facet for the patella (which was taphonomically lost). These pathological new facets show macroporosity and lipping and have an irregular granular appearance. When re-articulated, the leg twisted, with the femur angled antero-medially and the tibia antero-laterally. Given the extensive lipping and angle of false articulation, the flexibility of this knee would have been severely limited. In conjunction with this knee pathology, the right hand shows several osseous deformations. The hamate had ankylosed with the 4th metacarpal and the trapezoid with the 2nd metacarpal. The two other carpals available for analysis were so deformed as to be near unrecognizable. The phalanges were relatively unaffected, although one bone was too deformed for accurate identification; it could be a phalanx, metacarpal, or the fusion of multiple hand bones. Throughout the skeleton, anomalies which were likely secondary to these joint pathologies could be observed. The humeral heads were angled more superiorly than normal, and the auricular surfaces on both os coxae and sacrum were more oblong than ear-shaped with granular new bone. The extent of the primary and possible secondary pathological lesions implies that this woman had a chronic affliction. These joint pathologies would have had a severe impact on her life, as she would have required a cane at the very least to achieve some mobility. Her right hand would have been stiff and unable to perform many tasks. She was buried in zone 3, the proposed general cemetery area. SK80 was included in the stable isotope study to assess whether her pathological condition altered her role in society to such an extent that her diet differed from the rest of the population.

The second individual, SK129, was a middle-aged (35-50) woman buried in zone 4 (i.e., the potential high-status zone).She showed severe pathological lesions in several locations on her skeleton (Fig. 5). Lesions occurring in het vertebrae, sacrum, os coxa and cranium had a lytic, starburst-like appearance. On her cranium specifically, the lesions have a hollowed-out appearance, with the outer cortical surface both ecto- and endocranially less resorbed than the trabecular bone in between. Two vertebrae also show unstructured new bone formation in the vertebral body, with the new bone having a chalky, brittle appearance. These vertebrae are heavy compared to the vertebrae where bone erosion has occurred (for instance, the complete L5 weighed 11.3g whereas the L4, of which only the body was preserved, weighed 16.8g. Both had been cleaned

35 For an overview of all pathological conditions encountered in this skeletal collection, see Palmer 2018 in Bruggeman *et al.* in prep.

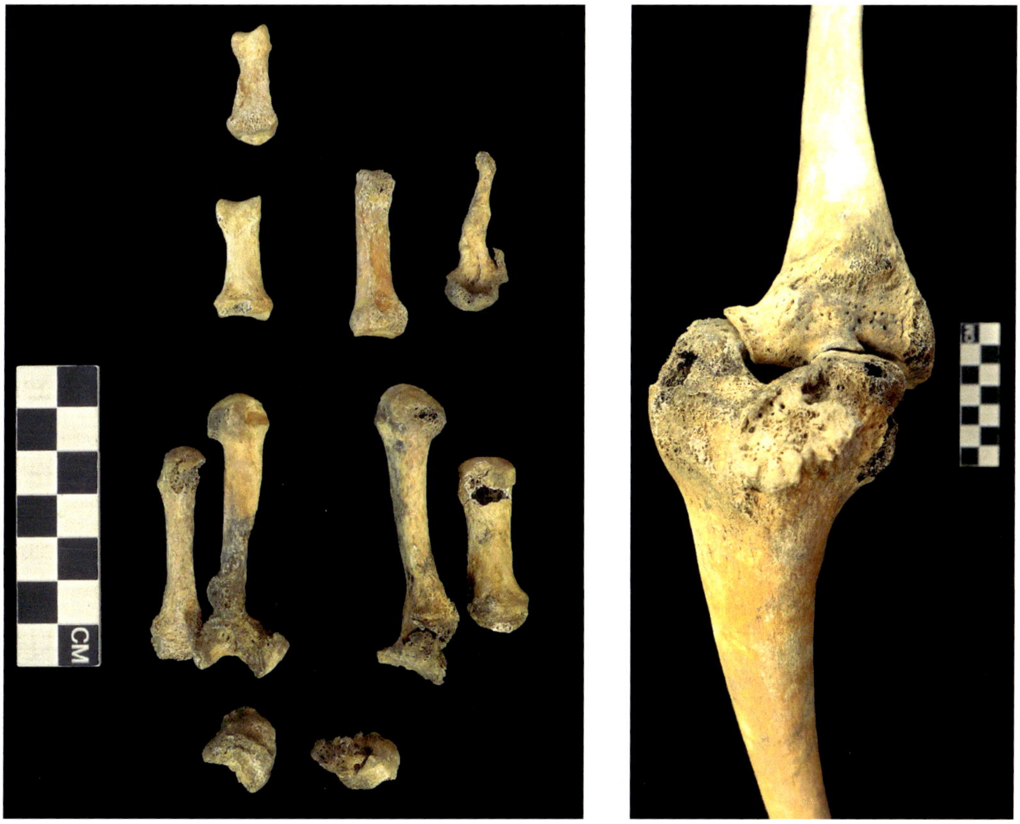

Fig. 4: Right-hand bones and knee of SK80. Note the fused wrist and hand bones, the deformed phalanx/metacarpal, the angle of the knee, the outward twist of the lower leg, and the pathological new facet for the patella on the outside of the femur.

through sonication to remove soil particles). Her femora were also affected, particularly on the right anterior diaphysis and near the femoral heads. The type and location of the lesions are concurrent with metastatic cancer,[36] but the exact type of cancer cannot be determined. However, the osseous metastasis of cancer is most common in breast cancer, being present in 60-70% of cases.[37] This type of cancer is not unlikely given her age and sex. On both legs, dark green-grey stains were visible at regular intervals on tibiae and femora. This could point to a brace with metal fittings, which would have allowed her some mobility despite her widespread, severe pathology. This woman's life would have been greatly affected by this pathology. Both the original cancer and secondary metastatic osseous pathology would have severely impaired her physical abilities. However, the extent of the lesions shows that she lived with this disease for quite some time, and the possible braces point to care being given by the community.

36 Mundy 2002, 585; Lieverse *et al.* 2014, 18.
37 Guise *et al.* 2006, 6213s.

This is a close parallel to a skeleton excavated at St. Martin's Church, also a woman with metastatic carcinoma buried in the high-status area of the site, i.e., within the church. Her lesions were also extensive, illustrating that she, too, lived with the disease for some time and in a physical state which would have required assistance from others. Although it is unlikely that the socio-economic position of these two women had any bearing on them getting cancer, their social status might have given them access to better care, which would have allowed them to live longer

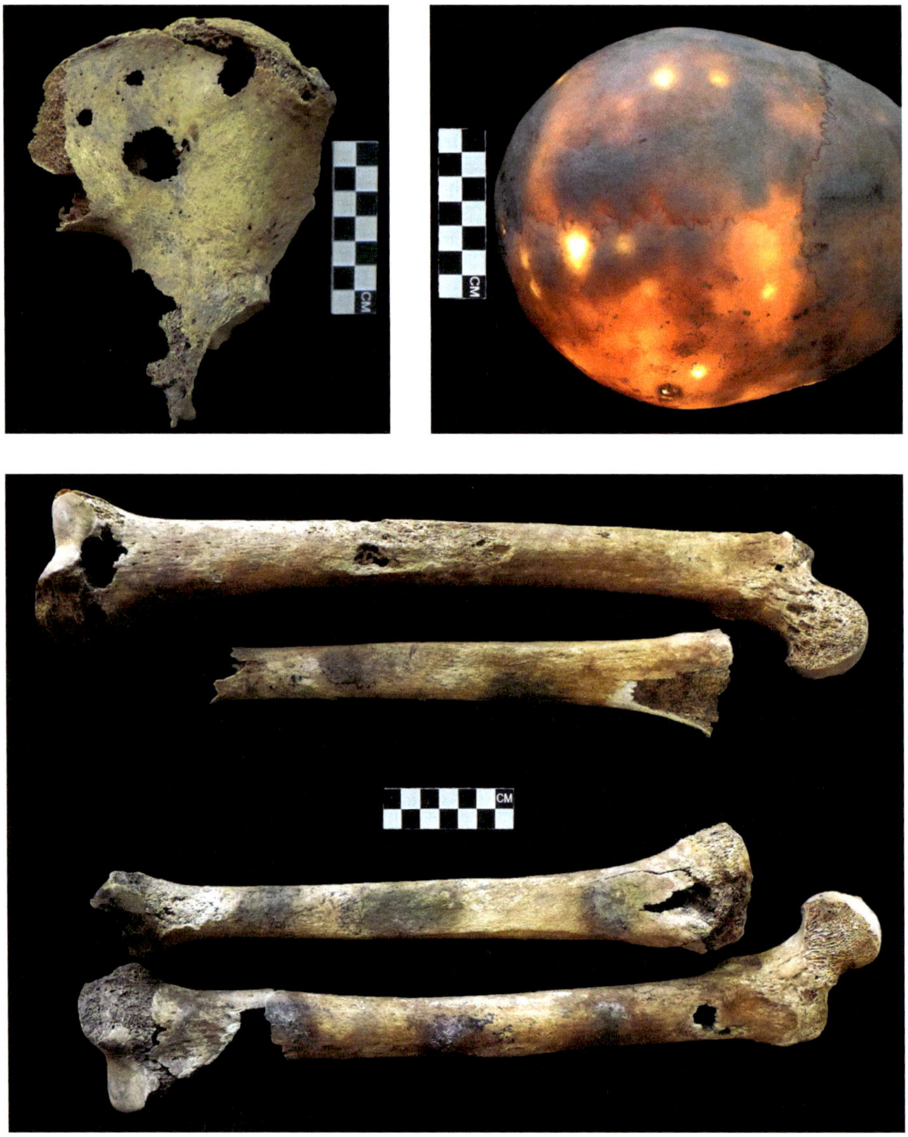

Fig. 5: Skull, right os coxa and leg bones of SK129. A light source placed endocranially shows the endosteal lesions in both parietals (superior view). Osteoclastic lesions in the right os coxa with a hollowed out interior are typical of metastatic carcinoma. The leg bones show a pattern of staining which could be indicative of a brace. Note also the metastatic lesion on the anterior diaphysis of the right femur.

despite the absence of any effective medical treatment at the time. Aside from this similarity, it must be noted that paleopathological cases of cancer are rare. To my knowledge, these women are the first archaeological cases of cancer from Belgium. It is remarkable that two individuals from this small area and limited time period could be diagnosed. Some types of cancer, including breast cancer, have genetic risk factors.[38] Therefore, one possible explanation for this is that the small gene pool suggested by historical records (cfr. supra) contained a gene which resulted in a higher risk of cancer in this population or in some of its families.

Dietary isotopes

Diet is intrinsically linked to socio-cultural environment and economic status. It is hypothesized that nuns and lay people were buried in the excavated area, with zone 1 being primarily reserved for high-ranking nuns and zones 2 and 3 for the general population. A bone collagen sample was taken from 50 individuals. Sample selection was based primarily on burial location, with representative samples taken from the three burial zones to analyze whether burial location was determined by social factors. For each burial cluster, all layers were sampled to analyze potential chronological changes in diet. Some individuals were also sampled because they had a deviant burial context, i.e., orientation or position in the grave. SK80 was included to evaluate whether she had a different diet from the rest of the population, given her physical impairment. To evaluate sex and age differences in diet, individuals were chosen to represent all adult age categories for both sexes. Thus, a total of 25 women and 25 men were selected, some from each adult age category.

These samples were processed and analyzed for the stable isotopic ratios of carbon and nitrogen. Ratios of ^{13}C versus ^{12}C are represented as $\partial^{13}C$, ratios of ^{15}N versus ^{14}N as $\partial^{15}N$ in amounts pro mille relative to the relevant standards. These isotopes give an indication of the type of plant that was consumed ($\partial^{13}C$) and the amount and potential type of animal protein that was consumed ($\partial^{15}N$).[39]

Results show a marked variation in nitrogen isotopic values, with $\partial^{15}N$ ranging from 9.6 to 13.5 pro mille (the $\partial^{13}C$ range was more limited, -20.72 to -19.45 pro mille) (Fig. 6). This range was partially caused by a difference in dietary isotopes between the burial clusters. Specifically, zone 1 (average $\partial^{13}C$ was -19.83‰, average $\partial^{15}N$ was 12.65‰, n=3) had a higher $\partial^{15}N$ isotopic signature than zone 2 (average $\partial^{13}C$ was -20.12‰, average $\partial^{15}N$ was 10.95‰, n=9) and zone 3 (average ∂13C was -20.18‰, average $\partial^{15}N$ was 11.04‰, n=37). Within zones 2 and 3, no differences in isotopic signature were found between the stratigraphic layers. The woman with the severe knee pathology had a diet that was within the normal range of the population (Fig. 6). When all the data are plotted, two individuals stand out due to their high $\partial^{15}N$ values (top right corner of Figure 6). These values represent two women, estimated to be between 35 and 50 years old. Both were buried in zone 1, i.e., well separated from the other burial clusters. The third individual sampled from zone 1, a 50+-year-old women, had isotopic values more in line with the rest of the population ($\partial^{13}C$ -20.44‰, $\partial^{15}N$ 11.17‰).

---

38 Turnbull & Rahman 2008, 321.

39 See Lee-Thorp 2008 for an overview of the field of dietary stable isotope analysis.

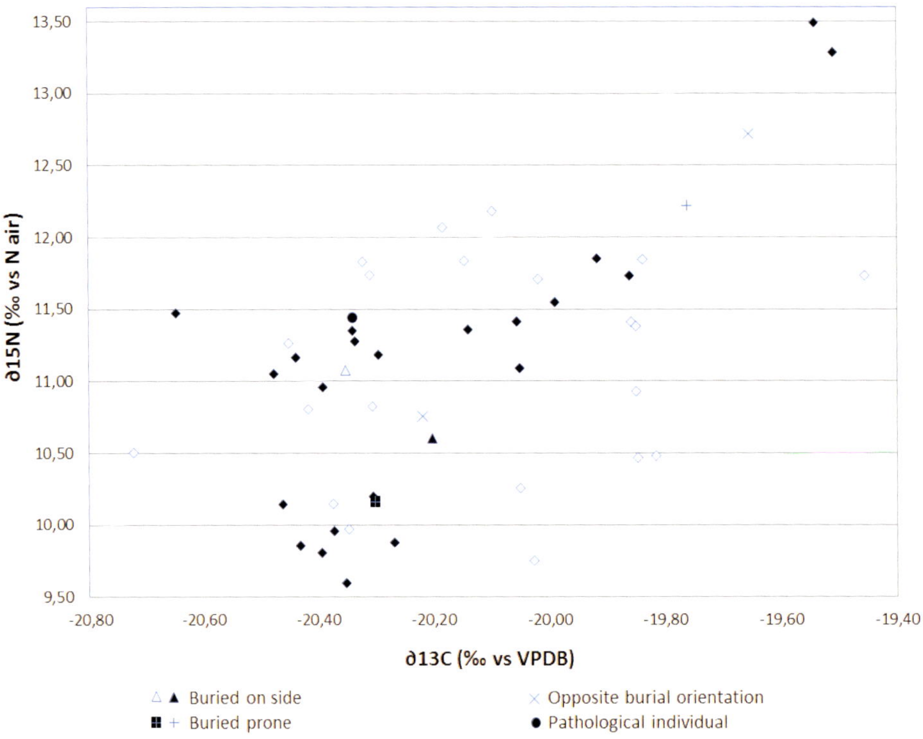

Fig. 6: ∂13C and ∂15N values of 50 adult individuals from the 1450 Louis D'haeseleerstraat excavation.
black – woman ; blue – man
Δ – an individual buried on their side
x – an individual buried with their head to the northeast
+ – an individual buried lying prone
o – the individual with the pathological knee and hand condition
◊ – an individual buried with their head to the southwest, on their back

	n	$\partial^{13}C$ (‰ vs VPDB)	$\partial^{15}N$ (‰ vs N_{air})
Younger women	14	-20.24	10.91
Older women	11	-20.18	11.20
Younger men	11	-20.14	10.92
Older men	14	-20.05	11.41

Table 1: Average isotopic values per age and sex category.

There are no clear differences between men and women in this sample (Fig. 6). The female average is slightly lower ($\partial^{13}C$ -20.22‰ and $\partial^{15}N$ 11.04‰) than the male average ($\partial^{13}C$ -20.09‰ and $\partial^{15}N$ 11.20‰) (see also Fig. 7). To achieve a sample that was comparable to other isotopic research from Aalst (cfr. infra), individuals aged 18-35 were grouped as 'younger women/men' and individuals aged 35+ as 'older women/men'. These averages show that while no large dietary differences between the sexes were present, based on the $\partial^{15}N$ values, there was a slight increase in animal protein intake with age.

When these stable isotopic values were compared to the stable isotopic data from the Hopmarkt site, the Hopmarkt samples showed similar diversity in diet in the ∂15N ratios, if slightly less variation than at the Louis D'haeseleerstraat. On average, isotopic values were higher at the Hopmarkt site, especially for males. This suggests that the diet of people buried there was richer, i.e., higher in animal protein. This supports our hypothesis that zones 2 and 3 of the Louis D'haeseleerstraat site formed the general cemetery of this convent, where the relatively lower class population was buried. The sexual differentiation seen at the Hopmarkt, with older males, and to a lesser extent younger males, showing evidence of a richer diet, is not seen at the Louis D'haeseleerstraat excavation. At this site, the highest values were assigned to two women. Given that the Hopmarkt was a male convent and the Louis D'haeseleerstraat a female convent, and that the Louis D'haeseleerstraat site contained more females than males, whereas the Hopmarkt cemetery contained more males than females, we can conclude that nuns were buried at the Louis D'haeseleerstraat and that high-ranking nuns were buried in zone 1.

Of the deviant burial positions, one individual buried with their head to the northeast stands out. This 35-50-year-old man had the highest $\partial^{15}N$ after the two women mentioned in the previous paragraph (Fig. 6). It can be hypothesized that he was a priest. In Catholic burials, high-ranking clerics were buried in the opposite orientation than lay people, so that on the Day of Judgment they would be facing their flock when they rose from the grave. The second man buried in the opposite orientation from most of the individuals was also middle aged and buried in zone 2. His stable isotopic values fell within the average range of the population. The dietary isotopes of the rest of the individuals buried in deviant positions also did not diverge significantly. A possible explanation for these deviant burials with average dietary isotopic values is that mistakes were made in their burial. It was not unheard of that some coffins and shrouded bodies got turned around by mistake in the process of burial. No clear explanation presents itself for the man and woman buried lying on their side. The man was almost fully stretched out, and this might

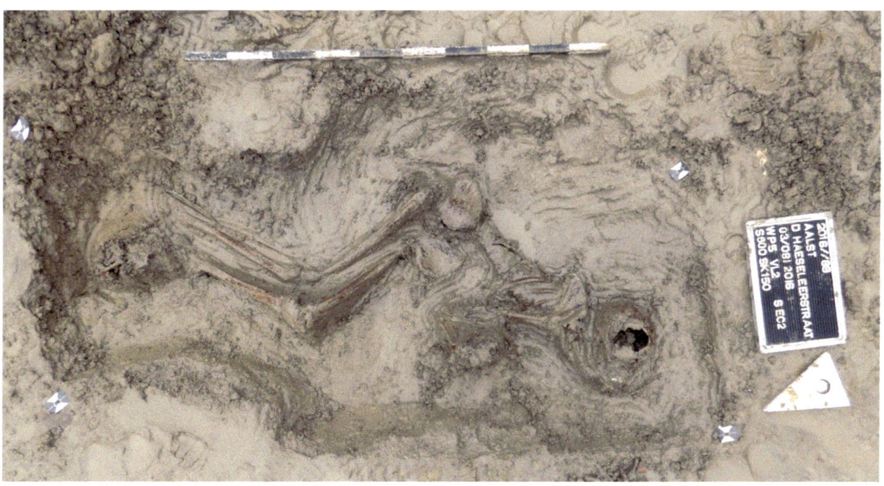

Fig. 7: SK150 with a deviant burial position (photo courtesy of All-Archeo bvba).

have been a burial error. The woman (17+/-2 years old), however, was curled up on her side in such a way that this explanation is unlikely (Fig. 7). Osteological analysis revealed that at the time of death there was active periosteal new bone formation on both distal tibiae and on the medial end of the left clavicle. This indicates that she was experiencing some form of physical stress in the period prior to death. Furthermore, she showed several asymmetries in her spinal column which could have resulted in abnormal posture. Thus, it can be hypothesized that her burial position potentially reflects her spinal pathology.

In summary, the dietary stable isotope data added unique information to our understanding of the population of the Louis D'haeseleerstraat site and the social differentiation in burial location. Two women buried in a distinct separate zone of the site had consumed significantly more animal protein than the rest of the sample individuals. In this socio-historic context, marine fish was an important source of animal protein,[40] and given the reservoir effect of the marine environment on fish nitrogen values, seafood consumption likely contributed to the elevated ∂^{15}N ratios. This dietary difference, combined with their separate burial location within the convent, might mean that these women were nuns, possibly of a high rank. It also indicates that this area was distinct from the general cemetery. The dietary isotopes thus support the hypothesis that zones 2 and 3 at the Louis D'haeseleerstraat cemetery represent the general cemetery associated with the convent, whereas zone 1 represents a high-status burial location, most likely the cloister garth from a previous building phase or an earlier church.

Conclusion

The osteoarchaeological data presented here provide information on burial preferences both within the main site of the female convent at Louis D'haeseleerstraat, as well as between the different burial contexts available to the citizens of post-medieval Aalst. The burial pattern revealed during excavation, with a large well-organized area of burials (zones 2 and 3) and one sequestered area (zone 1), suggest that the larger area represented the general cemetery. Osteobiographic data, which show that the smaller, separate area held mainly females whereas the other burial area held all ages of individuals from both sexes, corroborates this hypothesis. The addition of isotopic data, which showed a distinct dietary isotopic signature for the individuals buried in zone 1, meaning that they enjoyed a rich diet with more marine fish, confirms that this zone contained the high-status burials of the Louis D'haeseleerstraat excavation.

When the isotopic data were compared to those gathered for the high-status individuals of the convent excavated at the Hopmarkt and analyzed by Quintelier *et al.* (2014), it was clear that while the high-status females (probably nuns) of the Louis D'haeseleerstraat site had isotopic signatures very similar to the male clerics of the Hopmarkt, the general cemetery population had a diet lower in animal protein than these clerics and high-status individuals. In the Hopmarkt, the average male ∂^{15}N was 12.3 and the average female ∂^{15}N was 11.4, whereas at the Louis D'haeseleerstraat site, the average male ∂^{15}N was 11.2‰ and the average female ∂^{15}N was 11.04‰. When the zone-1 women are excluded from the data, the average female ∂^{15}N is 10.82‰.

40 Van Neer *et al.* 2016, 9; Ervynck *et al.* 2004, 233-237.

The demographic composition of the Louis D'haeseleerstraat population, with its high number of subadults, contrasts with the Hopmarkt. This supports the hypothesis of De Groote *et al.* (2011) that children were more often buried in the general cemetery than in the cloister alleys or cloister garden.

Finally, the data gathered here provide a unique insight into disease in the past and how this post-medieval society treated those who were, due to physical impairments, unable to function 'normally'. SK80, a woman with impairments to the right hand, which would have severely limited the use of her arm, and lesions to the right leg, which would have prevented her from walking normally, ate the same general diet as the other individuals in her community. SK 129, a woman who suffered from widespread metastatic carcinoma, probably had braces that would have helped her retain some mobility, as indicated by stains on her leg bones, which may be a vestige of the metal clasps of braces. The presence of two women with metastatic carcinoma in this small post-medieval town also suggests that a genetic factor might be at play and adds unique and valuable data to our growing understanding of the history of cancer, further supporting the hypothesis that cancer is not a disease of modernity.

This research demonstrates the value of comparing osteoarcheological data both between different sites from the same historical period and within a single archaeological site. In the current archaeological landscape, with an ever-increasing body of data from excavation reports and isolated sites, this three-site comparison underlines the need for larger studies to fully understand the burial dynamics and physical reality of life within past urban environments.

Acknowledgements

I would like to thank Drs. Jordi Bruggeman and Dr. Natasja Reyns at All-archaeo bvba for allowing me to analyze the Louis D'haeseleerstraat collection, and Kim Quintelier at the Flemish Heritage Institute for allowing me to analyze the Hopmarkt and St. Martin's Church collection.

Bibliography

Aerts, E., 1999: 'Hop en bier. Handelsrelaties tussen Aalst en Lier (17[de]-18[de] eeuw)', *Het Land van Aalst,* 51, 101-126.

Bruggeman, J., Coremans L., Claessens, L. & Reyns, N. in prep.: *Archeologische opgraving Aalst – Louis D'Haeseleerstraat. Annunciaden- en Theresianenklooster,* (met bijdrage van Jessica Palmer), Temse/Bornhem (Rapporten All-Archeo bvba 316).

Buckberry, J.L. & Chamberlain, A.T., 2002: 'Age Estimation from the Auricular Surface of the Ilium: A Revised Method', *American Journal of Physical Anthropology* 119, 231-239. DOI: 10.1002/ajpa.10130

Callebaut, D., 1983: 'De topografische groei van Aalst of hoe een Zelhof een gebastioneerde stad werd', *Archaeologia Belgica. Miscellanea Archaeologica in honorem H. Roosens*, 255, 227-249.

Courteaux, F. & Martens, D., 1973: 'Het leven in de stad', *Het Land van Aalst,* 25(5), 258-263.

De Brouwer J., 1968: *Demografische evolutie in het Land van Aalst 1570-1800,* Pro Civitate Historische Uitgaven, Brussel.

De Groote, K., 2010: 'The Contribution of Archaeological Sources to the Research of the Formation of Towns: The Example of Aalst, a Border Town in the County of Flanders', in: K. De Groote, D. Tys & M. Pieters (eds.): *Exchanging Medieval Material Culture: Studies on Archaeology and History Presented to Frans Verhaeghe*, Brussel (Relicta Monografieën 4), 249-266.

De Groote, K. & Moens, J., 1999: 'Noodonderzoek in de St-Martinuskerk te Aalst (O.-Vl.)', *Archaeologia Mediaevalis*, 28, 104-105.

De Groote K., De Maeyer W., Moens J., Quintelier K., Van Cleven F., Vanden Berghe I. & Vernaeve W., 2011: 'Het Karmelietenklooster van Aalst (Prov. Oost-Vlaanderen) (1497-1797). Het Gebouwenbestand, de Begravingen en het Fysisch-Antropologische Onderzoek', *Relicta* 8, 83-250.

De Groote, K., Moens, J. & Quintelier, K., 2018: 'The Carmelite Monastery in Aalst, Belgium, Province of East Flanders (1497-1797): An Urban Burial Ground in a Monastic Environment', in R.M.R. van Oosten, R. Schats, K. Fast, N. Arts & J. Bouwmeester (eds.), *The Urban Graveyard: Archaeological Perspectives*. Leiden: Sidestone Press, 219-238.

De Maeyer W., Van Cauwenbergh S., Klinkenborg S., Taelman E. & Cherretté B., 2014: *Aalst Hopmarkt – fase 2 Onderzoek van de Pandgangen en de Poel*, Sint-Lievens-Houtem (Solva Archeologie rapport 25).

De Schryver S., 2001: *Aspecten van sociale mobiliteit Binnen de 18de-eeuwse Aalsterse Ambachtswereld. Een prosopografische benadering*, (unpublished thesis, Ghent University).

Ervynck, A., Van Neer, W. & Pieters, M., 2004: 'How the North Was Won (and Lost Again): Historical and Archaeological Data on the Exploitation of the North Atlantic by the Flemish Fishery', in: R.A. Housley & G. Coles (eds.), *Atlantic Connections and Adaptations: Economies, Environments and Subsistence in Lands Bordering the North Atlantic*. Oxford: Oxbow, 230-239.

Ferembach, D., Schwindezky, I. & Stoukal, M., 1980: 'Recommendation for Age and Sex Diagnoses of Skeletons', *Journal of Human Evolution* 9, 517-549. https://doi.org/10.1016/j.jchb.2005.07.002

Guise, T.A., Mohammad, K.S., Clines, G., Stebbins, E.G., Wong, D.H., Higgins, L.S., Vessella, R., Corey, E., Padalecki, S., Suva, L. & Chirgwin, J.M., 2006: 'Basic Mechanisms Responsible for Osteolytic and Osteoblastic Bone Metastases', *Clinical Cancer Research* 12, 6213-6216. DOI: 10.1158/1078-0432.CCR-06-1007

Işcan, M.Y., Loth, S.R. & Wright R.K., 1984: 'Metamorphosis at the Sternal Rib End: A New Method to Estimate Age at Death in White Males', *American Journal of Physical Anthropology* 65, 147-156. DOI: 10.1002/ajpa.1330650206

Le-horp J.A. 2008. On isotopes and old bones. Archaeometry 50:925-950.

Lee-Thorp, J.A., 2008: 'On Isotopes and Old Bones', *Archaeometry* 50, 925-950. https://doi.org/10.1111/j.1475-4754.2008.00441.x

Lieverse, A., Temple, D.H. & Bazaliiskii, V.I., 2014: 'Paleopathological Description and Diagnosis of Metastatic Carcinoma in an Early Bronze Age (4588+34 Cal. BP) Forager from the Cis-Baikal Region of Eastern Siberia', *PLoS ONE* 9(12): e113919. https://doi.org/10.1371/journal.pone.0113919

Maat, G.J., 2001: 'Diet and Age-at-Death Determinations from Molar Attrition: A Review Related to the Low Countries', *Journal of Forensic Odontostomatology* 19(1), 18-21.

McCormick, W.F., Stewart, J.H. & Greene, H., 1991: 'Sexing of Human Clavicles Using Length and Circumference Measurements', *American Journal of Forensic Medicine and Pathology* 12, 175-181.

Meindl, S. & Lovejoy, O., 1985: 'Ectocranial Suture Closure: A Revised Method for the Determination of Skeletal Age at Death Based on the Lateral-Anterior Sutures', *American Journal of Physical Anthropology* 68, 57-66. DOI: 10.1002/ajpa.1330680106

Mundy, G.R., 2002: 'Metastasis: Metastasis to Bone: Causes, Consequences and Therapeutic Opportunities', *Nat. Rev. Cancer* 2, 584-593. DOI: 10.1038/nrc867

Palmer, J.L.A., 2014: Kort Rapport. Aalst-Hopmarkt 2011: Fysisch Antropologische Analyse. Unpublished osteological report.

Palmer, J.L.A., 2016: Kort Rapport: Aalst-Sint-Martinuskerk: Fysisch Antropologische Analyse. Unpublished osteological report.

Palmer, J.L.A, Quintelier, K. & Waters-Rist, A.L., 2017: 'A Probable Case of Metastatic Carcinoma from Post-Medieval Belgium', Poster presented at the 44th Annual North American Meeting of the Palaeopathology Association (April 17-19, 2017), New Orleans.

Phenice T.W., 1969: A Newly Developed Visual Method of Sexing the Os Pubis. *American Journal of Physical Anthropology* 30, 297-302. DOI: 10.1002/ajpa.1330300214

Quintelier, K., Ervynck, A., Müldner, G., Neer, W., Richards, M.P. & Fuller, B.T., 2014: 'Isotopic Examination of Links between Diet, Social Differentiation, and DISH at the Post-Medieval Carmelite Friary of Aalst, Belgium', *American Journal of Physical Anthropology*, 153, 203-213. doi:10.1002/ajpa.22420

Schaefer, M., Black S. & Scheuer L., 2009: *Juvenile Osteology: A Laboratory and Field Manual*. San Diego, CA: Academic Press.

Scheuer, L. & Black, S., 2000: *Developmental Juvenile Osteology*. San Diego, CA: Academic Press.

Stewart, T.D., 1979: *Essentials of Forensic Anthropology*. Springfield, IL: Charles C. Thomas.

Steyn, M. & Işcan, M.Y., 1999: 'Osteometric Variation in the Humerus: Sexual Dimorphism in South Africans', *Forensic Science International* 106, 77-85.

Suchey, S. & Brooks, J.M., 1990: 'Skeletal Age Determination Based on the Os Pubis: A Comparison of the Acsádi-Nemeskéri and Suchey-Brooks Methods', *Human Evolution* 5, 227-238.

Turnbull, C. & Rahman, N., 2008: 'Genetic Predisposition to Breast Cancer: Past, Present, and Future', *Annual Review of Genomics and Human Genetics* 9(1), 321-345.

Van Neer, W., Ervynck, A., Wouters, W., Muylaert, L., Barrett, J., Richards, M. & Johnstone, C., 2016: 'The Rise of Seafish Consumption in Inland Flanders (Belgium)', in: J. Barret & D. Orton (eds.), *Cod and Consequences: The Archaeology and History of Medieval Sea Fishing*, Oxford: Oxbow, 156-171.

Taking sides

An osteoarchaeological analysis of human skeletal remains from the south and north sides of St. Andrew's Church (Andreaskerk) in Hattem, the Netherlands

Barbara Veselka & Michael Klomp

Introduction

Traditionally, the preferred location for burial was inside the church, but this was often only affordable for the elite. Therefore, individuals of low to middle socioeconomic status were buried in the churchyard. Here too, some locations were preferable over others. The best location was close to the church on the 'warm' south side, whereas being buried on the 'cold' north side further away from the church was considered undesirable.[1] This chapter presents the results of the ostoarchaeological analysis of the skeletal collection from the Andreaskerk (St. Andrew's Church) in Hattem, the Netherlands, providing a unique opportunity to assess human remains from both sides of the church. In addition, the results of this analysis will be compared to three other contemporaneous populations: individuals from the cemetery of St. John's Church in Roosendaal (n = 60),[2] individuals from inside St. John's Church in Gouda (n = 45),[3] and individuals from the cemetery of the Keyserkerk in Middenbeemster (n = 125).[4] Such a study allows for the population of Hattem to be compared to a small urban population of low to middle socioeconomic status (Roosendaal), a population of high socioeconomic status (Gouda), and a rural population of low to middle socioeconomic status (Middenbeemster), enabling an assessment of differences and similarities between various contemporaneous sites.

1 Grolman 1923, 388.
2 Veselka 2015a, 3.
3 Veselka 2015b, 4.
4 Lemmers *et al.* 2013, 35.

The church and its cemetery

In 2015, renovations of the church square in Hattem required an excavation of parts of the cemetery of the Andreaskerk. Hattem, a small town near the large city of Zwolle, enjoyed prosperous times up to the 17th century because it was part of the Hanseatic League, but after the Spanish War and several periods of French occupations, experienced an economic decline.[5] The main economic activities of its inhabitants were agriculture and the transport of goods to neighbouring villages.[6] The Andreaskerk, also known as the Large Church, dates to the 12th century and was initially a small chapel. The current Gothic church was built in 1380 to 1390 AD. The church was Catholic, but following the 16th-century Reformation, became Protestant.[7] The cemetery of the Andreaskerk is believed to have been in use from 1190 to 1829 AD, but based on some of the grave finds (*i.e.* coins and buttons), combined with the stratigraphy of the trenches, the individuals have been dated only from the 17th to the 19th century. Figure 1 shows the location of the four trenches on either side of the church that were excavated, two on the south side and two on the north.

A total of 133 individuals has been excavated in the graveyard of the Andreaskerk. The majority of individuals were buried in a west-east orientation, a traditional Christian custom ensuring the deceased would be able to rise to meet the returning Jesus on Judgment Day in the east. Priests, on the other hand, were buried in an east-west orientation so that they would be able to address the risen believers, together with Jesus.[8] However, several individuals were buried in the opposite direction, east-west, or even perpendicular to most individuals. In particular, the orientation of the non-adults was less consistent. It has been suggested that the grave diggers had to economize space to accommodate the large number of individuals that needed to be buried in the churchyard and so employed various orientations.

Although discolouration of the soil suggests coffin burials for all individuals, confirmed by the presence of some coffin handles, no wood has been preserved. A limited number of grave finds accompanied the deceased, consisting of a button, a coin, and some pottery sherds. The grave of one individual buried in an east-west orientation (the opposite of what would be expected), contained a small jar, which has been x-rayed to assess the contents. The jar did not contain any objects, but samples of soil in the jar will be analysed to determine if the jar was empty or filled when buried. This could possibly enhance our knowledge of burial rituals and provide more information on the socioeconomic status of the individual.

Past Hattem individuals

The excavated human remains from the cemetery of the Andreaskerk are merely a fraction of the individuals buried there, which have been estimated to be around 22,855,[9] and even a smaller part of the past population of Hattem. In addition, the location and nature of the renovation activities influenced the sample of individuals that were excavated. In the case of Hattem, excavation on two sides

5 Sypkens Smit 1964, 43-44.
6 Koridon 1985, 23-28.
7 Sypkens Smit 1964, 40-41.
8 Grolman 1923.
9 Pers. comm. G. Kouwenhoven; http://streekarchiefehh.blogspot.nl/2015/

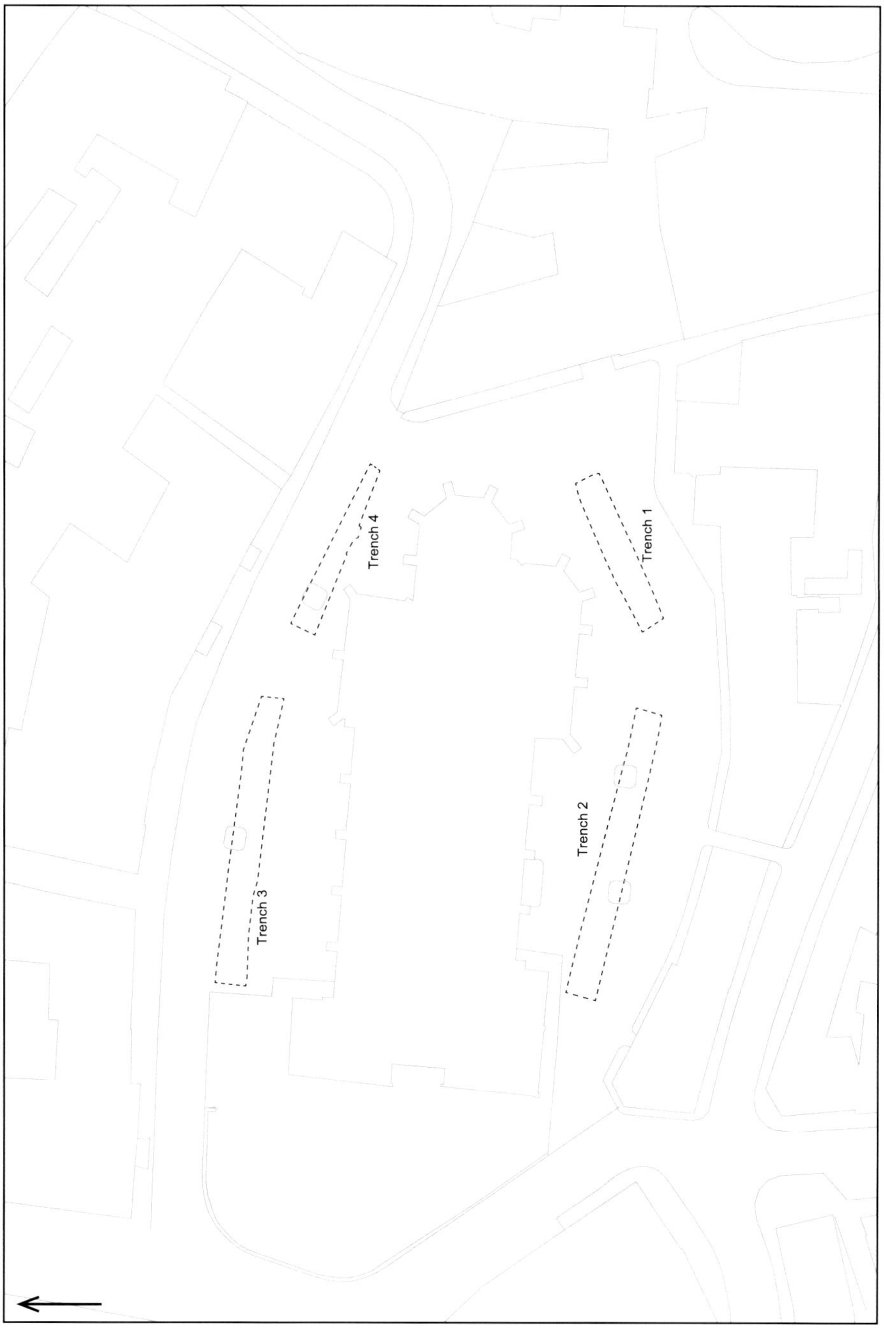

Fig. 1: Map of the church and the location of the four trenches.

of the church was required: the north and south sides. Usually, the north side was considered to be the 'cold side', reserved for poor people who were buried at a distance from the church.[10] In some cemeteries, stillborn babies, perinates, and young infants, were not allowed to be buried in the sacred ground of the cemetery, but were buried elsewhere, whether in a specially designated area of the cemetery or beyond the perimeter of the cemetery.[11] In other cemeteries, like the one from the Andreaskerk, the non-adults were buried amongst the adults. A total of 133 individuals come from trenches on the north (n = 67) and south sides (n = 66) of the church and were analysed for this paper.

Age-at-death

Age-at-death was estimated using a combination of several age-determination methods. For non-adult individuals, growth and development of certain parts of the skeleton were assessed, such as dental eruption,[12] dental development,[13] stage of epiphyseal fusion of the long bones,[14] long bone length,[15] and the length of the clavicle.[16] In adults, because growth has ceased, the stage of degeneration and ossification for certain parts of the skeleton could be assessed. These include the pubic symphysis,[17] the auricular surface,[18] the stage of cranial suture closure,[19] and the morphology of the sternal rib ends.[20]

The majority of individuals (n = 56) had an age-at-death between 36 and 49 years (middle adult). Twenty-eight individuals were non-adult. Two adult individuals had an age-at-death of at least 35 years and of four individuals the age-at-death estimation was 18+ years. Figure 2 shows the age distribution of the Hattem population.

As mentioned, the excavation of the cemetery of the Andreaskerk took place on two sides of the church, the north and south. The difference in age distribution of the two sides is statistically significant ($X^2 = 8.179$, $p = 0.042$). More non-adults were buried on the north side than on the south side, and all the non-adults younger than three years of ages were buried on the north side. This suggests that the 'cold' side was preferred as a burial location for the youngest non-adults. Although the north side was considered the least desirable side of the church in which to be buried, young children, infants, and perinates were buried in the cemetery in sacred ground among the adults, suggesting that the Hattem inhabitants considered these non-adults to be part of society and deserving of a burial with the rest of the deceased, as opposed to other traditional practices in which young infants and perinates were not allowed to be buried in sacred ground.[21]

---

10 Grolman 1923.
11 Grolman 1923.
12 Uberlacker 1979.
13 Demirjian *et al.* 1973; Liversidge *et al.* 1963; Moorrees *et al.* 1963.
14 Schaefer *et al.* 2009.
15 Maresh 1970.
16 Black and Scheuer 1996.
17 Brooks and Suchey 1990.
18 Lovejoy *et al.* 1985; Buckberry and Chamberlain 2002.
19 Meindl and Lovejoy 1985.
20 Isçan *et al.* 1984; 1985.
21 Grolman 1923.

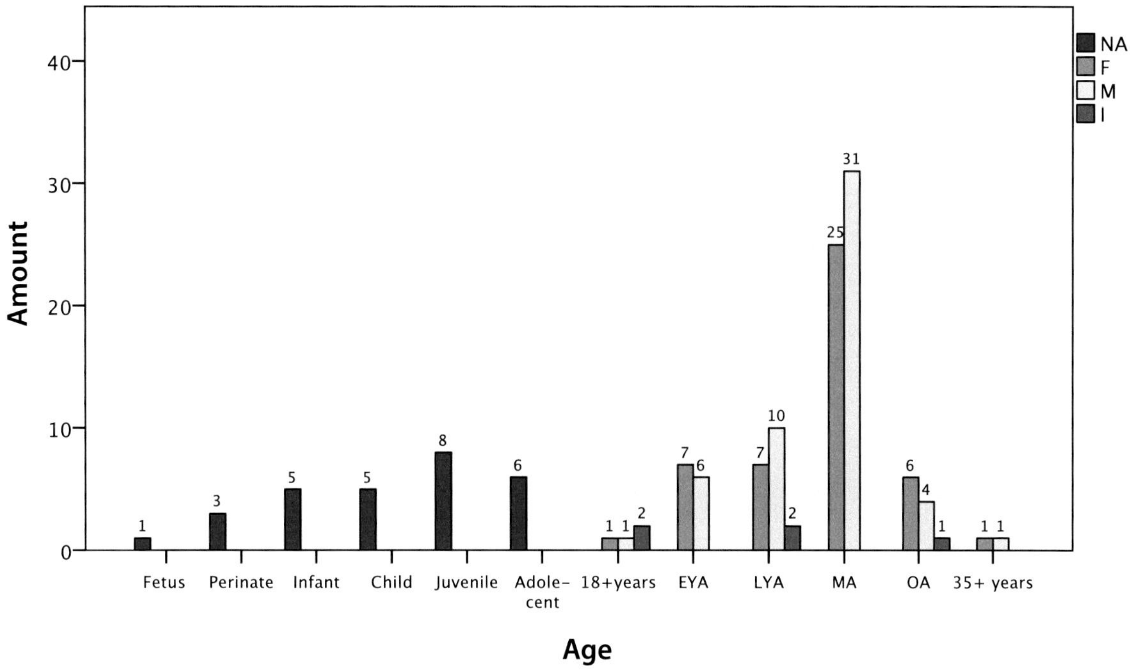

Fig. 2: Age distribution. Fetus (< 38 weeks in utero), Perinate (around birth), Infant (0-3 years), Child (4-6 years), Juvenile (7-12 years), adolescent (13-18 years) EYA = early young adult (19-25 years), LYA = late young adult (26-35 years), MA = middle adult (36-49 years), OA = old adult (50+ years). NA = not applicable, F = female, M = male, I = indeterminate.

Sex

The sex of an individual is estimated by using several methods that assess sexual dimorphic characteristics of specific parts of the skeleton according to the standards as described by the Workshop of European Anthropologists[22] and Buikstra and Ubelaker.[23] In addition, the Phenice traits were used, assessing the presence of the ventral arc, and the morphology of the ischiopubic ramus and the subpubic concavity.[24] The robusticity of the skeleton can also provide an indication of sex. Several measurements were taken from the clavicle,[25] the scapula,[26] the humerus,[27] and the femur.[28] Whenever possible, individuals were assigned to the categories 'F' (female) or 'M' (male). 'PF/PM' (probable female/male) was used if the sexual dimorphic characteristics were not clear or some of them were missing. If it was not possible to estimate sex, the category 'I' (indeterminate) was used. Only the sex of adult individuals was estimated. Current macroscopic methods for sex estimation of non-adults do not reach the necessary level of accuracy.[29]

22 WEA 1980.
23 Buikstra and Ubelaker 1994.
24 Phenice 1969.
25 McCormick *et al.* 1991.
26 Bainbridge and Genovés Tarazga 1956.
27 Steyn and Işcan 1999.
28 Stewart 1979.
29 Lewis 2007, 48.

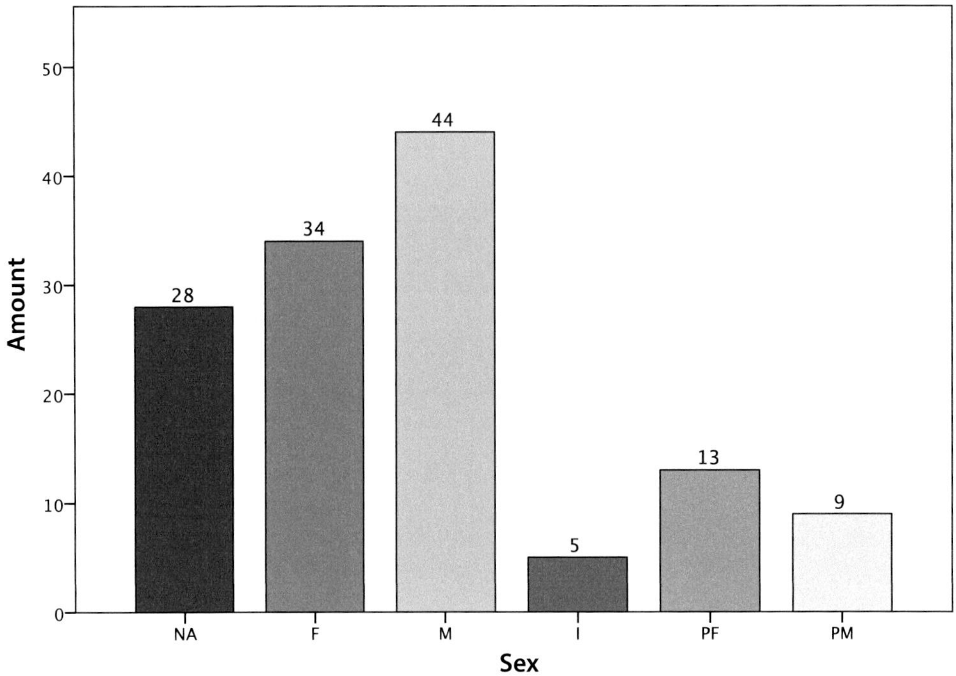

Fig. 3: Distribution of sex. NA = not applicable, F = female, M = male, I = indeterminate, PF = probable female, PM = probable male.

Figure 3 shows the distribution of sex. The sex of 28 individuals could not be determined because they were non-adult, and the sex of a further five individuals could not be estimated and they were assigned to the category 'I' (indeterminate). The difference in sex was not statistically significant ($X^2 = 0.360$, $p = 0.549$).

Stature

Stature was estimated using the methods of Trotter and Gleser[30] and Trotter,[31] which correlates one or more long bones and stature. Stature is determined by a number of factors, and it can provide information on living conditions and the diet of the population under study. It was possible to estimate the stature of a hundred adult individuals because one or more long bones were present. The statures were categorized to facilitate comparison. In addition, PF and PM were added to the F and M categories, respectively (figure 4). The average female stature was 161.5 cm and the statures varied from 153.6 cm to 172.9 cm. The average male stature was 171.4 cm and the statures varied from 162.7 cm to 182.6 cm.

There was no statistically significant difference in stature between individuals from the north side and the south side of the church ($F = 2.190$, $p = 0.779$), suggesting living conditions and diet were similar for adult individuals buried on either side of the church.

30 Trotter and Gleser 1958.
31 Trotter 1970.

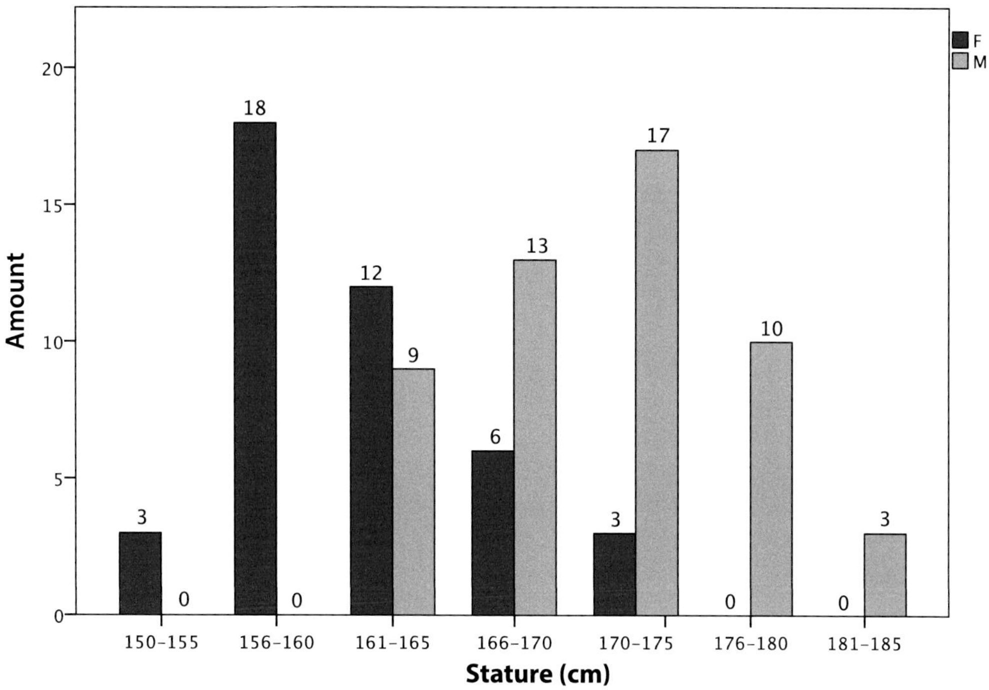

Fig. 4: Distribution of stature. F = female, M = male.

Table 1: Average statures of individuals from Hattem and three contemporaneous sites.

Site	Average female stature (cm)	Average male stature (cm)
Hattem	161.5	171.4
Roosendaal	159.7	170.9
Gouda	162.6	174.9
Middenbeemster	160.7	171.6

Table 1 presents the average statures of female and male individuals from Hattem compared with the average female and male statures of individuals from Roosendaal,[32] Gouda,[33] and Middenbeemster.[34]

These statures show that, on average, the females from Hattem were slightly taller than the ones from Roosendaal, but slightly shorter than the females of high socioeconomic status from Gouda. The averages of male statures display the same pattern. Hattem males, on average, were taller than the ones from Roosendaal, but shorter than the ones from Gouda. Both female and male average statures in Hattem are comparable to the average statures of Middenbeemster individuals. Although differences are minimal, the average statures of the Hattem individuals suggest slightly better living conditions and diet for these individuals than the

32 Veselka 2015a, 18.
33 Veselka 2015b, 26.
34 Lemmers *et al.* 2013, 43.

Pathologies		Hattem	Roosendaal	Gouda	Middenbeemster
Metabolic diseases	EH	45.6% (36/79)	41.6% (20/48)	21.1% (4/19)	13.0% (9/69)
	Residual rickets	23.9% (21/88)	13.5% (2/12)	12.5% (4/32)[1]	14.5% (29/200)[2]
Infections	NPB ribs	8.7% (9/103)	11.1% (5/45)	4.0% (1/25)	–
Trauma	Fractures	13.3% (14/105)	28.9% (13/45)	4.4% (2/45)	9.9% (7/71)
	Spondylolysis	3.9% (4/103)	6.7% (3/45)	0.0% (0/45)	3.2% (2/63)
	OD	13.3% (14/105)	13.3% (6/45)	6.7% (6/45)	7.0% (5/71)
	- OD foot	9.1% (7/77)	–	–	–

Table 2: Pathological anomalies observed in adult individuals in Hattem and three contemporaneous collections. EH = enamel hypoplasia, NPB = new periosteal bone, OD = osteochondritis dissecans, – = not noted in report.[1] Veselka 2019, 63-85; [2] Veselka et al. 2018b.

individuals from Roosendaal, but the stature of the Gouda individuals indicates that they seemed to have had access to better diets and most likely enjoyed better living conditions than the Hattem individuals.

Pathologies

Pathological anomalies were assessed using descriptions by Roberts and Manchester,[35] Rogers and Waldron,[36] Ortner,[37] and Waldron.[38] Pathologies can provide information on the disease burden of a past population, their living conditions, and diet. However, not all diseases affect bone and the majority of the acute and mortal diseases suffered by individuals cannot be determined from the skeletons. Therefore, the prevalent pathological anomalies are not representative of the actual disease burden within a population. For each pathology the true prevalence was noted, considering the number of individuals that could be observed for each pathological condition.

Table 2 provides an overview of commonly observed pathological anomalies in adult individuals from Hattem, Roosendaal,[39] Gouda,[40] and Middenbeemster.[41] Table 3 shows the same overview for non-adults. For enamel hypoplasia (EH), non-adults with only permanent dentition were added to the adult individuals. A complete overview of pathological anomalies in the Hattem population is provided in the site report.[42]

Metabolic diseases

The prevalence of enamel hypoplasia, a disruption in the deposition of tooth enamel, is indicative of one or more periods of disease and/or malnutrition (see figure 5). The percentage of adults with enamel hypoplasia was 45.6% in Hattem. No statistically significant difference in enamel hypoplasia prevalence was observed between Hattem individuals from the north and the south sides of the church ($X^2 = 1.038$, $p = 0.595$).

35 Roberts and Manchester 2005.
36 Rogers and Waldron 1995.
37 Ortner 2003.
38 Waldron 2009.
39 Veselka 2015a, 15-16.
40 Veselka 2015b, 17-18.
41 Lemmers *et al.* 2013, 46-47.
42 Veselka *et al.* 2018a, 11-13.

Pathologies		Hattem	Roosendaal	Gouda	Middenbeemster
Metabolic disease	EH	25.0% (4/16)	0.0% (0/15)	0.0% (0/4)	43.5% (10/23)
	Rickets	23.8% (5/21)	16.7% (2/12)[1]	66.7% (2/3)[2]	15.3% (9/59)[3]
Infection	NPB ribs	10.5% (2/19)	0.0 % (0/15)	0.0% (0/4)	-

Table 3: Pathological anomalies observed in non-adults. EH = enamel hypoplasia, NPB = new periosteal bone. 1 Veselka 2019, 63-85; 2 Veselka 2019, 63-85; 3 Veselka et al. 2015.

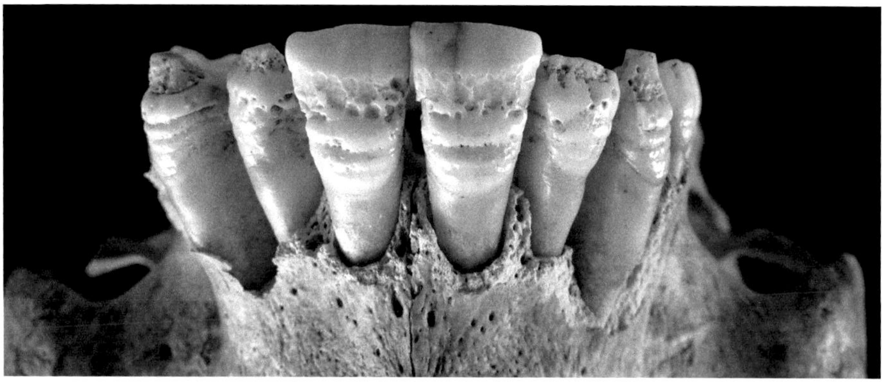

Fig. 5: Enamel hypoplasia visible as lines and pits in individual S130V138 (Human Osteoarchaeology Laboratory).

The percentage of enamel hypoplasia in Hattem individuals is comparable to the prevalence of enamel hypoplasia in Roosendaal, where 41.6% of the adults were affected.[43] The percentages in Middenbeemster[44] and Gouda[45] were much lower: 13.0% and 21.1% respectively. The relative high percentage of enamel hypoplasia in Hattem indicates that diseases and/or malnutrition frequently affected young children, as tooth enamel is formed in early childhood. However, the percentage of enamel hypoplasia in the Hattem non-adults was much lower than in the Hattem adults: 25.0%. This may be partly caused by a relatively small amount of non-adult individuals in the sample (n = 16).

The prevalence of vitamin D deficiency, which may be visible as bending deformities of certain parts of the skeleton, can be indicative of suboptimal living conditions and diet. Vitamin D is synthesized in the skin and induced by the ultraviolet B (UVB) radiation of sunlight. In addition, small amounts of vitamin D can be obtained by eating oily fish, beef liver, and egg yolk. Vitamin D is necessary for the mineralization of bone to make the skeleton durable enough to withstand muscular tension and gravity. The prevalence of vitamin D deficiency suggests inadequate exposure to sunlight and a diet low on vitamin D. Thus, the prevalence of vitamin D deficiency can provide information on daily activities and

43 Veselka 2015a, 15-16.
44 Lemmers *et al.* 2013, 46-47.
45 Veselka 2015b, 17-18.

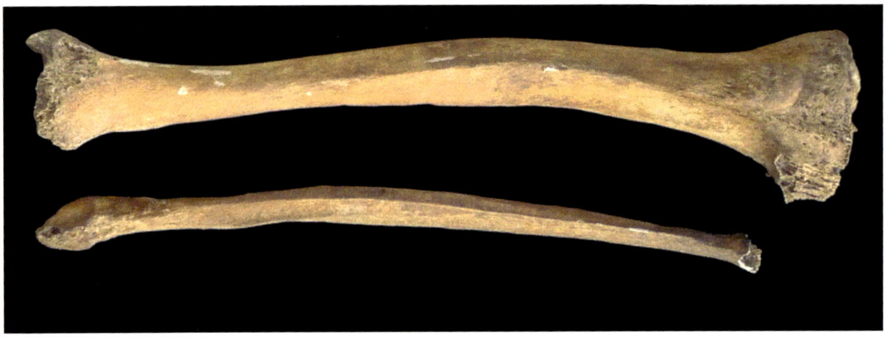

Fig. 6: Bending of tibia and fibula due to residual rickets in S066V073 (Human Osteoarchaeology Laboratory).

diet in past populations.[46] Residual rickets, visible as remnant bending deformities due to childhood vitamin D deficiency in the adult skeleton (see figure 6), was prevalent in the Hattem adults, with 23.9% of the adult individuals showing these deformities. Rickets lesions were observed in 23.8% of the non-adults.

The difference between affected adults from the north and the south sides of the church was not statistically significant ($X^2 = 0.192$, $p = 0.661$) nor was the difference in the prevalence of rickets for the north and south sides statistically significant ($X^2 = 0.643$, $p = 0.422$).

The percentage of residual rickets was lower in Roosendaal (13.5%), Middenbeemster (14.5%), and Gouda adults (12.5%). In the Hattem non-adults, the prevalence of rickets (23.8%) was higher than in Roosendaal (16.7%) and Middenbeemster (9.5%), but lower than in Gouda (66.7%).The prevalence of vitamin D deficiency in the Hattem population was relatively high compared to the other populations. The prevalence of rickets in the Gouda population seems very high comparatively, but the number of non-adults was relatively small ($n = 4$), which makes comparison difficult.

Infections

Most infections do not affect the skeleton and are not observable in archaeological remains. Infectious diseases that do affect bone will display similar non-diagnostic lesions, such as the formation of new periosteal bone. The prevalence of new periosteal bone on the ribs suggests irritation and/or inflammation of the respiratory tract and can be caused by several pathological conditions including pneumonia and tuberculosis. In 8.7% of the Hattem adults, new periosteal bone formation was observed on the ribs. The difference in the prevalence of new periosteal bone on the ribs of individuals from the two sides of the church was not statistically significant ($X^2 = 1.808$, $p = 0.405$). The percentage of new periosteal bone on the ribs of individuals in Roosendaal was 11.1%[47] and in Gouda, 4.0%.[48] (This lesion

46 Veselka 2019, 63-85.
47 Veselka 2015a, 15-16.
48 Veselka 2015b, 17-18.

was not noted in the Middenbeemster site report). The percentage in Roosendaal was higher than in Hattem, whereas the percentage of this pathological lesion was much lower in high-socioeconomic-status Gouda, suggesting that the prevalence of this anomaly, or lack thereof, provides information on living conditions.

Trauma

Several types of trauma, such as spondylolysis and osteochondritis dissecans, can be indicative of repetitive strenuous activities. Spondylolysis is the fracture of a vertebral arch, caused by additional stress, pressure, or falls. In Hattem, 3.9% of the adults were observed with this type of fracture. In Roosendaal,[49] 6.7% of the adults showed this lesion, and in Middenbeemster the prevalence of spondylolysis was 3.2%.[50] The Gouda individuals did not have this type of trauma.[51]

Osteochondritis dissecans is a pathological condition whereby one or more pieces of cartilage and the underlying bone within a joint break off. In Hattem, 13.3% of the adults showed this type of trauma. In Roosendaal, the percentage of osteochondritis dissecans was the same,[52] whereas in Middenbeemster, the percentage was 7.0%[53] and in Gouda 6.7% of the adults displayed this lesion.[54]

Although the relationship between fractures, living conditions, and socioeconomic status is complex, types of trauma that are generally attributed to hard and/or repetitive labor can provide information on daily activities and circumstances. Therefore, it is not surprising that in elite Gouda, where individuals were of a high socioeconomic status, no individual was observed with spondylolysis and the lowest percentage of osteochondritis dissecans was found.

Pipe notches

Although pipe notches are not necessarily pathological anomalies, they are discussed here. Figure 7 shows the type of dental wear caused by frequent clay pipe smoking.

Table 4 shows the distribution of pipe notches of males and females. The difference in pipe notch prevalence between individuals from the north and the south sides of the church was not statistically significant ($X^2 = 3.696$, $p = 0.158$).

For some time now, smoking a clay pipe has been considered to be a habit of the lower socioeconomic classes.[55] The prevalence of pipe notches in Hattem is relatively high (31.6%); in Roosendaal it was 35.5%[56] and in Middenbeemster, 21.3%.[57] Although Gouda was an important centre for the production of clay pipes, the elite individuals presented with a much lower percentage of pipe notches; only 6.7% of the adults showed this type of dental wear.[58]

---

49 Veselka 2015a, 15-16.
50 Lemmers *et al.* 2013, 46-47.
51 Veselka 2015b, 17-18.
52 Veselka 2015a, 15-16.
53 Lemmers *et al.* 2013, 46-47.
54 Veselka 2015b, 17-18.
55 Walker and Henderson 2010.
56 Veselka 2015a, 14.
57 Lemmers *et al.* 2013, 45.
58 Veselka 2015b, 16.

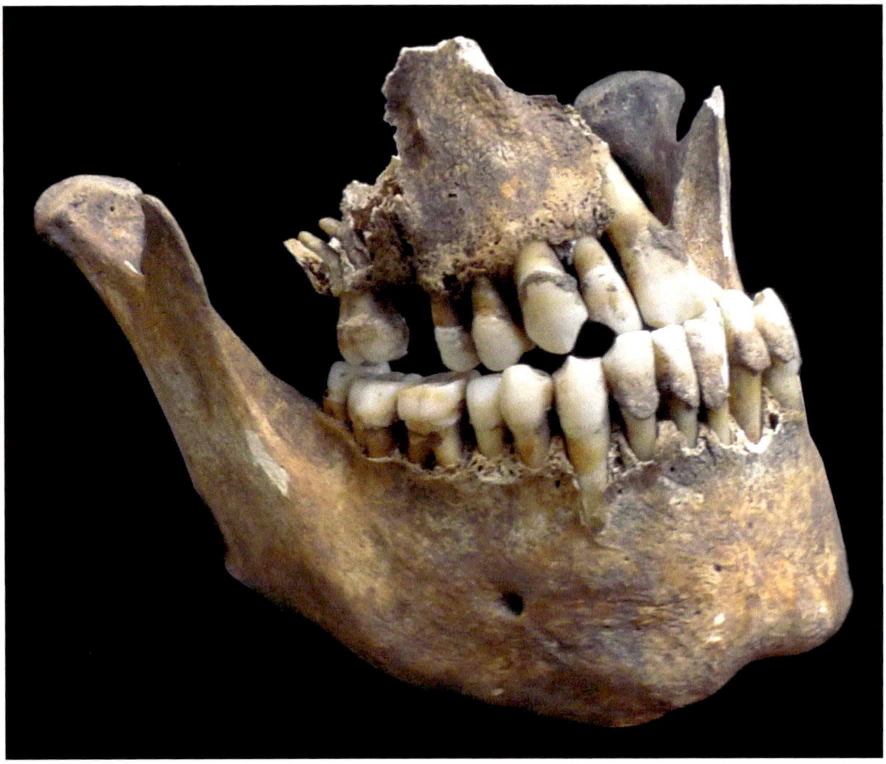

Fig. 7: Pipe notches of individual S015V011 (Human Osteoarchaeology Laboratory).

	N Individuals	Percentage	N Males	Percentage	N Females	Percentage
Pipe notches	25	31.6% (25/79)	24	60.0% (24/40)	1	3.2% (1/31)

Table 4: Distribution of pipe notches.

Conclusion

The results of the physical anthropological analysis suggest that the Hattem individuals were not of a high socioeconomic status. In contrast, in Gouda, the majority of individuals were of a high socioeconomic status and were buried inside the church.[59] The socioeconomic status of the individuals from Middenbeemster is postulated to have been mixed,[60] and the majority of the individuals from the Roosendaal collection are believed to have been of low socioeconomic status.[61] Based on the results of the osteoarchaeological analysis, the individuals from Hattem seem to have experienced better living conditions and diets than the individuals from Roosendaal, but clearly not as optimal as the individuals from Gouda. Historical sources report Hattem to have suffered from various occupations by the French in

59 Veselka 2015b.

60 Lemmers *et al.* 2013.

61 Van Gastel 1995, 107-119, 157, 229.

the 17th and 18th centuries that impoverished the small town.[62] The results of the osteoarchaeological investigation seem to confirm the decline in wealth as described by historical sources, although the living conditions and diet of the individuals from Roosendaal suggest a worse situation. Remarkable is the relatively high prevalence of vitamin D deficiency, as it is postulated that the availability of sunlight in 17th- and 18th-century Hattem would have been adequate. The town was relatively small and most daily activities concerned agriculture[63] and the transportation of goods along the river.[64] However, 23.9% of the adults show bending deformities due to childhood vitamin D deficiency, and 23.8% of the non-adults show rickets in an active or healing stage.[65] Further research should make it possible to assess the age of vitamin D deficiency onset and provide a better understanding of the development of vitamin D deficiency in this small urban center.

Although differences in socioeconomic status of the buried individuals existed, the results of the osteoarchaeological analysis were not statistically significant and it is postulated that the north side of the Andreaskerk may not have been reserved for only the lower socioeconomic classes. However, the younger infants and fetuses were only buried on the north side. Although this implies that the younger non-adults were considered a part of society and thus allowed burial in sacred ground, still the north side was their preferred burial location, which may be indicative of their relatively low socioeconomic status in general.

Bibliography

Bainbridge, D.R. & Genoves, S., 1956: 'Study of sex differences in the scapula', *Journal of the Royal Anthropological Institute* 86, 109-134.

Black, S. & Scheuer, L., 1996: 'Age changes in the clavicle: from the early neonatal period to skeletal maturity', *International Journal of Osteoarchaeology* 6, 425-434. DOI: https://doi.org/10.1002/(SICI)1099-1212(199612)6:5<425::AID-OA287>3.0.CO;2-U

Brooks, S. & Suchey, J.M., 1990: 'Skeletal age determination based on the os pubis: a comparison of the Acsádi-Nemeskéri and Suchey-Brooks methods', *Human Evolution* 5, 227-238. DOI: https://doi.org/10.1007/BF02437238

Buckberry, J.L. & Chamberlain, A.T., 2002: 'Age estimation from the auricular surface of the ilium: a revised method', *American Journal of Physical Anthropology* 119, 31-239. DOI: 10.1002/ajpa.10130

Buikstra, J.E. & Ubelaker, D.H., 1994: *Standards for data collection from human skeletal remains,* Favetteville (Arkansas Archeological Report Research Series 44).

Demirjian, A., Goldstein, H. & Tanner, J.M., 1973: 'A new system of dental age assessment', *Human Biology* 45, 211-227.

Grolman, H.C.A., 1923: 'Volksgebruiken bij sterven en begraven in Nederland', *Tijdschrift van het Koninklijk Nederlands Aardrijkskundig Genootschap* 40, 359-396.

62 Sypkens Smit 1964, 40-41, 50, 68.
63 Koridon 1985, 23-28.
64 Scheper 1984, 11-16.
65 Veselka 2019, 63-85.

Işcan, M.Y., Loth, S.R. & Wright, R.K., 1984: 'Metamorphosis at the sternal rib end: a new method to estimate age at death in white males', *American Journal of Physical Anthropology* 65, 147-156. DOI: 10.1002/ajpa.1330650206

Isçan M.Y., S.R. Loth & R.K. Wright, 1985: 'Age estimation from the rib by phase analysis: white females'. Journal of Forensic Sciences 30: 853-863.

Kouwenhoven, G., 2015: 'Archeologen graven lijk op bij de kerk van Hattem', blog Streekarchivaris Epe Hattem Heerde, http://streekarchiefehh.blogspot.com/2015/08/.

Koridon, L., 1985: 'Boeren binnen de vest', in: D. Kroese & Koridon, B. (eds.), *Attemer, wat e'j vrogger edaon?*, Hattem, 23-28.

Lemmers, S.A.M., Schats, R., Hoogland, M.L.P. & Waters-Rist, A.L., 2013: 'Fysisch antropologische analyse Middenbeemster', in: A. Hakvoort (ed.), *De begravingen bij de Keyserkerk te Middenbeemster*, Rotterdam (Hollandia Reeks 464), 35-60.

Lewis, M.E., 2007: *The bioarchaeology of children. Perspectives from biological and forensic anthropology.* Cambridge University Press: New York. https://doi.org/10.1017/CBO9780511542473

Liversidge, H.M., Herdeg, B. & Rosing, F.W., 1998: 'Dental age estimation of non-adults. A review of methods and principles', in: K.W. Alt, F.W. Rösing & M. Teschler-Nicola (eds.), *Dental anthropology, fundamentals, limits and prospects*, Springer: Vienna, 419-442.

Lovejoy, C.O., Meindl, R.S., Pryzbeck, T.R. & Mensforth, R.P., 1985: 'Chronological metamorphosis of the auricular surface of the ilium: A new method for the determination of adult skeletal age at death,' *American Journal of Physical Anthropology* 68, 15-28.

Maresh, M.M., 1970: 'Measurements from roentgenograms', in: R.W. McCammon (ed.), *Human growth and development*, Springfield: CC Thomas, 157-200.

McCormick, W.F., Stewart, J.H. & Greene, H., 1991: 'Sexing of human clavicles using length and circumference measurements', *American Journal of Forensic Medical Pathology* 12, 175-181.

Meindl, R.S. & Lovejoy, C.O., 1985: 'Ectocranial suture closure: a revised method for the determination of skeletal age at death based upon the lateral-anterior sutures', *American Journal of Physical Anthropology* 68, 57-66. DOI: 10.1002/ajpa.1330680106

Moorrees, C.F.A., Fanning, E.A. & Hunt, E.E., 1963: 'Age variation of formation stage for ten permanent teeth', *Journal of Dental Research* 42, 1490-1502. DOI: 10.1177/00220345630420062701

Ortner, D.J., 2003: *Identification of pathological conditions in human skeletal remains.* San Diego: Academic Press.

Phenice, T.W., 1969: 'A newly developed visual method of sexing the os pubis', *American Journal of Physical Anthropology* 30, 297-302. DOI: 10.1002/ajpa.1330300214

Roberts, C.A. & Manchester, K., 2005: *The archaeology of disease.* Ithaca New York: Cornell University Press.

Rogers, J. & Waldron, T., 1995: *A field guide to joint disease in archaeology.* Chichester: Wiley.

Schaefer, M., Black, S. & Scheuer, L., 2009: *Juvenile Osteology: A laboratory and field manual.* Academic Press, San Diego.
Scheper, A., 1984: "We moesten trekken in de lijn, wilden we in Hattem zijn", in: D. Kamp (ed.), *Hattemer, wat dee'j veur de kos?*, Hattem, 11-16.
Stewart, T.D., 1979: *Essentials of forensic anthropology, especially as developed in the United States.* Springfield: CC Thomas.
Steyn, M. & İşcan, M.Y,. 1999: 'Osteometric variation in the humerus: sexual dimorphism in South Africans', *International Journal of Forensic Science* 106, 77-85.
Sypkens Smit, M., 1964: *De Geschiedenis van de Stad Hattem.* Hattem: Schipper.
Trotter, M., 1970: 'Estimation of stature from intact limb bones', in: T.D. Stewart (ed.), *Personal identification in mass disasters*, Washington DC: National Museum of Natural History, 85-97.
Trotter, M. & Gleser, G.C., 1958: 'A re-evaluation of estimation of stature based on measurements of stature taken during life and of long bones after death', *American Journal of Physical Anthropology* 16, 79-123. DOI https://doi.org/10.1002/ajpa.1330160106
Ubelaker, D.H., 1979: *Human skeletal remains: excavation, analysis and interpretation.* Washington D.C.: Smithsonian Institute Press.
Van Gastel, L.J.P., 1995: *Roosendaal tussen platteland en stad.* PhD Thesis part A: 1770-1900 AD, University of Tilburg.
Van Poppel, F., Jonker, M. & Mandemakers, K., 2005: 'Differential infant and child mortality in three Dutch regions, 1812-1909'. *The Economic History Review* 58, 272-309. DOI: https://doi.org/10.1111/j.1468-0289.2005.00305.x
Veselka, B., 2015a: *Analyse van het menselijk skeletmateriaal uit Roosendaal, Tongerloplein, Sint-Janskerk, fysisch antropologische rapportage*, unpublished.
Veselka, B., 2015b: *Analyse van het menselijk skeletmateriaal uit de Sint-Janskerk te Gouda, fysisch antropologische rapportage*, unpublished.
Veselka, B., Hoogland, M.L.P. & Waters-Rist, A.L., 2015: 'Rural Rickets: Vitamin D deficiency in a post-Medieval Farming Community from the Netherlands', *International Journal of Osteoarchaeology* 25, 665-675. DOI: https://doi.org/10.1002/oa.2329
Veselka, B., Van der Merwe, A.E., Hoogland, M.L.P. & Waters-Rist, A.L., 2018: 'Gender-related vitamin D deficiency in a Dutch 19th century farming community', *International Journal of Paleopathology*, 23, 69-75. https://doi.org/10.1016/j.ijpp.2017.11.001
Veselka, B., 2019: *D-lightful Sunshine Disrupted: vitamin D deficiency as a method for the reconstruction of changes in sociocultural practices due to the reconstruction of changes in sociocultural practices due to industrialisation in 17th -19th century Netherlands*, unpublished PhD thesis, Leiden University.
Waldron, T., 2009: *Paleopathology.* Cambridge: Cambridge University Press, 118-137.
Walker, D. & Henderson, M., 2010: 'Smoking and health in London's East End in the first half of the 19th century', *Post-Medieval Archaeology* 44, 209-222. DOI: https://doi.org/10.1179/174581310X12662382629373
Workshop of European Anthropologists (WEA), 1980: 'Recommendations for age and sex diagnoses of skeletons', *Journal of Human Evolution* 9, 517-549.

The cursed side

A folk belief evidenced by documentary records in 's-Hertogenbosch (1782-1858)

Roos van Oosten

Introduction

While many studies on funerary customs have been published in the past decades,[1] none make reference to the folk belief of the 'cursed side' in relation to burial location. To learn more about this, we need to turn to a 1923 study published by Hermina Grolmann. In her article on folk customs, she discussed the fact that being buried on the south side of a church was much more popular that being buried on the north side.[2] After all, the sun never shone onto the north side and so this cold side was cursed. Grolmann refers to an 1874 publication[3] which incorporated information almost verbatim from a publication dating 1839.[4] The author of this latter article provides more detail.

> *The bodies of the village's [Vries, a small village in the province of Drenthe] most prominent residents are buried in the local church, and no persons of lower rank could obtain such a privilege. No villagers, however poor, would have their dead buried in the northern part of the churchyard, which lacks sunlight. There were no burials on that entire side except for the occasional passing stranger, beggar or soldier who met his death in this parish. He was relegated there as though he belonged to a different caste from the locals. The bulk of the parish was interred in the southern part of the churchyard, but only in a part of it. The burial pits furthest from the church were nearly empty, and those close to the church were crowded to excess. The accrual of bodies grew to a mound alongside the entire length of the church, which through time has grown progressively higher, and from which it is obvious that villagers who could not bury their dead inside the church wanted them to be as close to it as possible.*

---

1 For references to recent overview studies, see Van Oosten & Arts 2017.
2 Grolman 1923, 388.
3 Ter Gouw 1874, 124.
4 G.B.R. 1839, 140.

The author of the original 1839 source, who is only known by his initials G.B.R., notes that this custom was not limited to one village but was customary in the whole province of Drenthe. Grolman adds to this explanation that the north side was the 'cursed side' – 'the side of demons'.[5] Other references to such a folk belief are thin on the ground[6] and we wouldn't take it seriously if Portegies had not substantiated this folk belief with sound historical records in his study of St John's Cathedral in 's-Hertogenbosch. St John's was Catholic until 1629, then Protestant until 1811 and then it became Catholic again.[7] Portegies published his results in *Dood en begraven* (*Dead and Buried*) two decades ago (1999), following a partial excavation of the north side of the churchyard.[8] The book was briefly reviewed in the prestigious *BMGN – Low Countries Historical Review*[9] but received more acclaim in archaeological than historical circles. The study may have been quoted several times in the chapters of the *Urban Graveyard* publications, but the cursed side has remained largely overlooked. In this chapter I explore this folk belief evidenced from documentary records in 's-Hertogenbosch (1782-1858). Before doing so, funerals as an expression of social standing in the 19th century will be discussed.

First-class and sixth-class funeral processions and funeral locations

In the 18th and 19th centuries there were five or six burial classes,[10] and the funeral procession was an important class marker. A lot is known about the types of processions at St John's Cathedral from historical records studied by Portegies. Grand processions occurred in the evening as opposed to the day when lower-class funerals took place.[11] These stately funeral processions included mourning carriages (Fig. 1:A)[12] and many *lijkbidders,*(a kind of funeral undertaker)[13] and were accompanied by the prolonged ringing of the big church bells, as opposed to a short or no bell ringing for lower class burials (Fig. 1).[14]

While figure 1 shows an elite procession and two types of funeral processions of farmers, it does not show a sixth-class funeral. For this we must turn to a letter in a local Leiden newspaper, *Leidsch Dagblad,* dated April 11, 1889 written by someone who called himself 'Dr A'.[15] Dr A complained with disdain about 'an offensive

5 Grolman 1923, 388, note 7.
6 Kok (1970, 71-72), does not mention the source of this information. Given the words 'demon' and 'cursed', it may be Grolman 1923.
7 Van der Drift 2010, 155.
8 About this excavation: Van Genabeek 2017; Van Genabeek 2018.
9 Van Deursen 2001, 210.
10 The sixth class was also for the lower classes a disgrace, if they could afford it, they saved their entire life for a decent funeral. This can be seen in the well-known Dutch novel, *Camera Obscura,* 1839, in which Keesje, a poor old man, explained that he had saved three decades to be buried decently, to wear his own shirt rather than one provided by the church. To this end he had wrapped his savings of 12 guilders in a paper and kept them in a leather bag. Example also mentioned by Van Hoogdalem & Walle 2017, 138.
11 Portegies 1999, 105-106.
12 Portegies 1999, 125.
13 Portegies 1999, 108-109.
14 Portegies 199, 52, 53-54.
15 Van Hoogdalem & Walle 2017, 141-143.

Fig. 1: Six different processions: a) A noble funeral procession of carriages, b) A stately civil and merchant procession on foot, c) The procession on foot of the funeral of a young child, d) An Amsterdam procession of the funeral of a child, with a sledge, e) A procession of Holland farmers with carts, f) The usual procession of Holland farmers, in this case, the funeral of a woman who died in childbirth (Le Franq van Berkhey 1772, Plate XI).

scene in broad daylight',[16] a burial procession that took place between 8 and 9 in the morning, the usual time for low-class burials in Leiden. Historians Van Hoogdalem and Wallem identified this event as the burial of 37-year-old Anna Wilhelmina van Wegel who lived in Voorburg, but probably died in the hospital in Leiden.[17] The coffin was carried by two craftsmen on a low-slung bier (old Dutch, *berrie*) typical of a low-class burial, instead of on an elevated bier carried on shoulders (Fig. 1).[18] Worse in the eyes of Dr A was that the black mortcloth was faded and worn. It only covered the lid and not the sides of the coffin, and the wood of the coffin was rough and unpolished. To add to the pathos of the scene, only her mourning husband accompanied the coffin to the paupers' cemetery Heerenpoort at one of the town-wall bastions.

Besides the funeral procession, another important class marker was the burial location of the deceased. In Protestantism, the official church in the Netherlands following the Eighty Years' War, the concept of consecrated ground was not deemed as important, although burial inside the church was more prestigious than in the churchyard. In Protestant Alkmaar *c.* 1750, almost half of the burials took place inside the Grote Kerk; five decades later this number had decreased to a quarter.[19] Bitter explains this dramatic decrease as a result of steady, long-term economic decline and changing ideas on hygiene inspired by the Enlightenment.[20] These socioeconomic developments did not have the same impact in Protestant Zwolle or Catholic 's-Hertogenbosch. Instead, Zwolle witnessed the opposite: an increase in burials inside churches from 32% (1701-1747) to 41% (1767-1807).[21] St John's Cathedral in 's-Hertogenbosch faced a slow decrease in church burials from 39% in the 17th century (1631-1635) to 22% *c.* 1800 (1790-1810).[22] These divergent trends in church burials show that besides economic decline and changing ideas on hygiene, local factors must also have played a role, although what these factors might have been is not discussed in the relevant studies.

Within the church, burial costs differed considerably. This was already the case in the Late Medieval period, as Bonenkampová demonstrated in her study of the Oude Kerk in Delft, where the most expensive graves within the church cost five to six times more than the cheapest graves outside the church.[23] The cost depended on three factors: whether the deceased was an adult or a child, whether the grave was owned by the family or by the church and the location in the church, given that some spots were considered holier and hence, superior than others.[24] These three factors also determined the price differentiation in St John's Cathedral in the 18th century (Table 1), although in St John's, the price also depended on whether it was a normal grave or burial in a vault (*kelder*).[25]

16 Van Hoogdalem & Walle 2017, 141.
17 Van Hoogdalem & Walle 2017, 142.
18 This can be deduced from burial practices in 's-Hertogenbosch. See next paragraph.
19 Bitter 2013, 49; Bitter 2002, 221, Table 4.
20 Bitter 2018, 112.
21 Hagedoorn 1992, 33, 36-37.
22 Portegies 1999, 23, Table 1.
23 Bonenkampová 2013, 198, Table 2b
24 Bonenkampová 2013, 199.
25 Schuttelaars 2010, 57-58.

			Chancel	Elsewhere in the church
Rented plot	Vault	Adult		12
		Child		7
	Grave	Adult	18.0	9
		Child	8.5	4
Purchased plot	Vault	Adult		10
		Child		3
	Grave	Adult	4.5	6
		Child	1.5	2

Table 1: 1774 Burial costs in St John's Cathedral, in guilders. Data from Schuttelaars 2010, 57, table 1.

After 1811, burials in St John's Cathedral were forbidden.[26] While the national prohibition ended in 1813 (and again promulgated in 1829), the fact that St John's became Catholic again meant that the prohibition remained in place.[27] Schuttelaar does not explain whether this 'modern' determination stemmed from hygienic concerns among Catholics or from practical reasons.[28]

In the St John's churchyard, there was again a price differentiation. In 1782, the churchyard was divided in three areas: a small southern part (7% of the available area), a north-western area directly adjacent to the church wall (15%) and a north-eastern area (78%).[29] Being buried in the south plot was three times more expensive than in the north-east plot.[30] The most desirable and most expensive location on the north side was below the paved path (Fig. 2). Portegies supposes that this was because the path ran to the main altar.[31] At the Oude Kerk in Delft in medieval times, a burial location below the path was also the most desired. However, Bonenkampová, unlike Portegies, postulates that being buried near these pathways was sought after because they saw a lot of pedestrian traffic,[32] which meant that the living more often 'interacted' with the deceased and therefore the deceased remained more present in the memories of the living.

The type of mortcloth, bier and coffin used corresponded to the location of the burial at the St John's cathedral. The mortcloths that covered the coffin were of first-, second-, third-, fourth- and a fifth-class types. Only the most expensive morthcloths were used in burials in the south area of the churchyard, and many of the burials in the north-west part included the cheapest mortcloth (Fig. 2, Mortcloth graph Graph mortcloths). A similar pattern emerged in the type of bier and coffin used.[33] The shoulder bier was three times more expensive than

26 This first national prohibition went into effect in 1804, but the situation varied from town to town, Portegies 1999, 28-29.
27 Portegies 1999, 17, 119.
28 Schuttelaar 2010, 22, note 3.
29 Portegies 1999, 54 and discussed more elaborately on 178.
30 Portegies 1999, 184. On the price, see also 178.
31 Portegies 1999, 179-180.
32 Bonenkampová 2013, 199-200.
33 On coffins, see Portegies 1999, chapter 7; Van Genabeek 2018, 181, Fig. 13.

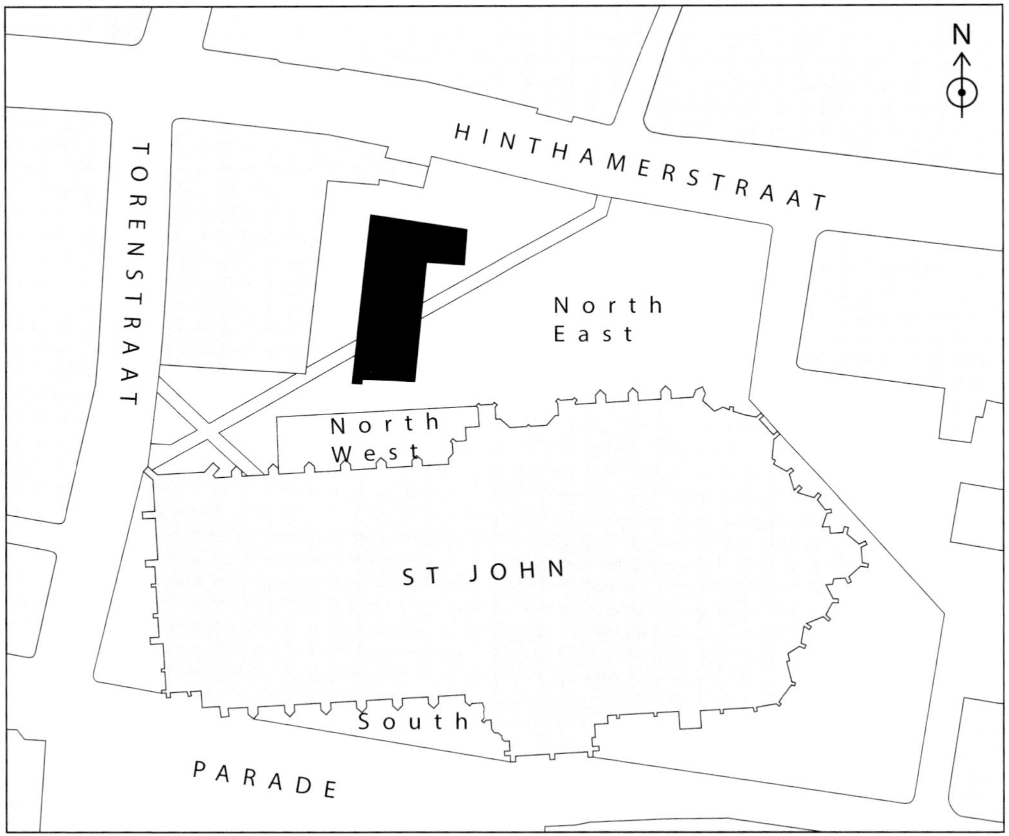

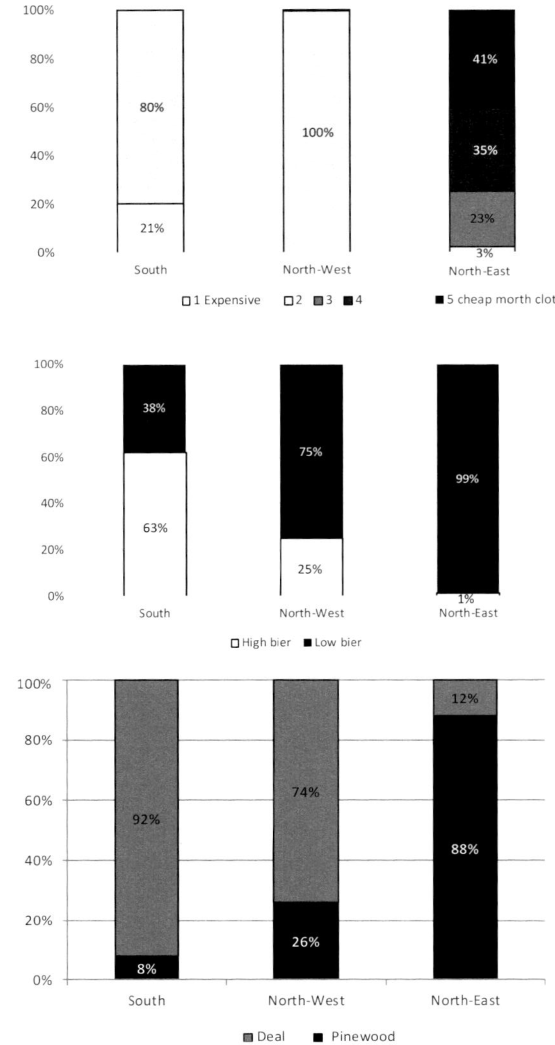

Fig. 2: St John's Cathedral and the three areas of the graveyard (1782-1852) and the location of the excavation in black. Figure after Portegies 1999, 179; Graph mortcloth 1822-1826, 1834, 1838, data from Portegies 1999, 119; Graph biers, 1793 and 1804, N=219 adults, data from Portegies 1999, 111-112, 152, n. 72; Graph coffins, 1793 and 1804, N=168 adults, data from Portegies 1999, 94. Map: Christian Smid, UvA-Kaartenmakers.

the hanging bier and was exclusively used for burials in the southern part of the churchyard, while the inexpensive hanging bier was exclusively used in burials in the north-west corner (Fig. 2, Bier graph). Medium-priced coffins made of deal were used for burials in the southern area of the churchyard, and the cheapest pine coffins were most often used for burials in the north-west corner (Fig. 2, Coffin graph). The data used for Figure 2 concern the period in which burials inside the church were also allowed. The most expensive oak coffins were probably used for burials in the church.

The biggest factor in determining the price of the coffin was the type of wood used. However, coffin regulations from 1675 and 1800 also detail other factors such as the thickness of the boards, whether several boards or only one board was used, the number and type of nails in the bottom and the lid, the length of the coffin, the 'blackness' of the coffin[34] and whether the coffin was polished both inside and out. The longest oak coffin (1.57-1.85 cm)[35] cost 222 *stuivers*, almost five times more than the cheapest pine coffin of the same length, which cost 46 *stuivers*. The medium-priced deal coffins cost 72 *stuivers*.[36] After 1800, coffins were inspected on Saturdays and the approval branded into the wood.[37]

First-class and sixth-class populations

Using documentary records, Portegies established that the three zones corresponded to three different populations. First, many more children were buried in the north-east area than in the other two zones. Second, the average age-at-death of the adults buried in the north-east was much lower than in the south. Third, more women than men were buried in the more expensive burial area (Table 1). While a high child mortality rate and a lower average age-at-death are clearly related to the lower class, the reason for the higher percentage of men in the cheapest area is not self-evident. Portegies hypothesized that this was the result of it being more difficult for a widow to pay for an expensive funeral for her late husband than it was for a widower to pay for his wife's burial. [38]

The dead of the cursed side

Portegies correlated the price differentiation of the south, north-west and north-eastern areas with the 'cursed side' belief.[39] It is remarkable that hardly any other written records remain of this custom, as folk beliefs in 's-Hertogenbosch and surroundings were recorded meticulously by the minister Hanewinkel, who travelled throughout the Meierij of 's-Hertogenbosch and described many, what in

34 Deal and pinewood coffins were painted black; oak ones were not. Portegies 1999, 89.

35 The longest coffin was 5.5 to 6.5 feet.

36 Details from Erfgoed 's-Hertogenbosch, Oud Archief inv.nr. A55 Stadsresoluties, 16-8-1675 fol 124r-127r. On coffins, see Portegies 1999, chapter 7.

37 Erfgoed 's-Hertogenbosch, Archief van het Gereformeerde Weeshuis inv. nr. 909, Contract met de Kistenmaker, 4-11-1800, 4. Such a difference in quality of wood was common in those days. In Alkmaar a 1777-price list included, from most expensive to cheapest, oak, deal, fir and pinewood (Bitter 2002, 229).

38 Portegies 1999, 186.

39 Portegies 1999, 184, 213.

	Source	N	Period	South	North-West	North-East
Burials	Portegies 1999, 183	N=7,055	1793-1858	5%	9%	86%
Children	Portegies 1999, 182-183, fig. 11; 205	N=5,799	1832, 1834, 1838, 1849-1858	Minority		45%
Adults: average age at death	Portegies 1999, 171	N=221	1793 and 1804	61 years	59 years	47 years
Women	Portegies 1999, 185		1793 and 1804	54%	56%	44%

Table 2: Population of the three areas of the graveyard of St John's Cathedral, based on historical data.

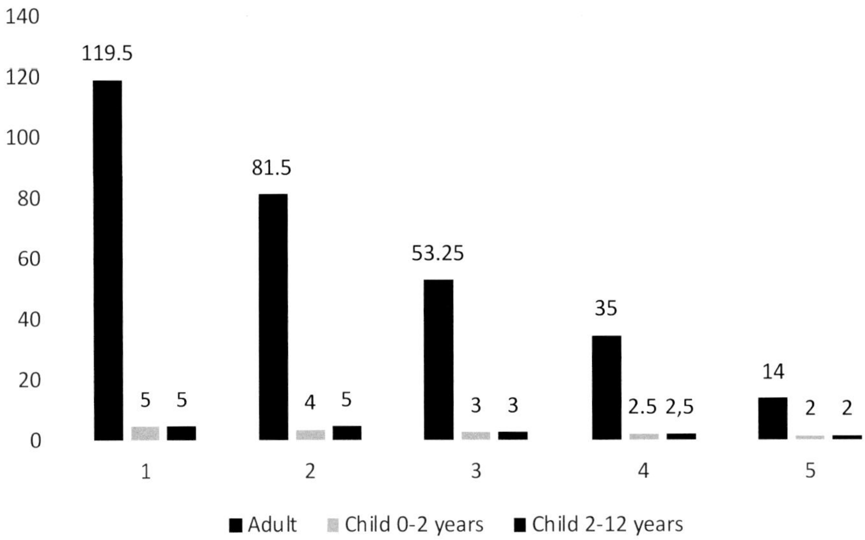

Fig. 3: Cost, in guilders, of first- to fifth-class burials of adults and children at the Orthen cemetery, d. July 11, 1862.

his eyes were despicable and ridiculous folk beliefs.[40] The only record of this belief seemingly is the price differentiation of burials.

The effect of the cost variation was that most burials took place in the north-east zone, the cheapest area (86%). The excavation of a trench in this area revealed the space-saving measures that were taken to accommodate all the burials (Fig. 1: black rectangular). In the excavated zone, five bodies were stacked in one plot, rather than the usual two.[41] The traditional orientation with the head to the west was not strictly followed here. Tapered coffins were alternatively oriented head to the west and head to the east to save space, and one fifth of the burials had a NE-SW or NW-SE orientation.[42] Whether this was different in the other zones cannot be known as these parts were not excavated.

40 Rooijakkers 1995, 98-102.
41 Van Genabeek 2018, 178.
42 Van Genabeek 2018, 177 fig. 10, 178, 179 fig. 12.

May 19, 1858, marked the date of the last burial in the churchyard of St John's. A day later the new cemetery in Orthen, outside the town walls, was already in service, although St John's Cathedral continued to manage the burials.[43] A fifth of the area was designated for Protestants and the rest for Catholics.[44] In 1862, St John's offered 'package deals' for first-, second-, third-, fourth- and fifth-class burials (Fig. 3). These interment options varied in the number of carriages in the procession, type of mortcloth used, and the number of undertakers in the procession. Interestingly, the location of the burial was not included in this offer.[45] In one fell swoop, the cursed side became a thing of the past.

Concluding comments

The burial records from St John's Cathedral (1782-1858) distinguish between three burial zones: the north-east, the north-west and the south. Portegies found that the north-east area was the cheapest, coldest and least desirable location to be buried in and was used by the low classes. He explains the low cost as being linked to the folk belief of a cold, or cursed, side. St John's north-east zone was also the most 'popular' because of its low cost. In other words, the church's price differentiation ensured that the least desirable location was the most 'popular'. As far as I can tell, the cold-side hypothesis has not been tested by historians at other locations. It is not clear whether this is a limitation of the data (burial records only rarely include the location of burial) or whether historians are disinterested. At the Oude Kerk in Delft, the burial records do include the location, and the analysis by Bonenkampová of over 3,058 burial records from the 15th century shows that the north-east side of the churchyard was more popular (40%) than the north-west side (23%) or the south side (37%). If the Oude Kerk in Delft applied similar prices to St John's Cathedral, with the north-east as the cheapest, its distribution pattern can be seen as a confirmation of the cold-side belief. If it didn't and the costs of the various locations were the same, the Delft case contradicts the cold-side belief.

Archaeologists are aware of the 'cold', or 'cursed', side.[46] However, this has not yet resulted in a commitment to systematically comparing north and south sides. Veselka and Klomp must be credited for testing it explicitly for the first time.[47] Their sample at St Andreas Church in Hattem is small, but confirms that the 'cold' north side was the most common burial location for the youngest non-

43 Portegies 1999, 196, 213.

44 'Begraafplaats Orthen' 2015.

45 Erfgoed 's-Hertogenbosch, Nieuw Archief Box 93, Omslag nr. 36 'Kerkhof', staat houdende de opgave v tarieven op kerkhoven in 's-Hertogenbosch, 'Kerkklokje-Officieel kerkelijke dienstregeling voor 's-Hertogenbosch'.

46 Bakx and Jongma (2013, 19) suggest that being buried on the north side of the Nieuwe Kerk was not popular because it was the shadowed side. Bakx and Jongma (2013) and Bult (2018, 135-138) describe the preliminary results from a test trench on the west side (214 coffins) and a smaller test trench on the north side (31 coffins) of the Nieuwe Kerk in Delft. The west side contained some coffins of high-quality wood (oak and beach) but mostly cheap coffins made of pine and larch. The north side contained better quality coffins. The density of burials was similar (Bakx & Jongma 2013, 25). As historical information is not plentiful and the dates of the graves on the north and west sides are not known, it is difficult to interpret the results.

47 Veselka & Klomp 2019, this volume.

adults. To irrefutably confirm the reality of a 'cursed', or 'cold', side historically and archaeologically will require a series of comparisons with larger data sets. Hopefully, new historical and archaeological research will take the 'cold-side' hypothesis on board.

Bibliography

Bakx, J.P.L. & S.H. Jongma, 2013: *Het grafveld van de Nieuwe Kerk in Delft. Archeologisch bureauonderzoek* (Delfste Archeologische Notitie 30), Delft.

'Begraafplaats Orthen', *Magazine Open Monumentedag* 2015, 47, available at Bossche-encyclopedie.

Bitter, P., 2002: *Graven en begraven. Archeologie en geschiedenis van de Grote Kerk van Alkmaar*. Hilversum (Published doctoral thesis University of Amsterdam).

Bitter, P., 2013: 'Begraven onder de zerken. Archeologisch en archiefonderzoek naar 18e- en vroeg-19e-eeuwse grafgebruiken in de Grote Kerk van Alkmaar', in: K. Goudriaan, P. Bitter & V. Bonenkampová (eds.), *Graven spreken. Perspectieven op grafcultuur in de middeleeuwse en vroegmoderne Nederlanden*, Hilversum, 37-51.

Bitter, P., 2018: 'Buried in Alkmaar: Historical and archaeological research on urban cemeteries', in: R.M.R. van Oosten, R. Schats, K. Fast & H.M.P. Bouwmeester (eds.), *The urban graveyard: Archaeological perspectives* (Urban Graveyard Proceedings 2) Leiden: Sidestone Press, 87-115.

Bonenkampová, V., 2013: 'Waren 'rijke stinkerds' rijk? De sociale stratificatie van de Delftenaren en hun graven in de Oude Kerk', in: P. Bitter, V. Bonenkampová & K. Goudriaan (eds.), *Graven spreken. Perspectieven op grafcultuur in de middeleeuwse en vroegmoderne Nederlanden*, Hilversum, 193-204.

Bult, E.J., 2018: 'Medieval and post-medieval cemeteries in and around the city of Delft: Thirty years of rescue archaeology', in: R.M.R. van Oosten, R. Schats, K. Fast & H.M.P. Bouwmeester (eds.), *The urban graveyard: Archaeological perspectives*, (Urban Graveyard Proceedings 2) Leiden: Sidestone Press, 117-164.

G.B.R. [full name unknown], 1839: 'Iets over de zorg der inwoners van Drenthe voor hunne doden', *Drentsche Volksalmanak,* 3, 130-145.

Grolman, H.C.A., 1923: 'Volksgebruiken bij sterven en begraven in Nederland', *Tijdschrift van het Koninklijk Nederlandsch Aardrijkskundig Genootschap*, 40, 359-396.

Hagedoorn, J., 1992: 'Dood en begraven', in: H. Clevis & T. Constandse-Westermann (eds.), *De doden vertellen. Opgraving in de Broerenkerk te Zwolle 1987-88*, Zwolle: Stichting Promotie Archeologie, 31-65.

Kok, H.L., 1970: *De geschiedenis van de laatste eer in Nederland*, Lochem: De Tijdstroom.

Le Francq van Berkhey, J., 1772: *Natuurlyke historie van Holland. Deel 3*, Amsterdam: Yntema en Tieboel.

Lesger, C. & M.H.D. Van Leeuwen, 2011: 'Residential segregation from the sixteenth to the nineteenth century: Evidence from the Netherlands'. *Journal of Interdisciplinary History* 42/3, 333-369.

Portegies, M., 1999: *Dood en begraven in 's-Hertogenbosch. Het Sint-Janskerkhof, 1629-1858*, Utrecht: Matrijs.

Rooijakkers, G., 1995: *Eer en schande. Volksgebruiken van het oude Brabant,* Nijmegen: SUN.

Schuttelaars, A., 2010: '"Hier leijt begraven…" Begraven, begravenen en grafzerken in de Sint-Jan van de middeleeuwen tot de negentiende eeuw', in: J. van Oudheusden & H. Tummers (eds.), *De grafzerken van de Sint-Jan te 's-Hertogenbosch*, 's-Hertogenbosch: Stiching ABC/Heinen, 21-78.

Ter Gouw, J., 1874: *De oude tijd*, Haarlem: Kruseman & Tjeenk Willink.

Van der Drift, R. J., 2010: 'Eigendomsrecht en locaties van de grafzerken in de Sint-Jan', in: J. van Oudheusden & H. Tummers (eds.), *De grafzerken van de Sint-Jan te 's-Hertogenbosch*, 's-Hertogenbosch: Stiching ABC/Heinen, 155-185.

Van Deursen, M., 2001: Book review of M. Portegies & H.L. Janssen, Dood en begraven in 's-Hertogenbosch. Het Sint-Janskerkhof 1629-1858, H.L. Janssen, ed. *BMGN – Low Countries Historical Review,* 116/2, 210. DOI: http://doi.org/10.18352/bmgn-lchr.5455

Van Genabeek, R., 2017: '1000 graven. Verschillen en overeenkomsten tussen archeologisch onderzochte begraafplaatsen in 's-Hertogenbosch (ca. 1275-1858)', in: R.M.R. van Oosten, R. Schats, N. Arts & H.M.P. Bouwmeester (eds.), *De stad en de dood. Archeologisch perspectieven,* Leiden: Sidestone Press (Urban Graveyard Proceedings 1), 45-76.

Van Genabeek, R., 2018: 'A thousand graves: Differences and similarities between archaeologically investigated burial grounds in 's-Hertogenbosch, the Netherlands (c. 1275-1858)', in: R.M.R. van Oosten, R. Schats, K. Fast, N. Arts, & H.P.M. Bouwmeester (eds.), *The urban graveyard: Archaeological perspectives*, Leiden: Sidestone Press (Urban Graveyard Proceedings 2), 165-196.

Van Hoogdalem, H. & K. Walle, 2017: 'Het armebolwerk. Of de geschiedenis van een vergeten begraafplaats', *Leids Jaarboekje*, 109, 131-154.

Veselka, B. & M. Klomp, 2019: Taking sides: An osteoarchaeological analysis of human skeletal remains from the south and north sides of St. Andrew's Church (Andreaskerk) in Hattem, the Netherlands, in: R.M.R. van Oosten, R. Schats, & K. Fast (eds.), *Urban graveyards: Archaeological perspectives from the Low* Countries, Leiden: Sidestone Press (Urban Graveyard proceedings 3), 139-153.

Acknowledgements

Marijke Janssen, afdeling Erfgoed, 's-Hertogenbosch for provinding scans of historical documents.

Methods of ageing and sexing human dry bone put to the test

Looking back on the 1987-1988 excavations in the Broerenkerk in Zwolle

Nico Aten & Hemmy Clevis

Introduction

In 1987, it was not self-evident that during a renovation of a large church, attention should be paid to physical anthropological research.[1] Then what inspired us to undertake an excavation of skeletons? At that time Hemmy Clevis was municipal archaeologist of Zwolle. His first encounter, maybe we should say confrontation, with skeletons had been in the large medieval city of Dordrecht. In the late 1970s, a trench had been excavated across the Grotekerksplein. As this was the highest point of Dordrecht, it was thought that remains of the earliest urban settlement might turn up in the section. The trench cut right across the former churchyard and its burials. Most of the coffins had been well preserved in the clay, and within many of the skulls the clay had even left three-dimensional casts of the brains, shrunk to a third of their original size. While the mechanical excavator cutting through the coffins produced the most peculiar noises, the excavation team had to stop the local youngsters from playing football with the skulls. And as expected, at the bottom of the section there appeared the earliest pottery finds of old Dordrecht, which was the original focus of the excavation.

Later on, in 1981, Clevis found himself involved in the excavation of the site of the Nonnenkerk at Nijmegen. The convent church was found to have many burial vaults with skeletons, within the church and outside. But the excavators' attention mostly went to the painted walls of the vaults. Still, the skeletons were salvaged, during which the team merely observed that some of the nuns had been

1 The full excavation has been published in a Dutch monograph (Clevis & Constandse-Westermann 1992). The data has been partially re-analysed for this first English article on the Broerenkerk excavation.

buried with their hands on the pubis and others not. No scientific questions were formulated with regard to these skeletons.

In January 1987, Clevis was appointed part-time archaeologist by the council of Zwolle. In the very same year a major challenge arose in the form of large-scale engineering works in the local Broerenkerk church. The building was going to have under-floor heating and an entirely new floor installed. Consequently, all of the tombstones in the church floor were to be removed. It was decided to survey all of the gravestones before they were discarded and to document them with photos and full descriptions. Moreover, installing the heating system also meant that more than half a metre of soil would be dug away. In one strip, the builders would even have to dig down over a metre for the technical installations. Would this necessitate an excavation? There was no certainty whatsoever about the depth at which burials might be encountered. Anyhow the subsoil was likely to be disturbed to a considerable depth by the pressure of heavy machinery. Excavation was thought to be the best option.

Aten had first embarked on skeletal analysis at the behest of the ROB, the national archaeological service (ROB, predecessor of the Cultural Heritage Agency of the Netherlands), dealing with the 871 individuals of the 9th to 13th centuries which had been excavated at Dokkum (province of Friesland). The ROB adopted a set of simple methods for establishing gender and estimating age, aimed at processing large quantities of skeletons at the least cost in a short space of time. These methods had earlier been applied at the Dordrecht excavation. Yet these methods had some distinct drawbacks: the reliability of the age determinations was doubtful, as estimating the age of adults was based only upon the degree of dental wear and the extent of cranial-suture closure. Aten was intrigued by the heated debates on estimating age-at-death in the mid 1980s. Bocquet-Appel and Masset argued that the traditional methods for estimating age had serious shortcomings because they tended to reproduce the age distributions of the skeletal series that the methods where derived from.[2] Indeed most of these methods, many of which had been in use for a long time, had never yet been tested on independent populations of known sex and age. Therefore, Aten wished to test the accuracy of methods of sex and age determination, especially on archaeological material, and started looking for a suitable reference population. An initial attempt to find useful reference material from the church of Berkel failed, because the numbering and position of the graves could not be ascertained. Luckily, Aten then received a call from Clevis, the newly appointed municipal archaeologist of Zwolle: things were afoot in the Broerenkerk! The last inhumations in the Dutch Reformed Broerenkerk had taken place in 1828, the year when burial inside churches was banned throughout the Netherlands. While affluent townspeople, such as magistrates, scholars or high-ranking military, would be buried in the main church, the Grote Kerk, members of the middle class, such as craftsmen, lower officials and military of lower rank were buried

2 Bocquet-Appel & Masset 1982; Bocquet-Appel 1986. For a summary, see for instance Chamberlain 2006, 84.

Fig. 1: View of Zwolle, anonymous, early 17th century, oil on canvas, collection City of Zwolle. The Broerenkerk is the double-nave building in the centre left of the painting.

in the Broerenkerk. Lower class people were buried outside the Broerenkerk.[3] Burial in Dutch Reformed churches was open to all denominations and therefore we find small numbers of Lutherans and Roman Catholics as well. What made the Broerenkerk an interesting test case was that the church archive still held a book of burials covering the final period of use (1819 to 1828), which also mentioned the grave numbers. It was still far from certain that identification of the skeletons would be possible, but it was definitely worth trying.

The excavation in the Broerenkerk (October 1987)

With some difficulty, the local authorities had made available an excavation budget of 80,000 guilders, a good 36,000 euros. As work progressed, sponsoring and subsidies for publicity (such as pamphlets and an exhibition), for scientific work and for publication provided additional funds, which raised the total to over 100,000 guilders (45,000 euros). The excavation would not have been possible without the help of some fifty volunteers, and three archaeology students who were going to work out aspects of the project into undergraduate theses. Three further researchers, not all of them paid, invested their time in processing the findings.[4]

The first step in the archaeological project was to reconstruct the numbering of the graves. Many of the slabs bore a grave number, but very few of them were still in their original positions. Yet it still proved possible to identify the original pattern of the rows and graves.

---

3 Hagedoorn 1992, 36-37.

4 Hemmy Clevis was the overall project leader. Monique Barwasser and Tineke Visser supervised the organisation of the excavation. Nico Aten did the technical supervision. Trinette Constandse-Westermann ensured scientific assistance. At that time she was employed as assistant professor at the University of Amsterdam. The archaeological institute of the University of Amsterdam was then known as the Albert Egges van Giffen Instituut voor Prae- en Protohistorie (IPP).

Fig. 2: Interior of the Broerenkerk during excavation, seen from the vaulting.

At the same time, the historian Jaap Hagedoorn set to work on the data from the burial records[5]. During the excavation and the subsequent anthropological analysis he informed his fellow researchers only about which graves had been used between 1819 and 1828, and how many adults and children had gone into each burial space. This minimum of information was important in order to position the excavation trenches in such a way as to include the maximum number of identifiable skeletons, and especially those of children. The anthropological analysis of the recovered skeletons would thus be performed blind. Only after completion would the results be matched up with the identity of the individuals, whose name, sex, age, and often also occupation would then be revealed.

Besides the methodological aspect of sex and age determinations, the study might also offer an impression of the health of part of the population of Zwolle in the early 19th century and before. For this purpose, it was necessary to recover as many skeletons as possible, both identifiable and non-identifiable. In the time allotted, about a third of the church interior could be excavated.

Since skeletons can only be excavated manually, many hands were needed. Volunteers were recruited through ads in the local newspaper. These volunteers were given a brief course in skeletal anatomy, as well as verbal and written instructions on how to record and lift skeletons. For this excavation, a bespoke recording system with specific forms had been devised. The soil would be removed in layers by shovel, down to the first signs of a burial, usually appearing in the form of dark stains marking the vertical sides of a coffin. The skeleton would then be exposed with trowel and brush, leaving the articulation intact for *in-situ* measurement. The skeletons were not drawn, but all were photographed. When they were lifted, certain parts were packed separately for ease of subsequent determination and for

5 Hagedoorn 1992, 31-65.

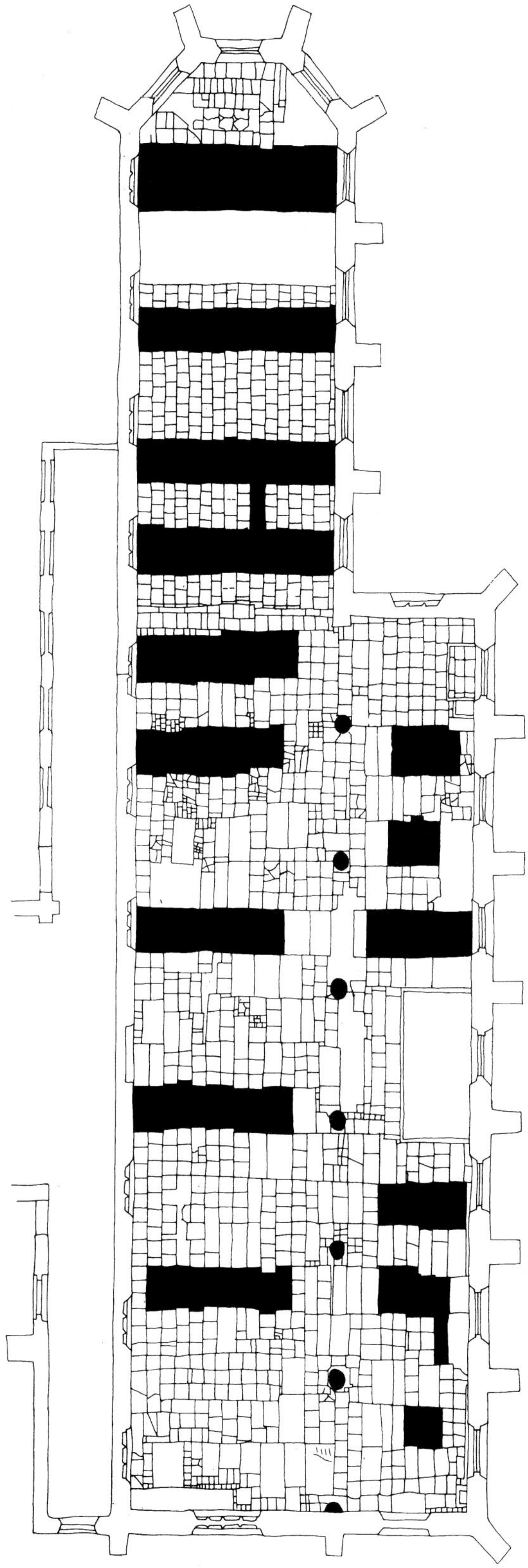

Fig. 3: Location of the excavation trenches within the Broerenkerk.

position of arms and hands	numbers	percentage
arms on pelvis, hands loose	73	26.9
arms alongside body	43	15.9
arms crossed on pelvis	35	12.9
arms crossed on chest or abdomen	24	8.9
hands clasped on pelvis	19	7.0
left arm alongside body, right arm on pelvis	16	5.9
right arm alongside body, left arm on pelvis	11	4.1
left arm on chest or abdomen, right arm on pelvis	8	3.0
left arm alongside body, right arm on chest or abdomen	8	3.0
left arm on pelvis, right arm on chest or abdomen	8	3.0
arms on pelvis, hands on top of each other	7	2.6
arms on chest or abdomen, hands clasped	5	1.8
arms on chest or abdomen, hands loose	4	1.5
right arm alongside body, left arm on chest or abdomen	1	0.4
other positions	9	3.3

Table 1: Position of arms and hands (N=271) of the excavated bodies from the Broerenkerk, dating from the 18th and early 19th centuries.

protection of the dentition: right hand, left hand, right foot, left foot, mandible and skull. The skeletons were laid out to dry in a separate, adjoining space with a blow heater. Special attention was given to small finds associated with individual burials; these were collected separately. All other finds, not relatable to specific burials, were numbered according to grave row.

The trenches had a width of two metres and a maximum depth of two and a half metres. The loose sandy soil in the topmost metre was very dry, so the sides had to be shored up. Soon it was apparent that in the late 17th or early 18th century, the church had been entirely cleared out to a depth of 1.90 to 2.10 m and filled up with fresh sand, to a level somewhat above the old level. As a result, earlier burials appeared only at a greater depth. Because of the raised floor and the centuries of use, a single grave pit might contain five, six, or even seven superimposed burials. All of the dead had been buried in coffins.

Coffins were rectangular (not tapered) in shape, and as far as identifiable were held together with nails. It was observed that the interior of several coffins was covered with black paint or pitch. Two metal handles at each long side were seen on five coffins only. The bodies were buried supine, with the head to the west. The orientation of a few bodies was opposite. This deviating orientation is usually interpreted as the burial of a priest;[6] however, there is no evidence for this explanation in the Broerenkerk. Maybe the body's orientation was not considered important; or during transportation of the rectangular coffin confusion arose as to what was the head end. The position of the arms of 271 bodies was recorded (Table 1). It should be remembered that during transportation of the coffin and in the course of decomposition, the position of arms may have shifted.

6 Bitter 2002, 255.

Burial attire

While virtually no remains of clothing were found, large numbers of pins were encountered. This suggests that the majority of the dead were buried in shrouds that were fastened with copper pins. Less frequently bone buttons were found, in one case still in a row down the front of the chest. Beside the pelvis of one skeleton, an empty leather purse was found. A baby was wrapped in a woollen blanket that was preserved in the soil. Occasionally, badly corroded metal was observed on a skull, probably remnants of a maiden crown or another hair ornament. Not only were garment remains thin on the ground, jewellery too was exceptional: in one case a ring on a right-hand finger, several times a simple earring; once a gold earring and twice a silver hairpin. A rosary was found on the chest of a Beguine. In the coffin of a young child lay an earthenware marble. Although many coins were found, just three were related to specific burials: one coin lay on the edge of a coffin, one coin inside a coffin and one coin on the left arm inside a coffin. In two cases, coins had been placed on the eyes. One of these two bodies was a 32-year-old silversmith, buried in 1826.

Little is known about late-medieval and post-medieval grave goods. According to Hirsch, it was common practice in the 17th century to include objects, in particular coins, in the grave: a remnant of an old custom of giving the deceased gold and other precious jewellery. This was done to placate the dead ancestor while ensuring that the possessions of the deceased were redeemed.[7] The explanation that this was a coin for Charon the ferryman who according to Greek mythology carried the souls to the realm of the dead, or a penny for St Peter, may have been subsequently attached to this custom, when people no longer understood its original meaning[8]. Placing coins on the eyes has been explained as a way to prevent the return of the soul to the head. Later it may have been regarded as a means to keep the eyes closed and create a sleeping impression.[9] The meaning has remained unclear; however, the cases from the Broerenkerk were among the earliest archaeological evidence to show that this custom was still practised in the 19th century.[10] By now, similar finds of coins on the eyes have been described in Alkmaar and Middenbeemster as well.[11]

Near some skeletons many arthropod remains were found. Huge concentrations originated from millipedes, 'coffin-flies' (*Conicera tibialis)* and 'graveyard beetles' (*Rhizophagus parallelocollis)*. These species, as well as the encountered *Trichonyx sulcicollis*, are also known from other 19th-century burials. Next to other arthropod species recorded for the first time, these all have in common that several generations may live below the ground and they are able to reach a decomposing body from the surface.[12]

---

7 Hirsch 1921, 36.

8 *ibid.*

9 Hirsch 1921, 37.

10 Aten 1992a, 27.

11 Alkmaar: Bitter 2002, 265-266; Bitter 2018, 109-110. Middenbeemster: Van Spelde 2018, 328, fig. 18.

12 Hakbijl 2000.

Fig. 4: A 32-year old silversmith, buried in 1826, whose eyes were covered with copper coins.

The physical-anthropological research

The recovered skeletal material fell into three categories.

- Series A comprised 141 individuals buried during the period 1819-1828, who could all be identified from the burial records.
- Series B was made up of 388 individuals who could not be identified, largely dating from the 18th and early 19th centuries.
- Series C consisted of about 500 individuals whose buried remains were no longer articulated.

The finds were processed according to the methods for sex and age determination that were at the time applied by the ROB. These methods were:

- sex determination based upon the cranium and pelvis as devised by the *Arbeitsgruppe europäischer Anthropologen*[13]. The ROB only recorded a total score for all features combined rather than scores for each feature separately;
- sex determination by measuring the widest diameter of the caput femoris;
- age determination based upon the degree of dental wear, using the scheme by Brothwell[14];

13 *Arbeitsgruppe europäischer Anthropologen* 1979.
14 Brothwell 1981, 72.

- age determination by using the dental chart of Ubelaker[15];
- age determination based upon the closure of cranial sutures, using the scheme of Vallois[16];
- age determination based upon the degree of fusion of the epiphyses, using the scheme of Brothwell[17];
- age determination based upon the length of long bones, using the scheme of Stloukal and Hanáková[18].

The selection criteria for these methods were that they could be applied rapidly, with a minimum of technical equipment, and, if possible, even in the field and on fragmented material. As said before, the aim was to develop a cheap way of processing large numbers of individuals from archaeological contexts. The Broerenkerk material was also subjected to some older and newer methods (see below), which were expected to produce more reliable results while still meeting the criteria. Microscopic and chemical analyses were therefore ruled out. Moreover, only non-destructive methods were used, in view of the material's future potential as a reference collection.

Accuracy and reliability in sex determination: the pelvis

Were the methods for sex and age determination effective? The first method to be put to the test was the commonly used sex determination developed by Acsádi en Nemeskéri, supplemented and expanded by the *Arbeitsgruppe europäischer Anthropologen*.[19] The method is based on the morphological differences between the male and female pelvis. Fourteen single features were given a score on a five-point scale ranging from -2 (hyperfeminine) to +2 (hypermasculine). The scores of the single features were weighted and expressed in an overall score, the degree of sexualization. Tables 2A and 2B show that the degree of sexualization of 86 adult individuals, based on morphological differences of 14 features of the pelvis, in 85% of cases correctly matched the identities from the burial records.

known sex	degree of sexualization			total
	< 0	0	> 0	
male	2	3	32	37
female	41	1	7	49
total	43	4	39	86

Table 2A: Results of sex determination based on morphological differences of the pelvis on skeletons of known sex (Series A).

n = 86	percentage
correspondence	85%
indeterminate	5%
no correspondence	10%

Table 2B: Comparison of the degree of sexualization with historically documented sex.

15 Ubelaker 1978, 47.
16 Vallois 1937, 502.
17 Brothwell 1981, 66.
18 Stloukal & Hanáková 1978.
19 *Arbeitsgruppe europäischer Anthropologen 1979.*

female and male traits of the pelvis	weight	n	D	p
p<0.05, significant				
arc composé	2	78	0.508	0.000
sulcus praeauricularis	3	72	0.618	0.000
incisura ischiadica major	3	70	0.582	0.000
shape of the foramen obturatum	1	36	0.611	0.002
width of the corpus ossis ischii	1	82	0.373	0.007
tuber ischiadicum of the corpus ossis ischii	1	58	0.443	0.007
angulus pubis	2	23	0.623	0.025
p>0.05, not significant				
muscle attachments of the os coxae	1	53	0.360	0.064
shape of the os coxae	1	48	0.379	0.064
pelvis minor	½	30	0.420	0.144
fossa iliaca	1	51	0.248	0.415
rim of the foramen obturatum	1	40	0.200	0.819
pelvis major	½	31	0.158	0.992
crista iliaca	1	50	0.120	0.994

Table 3: Significance (p) of the distance (D) between the distributions of the scores for historically documented males and females per single pelvic trait (Series A) (Kolmogorov-Smirnov, SPSS).

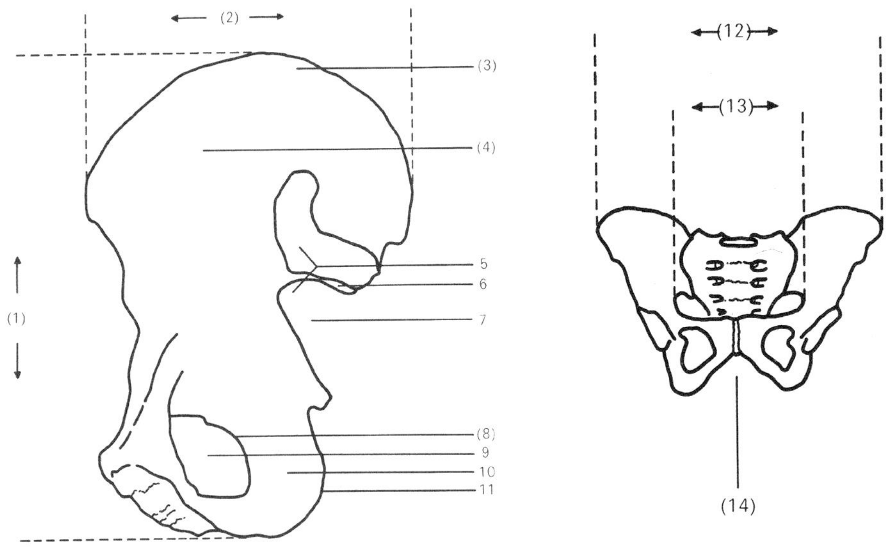

Fig. 5: Morphological features of the pelvis used in determination of sex; 1 and 2 shape and muscle attachments of the os coxae, 3 crista iliaca, 4 fossa iliaca, 5 arc composé, 6 sulcus praeauricularis, 7 inscisura ischiadica major, 8 rim of the foramen obturatum, 9 shape of the foramen obturatum, 10 width of the corpus ossis ischii, 11 tuber ischiadicum of the corpus ossis ischii, 12 pelvis major, 13 pelvis minor, 14 angulus pubis.

morphological traits of the pelvis	true distribution according to burial records			found distribution according to degree of sexualization				bias
	female	male	ratio	< 0 female appearance	0	> 0 male appearance	ratio	
width of the corpus ossis ischii	47	35	1.34	24	16	42	0.57	2.35
sulcus praeauricularis	39	33	1.18	27	8	37	0.73	1.62
arc composé	43	35	1.29	33	12	33	1.00	1.23
rim of the foramen obturatum	20	20	1.00	13	11	16	0.81	1.23
tuber ischiadicum of the corpus ossis ischii	30	28	1.07	23	11	24	0.96	1.12
incisura ischiadica major	39	31	1.26	34	9	27	1.26	1.00
pelvis minor	14	16	0.88	11	8	11	1.00	0.88
shape of the os coxae	25	23	1.09	22	10	16	1.38	0.79
crista iliaca	25	25	1.00	25	6	19	1.32	0.76
fossa iliaca	26	25	1.04	24	11	16	1.50	0.69
angulus pubis	10	13	0.77	8	8	7	1.14	0.67
muscle attach-ments of the os coxae	27	26	1.04	24	14	15	1.60	0.65
shape of the fora-men obturatum	18	18	1.00	17	10	9	1.89	0.53
pelvis major	13	18	0.72	14	7	10	1.40	0.52

Table 4: The bias towards a female or male degree of sexualization, per single feature of the pelvis (Series A).

For every single feature an assessment was made as to whether the scores were truly indicative of the difference between male and female. To this end, a Kolmogorov-Smirnov test was used. It turned out that seven of the fourteen features failed to bring out any significant difference ($p>0.05$) beteween male and female. The features in Table 3 are ranked according to their p value.

Remarkably, the three features of the pelvis that best mark the difference between male and female (the top three features in Table 3) are those features that are most suited to archaeological material. As a result of their specific location on the pelvis, they are less prone to disintegration of the bone.

Besides the power of single features to distinguish between male and female, also a possible bias towards male or female was investigated. The found female-male ratio is compared to the known female-male ratio from the historical record. By dividing them, a bias towards male sexualization results in a score >1, whereas a bias towards female sexualization results in a score <1. If there were no bias at all, the found ratio divided by the known ratio should be 1.The results are shown in Table 4.

The bias that arises from applying morphological criteria may have various causes. First, the skeletal population may have specific morphological characteristics. The population as a whole may be more robust or more slightly built. Secondly, the skills and experience of the physical anthrolopogist affect the outcome. To obviate this at the Broerenkerk site, first a test series was determined by four researchers, after which one researcher assessed all the skeletons. Thirdly, there may be structural errors in the applied methods. Any such errors can only be made visible by applying the method to populations of known sex.

known sex	degree of sexualization			total
	< 0	0	> 0	
male	12	-	32	44
female	61	1	2	64
total	73	1	34	108

Table 5A: Results of sex determination based on morphological differences of the cranium on skeletons of known sex (Series A).

n = 108	percentage
correspondence	86%
indeterminate	1%
no correspondence	13%

Table 5B: Comparison of the degree of sexualization with historically documented sex.

female and male traits of the cranium	weight	n	D	p
p<0.05, significant				
glabella	3	90	0.667	0.000
protuberantia occipitalis externa	2	98	0.635	0.000
os zygomaticum, surface	1	90	0.620	0.000
arcus superciliaris	2	103	0.612	0.000
crista supramastoidea	2	100	0.583	0.000
os zygomaticum, shape	1	91	0.542	0.000
mandibula, total aspect	3	91	0.479	0.000
processus mastoideus	3	88	0.467	0.000
inclinatio frontale	1	98	0.445	0.000
planum nuchale	3	85	0.431	0.001
forma orbitae	½	82	0.422	0.002
margo supraorbitalis	½	102	0.317	0.015
mentum	2	90	0.320	0.022
processus zygomaticus	3	98	0.295	0.034
angulus mandibulae	2	82	0.314	0.036
p>0.05, not significant				
tubera parietalia	1	100	0.230	0.155
tubera frontalia	1	103	0.224	0.166
margo mandibulae	1	94	0.172	0.503

Table 6: Significance (p) of the distance (D) between the distributions of the scores for historically documented males and females per single cranial trait (Series A) (Kolmogorov-Smirnov, SPSS).

Accuracy and reliability in sex determination: the cranium.

The degree of sexualization could be determined for 108 individuals from Series A, based upon morphological differences of 18 features of the skull (Table 5A). When the degree of sexualization was compared with the known sex from the historical record, the correspondence turned out to be 86% (Table 5B).

Table 6 shows that three features of the cranium deemed to display differences between females and males yield a p value of over 0.05. In other words, these three are best omitted.

The female/male bias of the single traits of the cranium is somewhat larger than the bias of the pelvic traits. In particular, the features of the mandibula tend wrongly to suggest a more masculine appearance (Table 7). The results from a

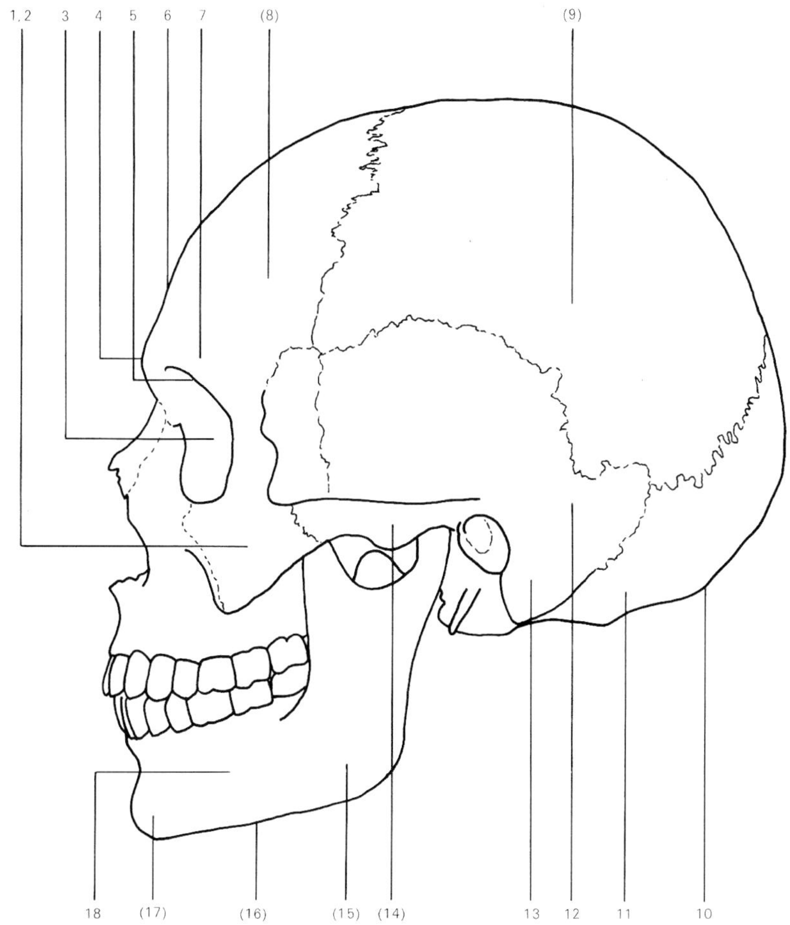

Fig. 6: Morphological features of the cranium used in determination of sex; 1 shape of the os zygomaticum, 2 surface of the os zygomaticum, 3 forma orbitae, 4 glabella, 5 margo supraorbitalis, 6 inclinatio frontale, 7 arcus superciliaris, 8 tubera frontalia, 9 tubera parietalia, 10 protuberantia occipitalis externa, 11 planum nuchale, 12 crista supramastoidea, 13 processus mastoideus, 14 processus zygomaticus, 15 angulus mandibulae, 16 margo inferior, 17 mentum, 18 total aspect of the mandibula.

morphological traits of the cranium	true distribution according to burial records			found distribution according to degree of sexualization				bias
	female	male	ratio	< 0 female appearance	0	> 0 male appearance	ratio	
mentum	51	39	1.31	17	27	46	0.37	3.54
margo mandibulae	54	40	1.35	17	43	34	0.50	2.7
mandibula, total aspect	51	40	1.28	25	29	37	0.68	1.89
margo supraorbitalis	62	40	1.55	34	29	39	0.87	1.78
angulus mandibulae	45	37	1.22	23	26	33	0.70	1.75
forma orbitae	48	34	1.41	23	31	28	0.82	1.72
inclinatio frontale	58	40	1.45	41	24	33	1.24	1.17
os zygomaticum, surface	54	36	1.50	40	26	24	1.67	0.9
crista supramastoidea	60	40	1.50	50	21	29	1.72	0.87
os zygomaticum, shape	55	36	1.53	45	24	22	2.05	0.75
planum nuchale	50	35	1.43	41	23	21	1.95	0.73
processus mastoideus	51	37	1.38	50	13	25	2.00	0.69
arcus superciliaris	62	41	1.51	53	29	21	2.52	0.6
glabella	54	36	1.50	51	19	20	2.55	0.59
processus zygomaticus	59	39	1.51	46	35	17	2.71	0.56
tubera frontalia	61	42	1.45	58	28	17	3.41	0.43
tubera parietalia	59	41	1.44	64	21	15	4.27	0.34
protuberantia occipitalis externa	55	43	1.28	60	28	10	6.00	0.21

Table 7: The bias towards a female or male degree of sexualization, per single feature of the cranium (Series A).

test of mandibulae in Dordrecht by Maat *et al.* reveal the same bias towards male appearance of the mandibulae.[20]

Still searching for simple methods applicable to archaeological material, we thoroughly investigated possibilities for sexing by means of metric distinctions. Use was made of measurements that were earlier employed sucessfully for sex diagnosis – for instance, a set of eleven cranial dimensions.[21] An optimised selection of just four of these dimensions[22] produced an accuracy of over 90 %, but given the frequency of damage to archaeological bone material, the usefulness of these parameters in archaeological practice will be limited.

20 Maat *et al.* 1997.

21 Based on the written instructions given by G.N. van Vark to the ROB. The applied measurements were XCB, ZYB, AUB, MDH, MDB, EKB, MLS, SOS, GLS, FOL, PAF, in accordance with the definitions formulated in Howells 1973.

22 ZYB, GLS, PAF, MDH.

measurement	males					females				
	n	mean	st. dev.	min.	max.	n	mean	st. dev.	min.	max.
F1	35	464.20	25.22	405	516	44	438.09	20.14	393	495
F2	35	460.57	25.16	401	510	45	433.53	19.38	391	490
F9	35	33.03	3.21	28	40	47	31.68	2.17	26	35
F10	35	28.29	2.23	24	33	47	25.94	1.86	21	29
F18	33	48.55	2.57	43.0	54.0	43	43.67	2.36	38.0	49
F19	33	47.71	2.58	42.5	52.0	35	43.06	2.57	37.0	49
F21	32	82.50	4.19	74	90	41	74.85	3.09	69	81
H1	35	335.83	16.75	300	368	41	312.24	10.01	287	336
H4	34	62.32	3.97	53	70	34	53.74	3.27	43	59
H9	32	45.28	2.17	38.0	49.0	42	39.32	1.94	35.0	44
H10	34	47.68	2.39	42.0	52.0	49	41.90	2.14	36.0	48
U1	31	260.84	13.57	232	291	25	234.04	9.29	219	254
R1	32	245.91	12.53	226	278	28	220.46	10.23	202	240
T1	35	376.54	22.21	333	421	42	359.50	19.13	322	406
T1A	34	383.09	22.23	336	431	44	365.41	19.51	330	412
Fi1	17	373.41	21.31	336	408	21	352.14	16.17	326	396

Table 8: Results of the measurements of the long bones (Series A). For the meaning of the codes, and the measuring instructions, see Martin & Saller 1957, 519 ff.

Accuracy and reliability in sex assessment: the long bones

For the postcranial skeleton the indices and discriminant analyses recommended by the *Arbeitsgruppe* were used, [23] supplemented with measurements of the long bones emplyed by Dittrick & Suchey[24, 25] and two measurements of the atlas and the axis.[26] With these data various discriminant analyses were performed. These fully confirmed the findings of Dittrick & Suchey, who also argued entirely on the basis of archaeological practice: the combination of parameters in the discriminant analyses fails to produce a better outcome than is attained by using individual measurements. Moreover, because of damage to the bones, the discriminant analyses are applicable to part of the archaeological material only. Surprisingly, a single measurement on the head of the humerus, measurement H 10 (vertical diameter), scored a correspondence of 90%. Some other single measurements yielded good results as well (Tables 8 and 9). Despite a greater susceptibility to damage of the material, this underlines the importance of simple measurements for rapid and reliable sex determination.

Finally, metric distinctions among children were examined. The possibilities are very limited because sexual dimorphism before puberty is hardly or not at all evident. Yet there is a difference in size; a value, however, much more determined

23 *Arbeitsgruppe europäischer Anthropologen* 1979.

24 Dittrick & Suchey 1986.

25 In contrast to Dittrick & Suchey, we did not follow Bass & Brothwell's definitions for the measurements, but only those of Martin & Saller 1957, 519 ff.

26 Hinck, Hopkins & Savara 1962.

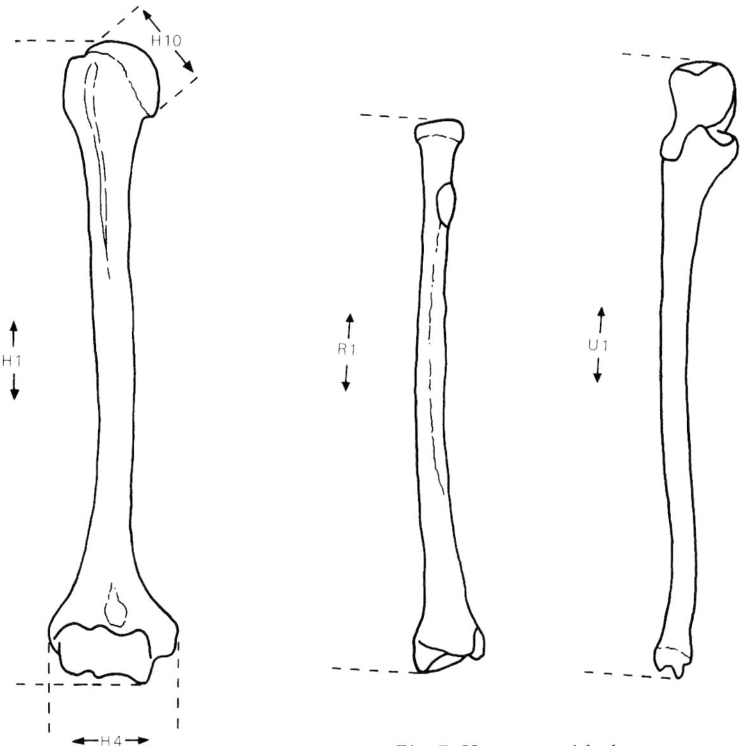

Fig. 7: Humerus with the measurements H1, H4 and H10 (not depicted is H9, the largest transversal diameter of the caput humeri); radius with the measurement R1; ulna with the measurement U1.

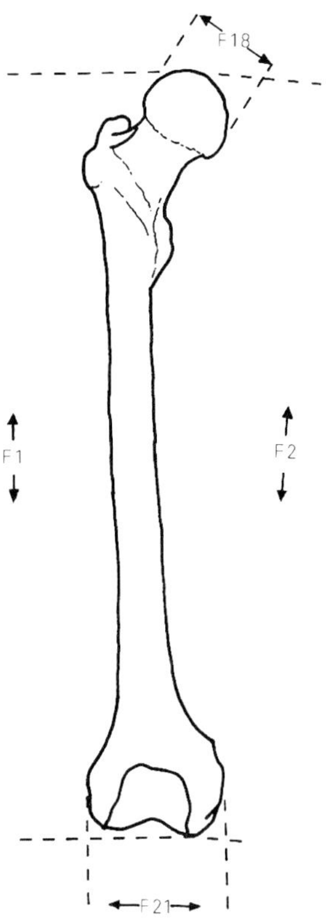

Fig. 8: Femur with the measurements F1, F2, F18 and F21 (not depicted are F9 transversal subtrochanteric diameter, F10 sagittal subtrochanteric diameter and F19 sagittal diameter of the caput femoris).

single variable	Dittrick & Suchey n	sectioning point in mm	% correct	Broerenkerk n	sectioning point in mm	% correct
H9	305	41.203	89.5	74	42.30	90.5
H10	318	44.343	89.0	83	44.79	90.4
R1				60	233.18	88.3
F18				76	46.11	88.2
U1				56	247.44	87.5
H4	332	59.323	85.2	68	58.03	86.8
F21	296	77.487	85.8	73	78.68	86.3
H1	303	313.871	79.5	76	324.04	84.2
F19				68	45.39	80.9
F2	288	430.201	80.2	80	447.05	72.5
F1	293	435.156	79.5	79	451.15	69.6
F9	350	29.348	55.1	82	32.36	57.3
F10	350	28.060	68.0	82	27.12	72.0
T1A				78	374.25	70.5
T1				77	368.02	70.1
Fi1				38	362.78	76.3

Table 9: Calculated single-variable sectioning points and the achieved percentage of correct sex determinations (Series A).

by age than by sex, and which therefore cannot be used for individuals of unknown age. An exception is the dentition, both the deciduous teeth and the permanent teeth, which is formed at one developmental stage and then no longer grows. Various researchers have tried to use differential tooth size.[27] Also differences in shape of the pelvis were examined.[28] Although the excavation strategy in the Broerenkerk was aimed at recovering as many historically identifiable child skeletons as possible, the number of measurements that could be performed on teeth and pelvises ultimately proved too small to allow us to test the efficacy of the applied methods.

Accuracy and reliability in age-at-death: cranium

The methods for age estimation turned out to be less accurate. The methods used by the ROB for adults, *viz.* the ectocranial closure of the sutures according to the scheme by Vallois and the dental wear according to the scheme of Brothwell, are presented by the *Arbeitsgruppe europäischer Anthropologen* as supplementary methods besides the so-called 'complex method'. In the case of our material from Zwolle, we used the then recently published method of Meindl & Lovejoy focusing on the ectocranial closure of sutures.[29]

27 For the Broerenkerk project we studied the methods of Ditch & Rose 1972, Black 1978 and Rösing 1983.

28 For an overview, see Schutkowski 1986. For the Broerenkerk project we used the measurements formulated by Weaver 1980 and Schutkowski 1987.

29 Meindl & Lovejoy 1985.

		Meindl & Lovejoy				Broerenkerk		
phase	**n**	**mean**	**st. dev.**	**range**	**n**	**mean**	**st. dev.**	**range**
'lateral-anterior system'								
0	42			-50	14	36.9	13.7	20-67
1	18	32.0	8.3	19-48	14	47.5	16.9	19-77
2	18	36.2	6.2	25-49	12	54.7	16.8	31-82
3, 4, 5	56	41.1	10.0	23-68	20	61.8	14.5	25-77
6	17	43.4	10.7	23-63	8	68.3	10.4	50-83
7, 8	31	45.5	8.9	32-65	7	73.4	7.1	68-89
9, 10	29	51.9	12.5	33-76	4	69.0	13.5	47-83
11 - 14	24	56.2	8.5	34-68	2	59.5	-	47-72
15	1				-	-	-	-
'vault system'								
0	24			-49	4	37.0	17.5	23-67
1, 2	12	30,5	9.6	18-45	7	38.1	15.5	19-60
3 - 6	30	34.7	7.8	22-48	22	48.9	16.7	25-83
7 - 11	50	39.4	9.1	24-60	19	60.3	14.5	33-77
12 - 15	50	45.2	12.6	24-75	12	66.5	12.0	47-78
16 - 18	31	48.8	10.5	30-71	4	76.5	6.7	68-83
19, 20	26	51.5	12.6	23-76	2	80.5	-	72-89
21	13			40-	1	70.0	-	-

Table 10: Results of the age estimation by the ectocranial aspect of the cranial sutures, following the method of Meindl & Lovejoy (Series A).

The Meindl & Lovejoy method is more refined and detailed than the scheme by Vallois and therefore enjoyed our preference. At the same time, our attention was drawn to the other methods presented by the same research team. Especially the method based on changes in shape to the facies auricularis is interesting for archaeologists because this part of the pelvis is generally better preserved in the soil than the more fragile facies symphysialis.[30] For the sake of comparison, however, also the facies symphysialis was examined.

Note was taken of the remarks and descriptions by Meindl *et al.*[31] but for practical reasons we nonetheless used the original subdivision by Todd[32] from which the method of Meindl *et al.* was derived. Besides, we used the method of Katz & Suchey.[33] The latter was promising, because in response to Meindl *et al.*, use had been made of a much larger reference collection with a greater age range for the development of the method.

The results of the age estimations according to these four methods are presented in Tables 10 to 13. In each instance, a row represents the average ages and in so far as known the range of ages encountered in the original reference collections during

30 Lovejoy *et al.* 1985.

31 Todd 1920.

32 Todd 1920.

33 Katz & Suchey 1986. In this instance use was made of the twelve plaster models associated with the method, which were kindly lent to us for a year by Dr G.N. van Vark, Groningen.

	Lovejoy *et al.*		Broerenkerk			
phase	**age**	**n**	**mean**	**st. dev.**	**min.**	**max.**
1	20 – 24	1	20.0		20	20
2	25 – 29	7	38.1	14.7	23	66
3	30 – 34	21	43.7	11.4	25	72
4	35 – 39	17	58.8	14.8	30	78
5	40 – 44	18	63.6	13.7	39	83
6	45 – 49	6	67.7	18.6	35	88
7	50 – 59	2	66.5	--	50	83
8	60 +	1	74.0	--	74	74

Table 11: Results of the age estimation by means of the facies auricularis, following the method of Lovejoy et al. (Series A).

	Todd		Broerenkerk			
phase	**age**	**n**	**mean**	**st. dev.**	**min.**	**max.**
1	18 – 19	2	22.0	--	19	25
2	20 – 21	1	20.0	--	20	20
3	22 – 24					
4	25 – 26	1	48.0	--	48	48
5	27 – 30	2	41.5	--	36	47
6	30 – 35	1	33.0	--	33	33
7	35 – 39	3	52.0	21.1	32	74
8	39 – 44	3	51.0	19.1	40	73
9	45 – 50	10	58.0	14.5	35	78
10	50 +	8	64.1	15.7	39	83

Table 12: Results of the age estimation by means of the facies symphysialis, following the method of Todd (Series A).

	Katz & Suchey			Broerenkerk				
phase	**n**	**mean**	**st. dev.**	**n**	**mean**	**st. dev.**	**min.**	**max.**
1	121	18.9	2.3	3	21.3	3.2	19	25
2	81	24.7	4.3					
3	43	28.8	5.9	6	39.3	6.9	32	48
4	153	36.8	9.6	5	60.0	14.4	36	72
5	241	51.0	13.6	9	56.3	17.9	35	83
6	100	62.7	12.4	6	68.7	9.8	55	82

Table 13: Results of the age estimation by means of the facies symphysialis, following the method of Katz & Suchey (Series A).

the development of the methods, and what values were found in the Broerenkerk material. Of all four methods it can be said that in the Broerenkerk material the average ages for almost all developmental phases were higher to substantially higher. In the estimation based on cranial sutures, the differences even in the early developmental stages (with entirely or almost entirely open sutures) are remarkably large. With the closure of cranial sutures, there is the problem that in many individuals this closure fails to occur until an advanced age.

In Meindl & Lovejoy's reference material, high age is markedly underrepresented, which is why this problem did not feature as much there as it does in the Broerenkerk material. And this although the phenomenon was discussed by several researchers even before 1985. Perizonius even posed the rhetorical question: "Do individuals with open sutures have more chance to grow old?"[34]

The results based on the facies auricularis are barely any better. In the earliest developmental stages the differences are somewhat less pronounced than with those of the cranial sutures, but beyond phase 3 the average ages in the Broerenkerk material steeply rise, and the standard deviation per developmental stage is large, whereas for later stages the average ages are far less divergent. A similar picture arises from age estimation based on the facies symphysialis, although the results seem somewhat more favourable. In the age estimation methods by Katz & Suchey the range among the higher age groups is a bit narrower. When judging the methods based on the facies symphysialis, we are hampered by the number of individuals that must be excluded because of damage: some developmental stages are no longer represented, so that no full and reliable picture of the method's efficacy can be achieved.

Accuracy and reliability in age-at-death: dental wear

Age estimations were made also from dental wear[35]. Here the age classes were 18 to 25, 25 to 35, etc. For the 37 males there were just 6 correct scores, and among the 43 females only 11. Nonetheless, the degree of dental wear produced a better result than any of the other methods[36]. Moreover, age estimation on the basis of dentition is, for archaeologists, an invaluable method in the case of unfavourable soil conditions. In peaty soils and in loess it often is observed that all that remains of a skeleton is the enamel caps of the teeth. The example of the Carolingian cemetery of Inden shows that these caps still allow an age analysis of all burials.[37] Though such research does make extraordinary demands on excavation technique.

The Broerenkerk study clearly illustrated the methodological problems concerning the age estimation of adult individuals. It is a fundamental problem in virtually all methods of age diagnosis, that they approach the issue through degenerative processes acting on the skeleton. These in their turn are strongly affected by extraneous factors such as living conditions and physical strain, and are therefore highly variable and up to a point specific to populations. In general it can be said to be highly inadvisable to use methods of age estimation that have not been previously tested on an independent population. For such a test, or in fact a calibration, the Broerenkerk population is too small. Nonetheless, more recent

34 Perizonius 1983, 215.
35 The data were gathered in 1988 by Tjeerd Pot and Wilbert Bouts.
36 Bouts *et al.* 1992, Constandse-Westermann 1997.
37 Unselt *et al.* 1995.

further research on the Broerenkerk material has demonstrated the special value of dental wear for age assessment, especially when it comes to older individuals.[38]

All of this of course is in stark contrast to the age diagnosis of childern's skeletons, which is based on various aspects of a child's physical development. Here too extraneous factors play a part, but because growth proceeds rapidly in a relatively brief period of some 20 years, there is far less variability. All of the tested methods (using the development of deciduous teeth and permanent teeth[39], body length[40], or closure of the epiphyses[41] produced satisfactory results. However, although the excavation strategy was aimed at recovering as many children as possible whose age and sex could be gleaned from the burial records, the eventual number of child skeletons was too small to allow their reliable statistical testing against the documentary sources. Therefore a discussion of the child skeleton study falls beyond the scope of this article.

Stature

In 1987 barely any data was available about the stature or body length of Dutch skeleton populations. The Broerenkerk material might be able to close the temporal gap between the 17th- and 18th-century material from Spitsbergen and Leiden on the one hand and the 19th- and 20th-century historical records on the other.[42] The research into stature, like that into sex determination and age estimation, was now also considered from a methodological perspective. To this end, multiple methods were examined, and the differences between males and females were studied.

In the Broerenkerk project, both the *in situ* measurements of overall body length, and body length inferred from the long bones were given consideration. Both methods have significant pros and cons. The ratio of the length of the limbs to overall stature may vary considerably among individuals and among populations. The most important advantage of measuring the length of a skeleton *in situ* is that it is unaffected by the variable proportions of limb lengths to stature. A great drawback however is that body length *in situ* is affected by taphonomic processes. Especially in an urban cemetery, with multiple superimposed coffins, major displacements of body parts may be expected in the course of and following decomposition. While making observations in the field one should therefore take into account such displacements, and their potential effect on the measurements should be assessed and recorded. Formulas used for the reconstruction of stature on the basis of the length of long bones, in each instance reflect the population from which they were developed. Since the body proportions of an archaeological skeleton population are unknown to start with, it is up to the researcher to decide which formula is applied. As a result, a variety of formulas are in circulation, which hamper objective comparison between different studies. Another drawback of the use of formulas is that these

38 Mays 2002; 2014.

39 According to Ubelaker 1978.

40 According to Stloukal & Hanáková 1978.

41 According to *Arbeitsgruppe europäischer Anthropologen* 1979, 15.

42 Maat 1981; 1982

	n	mean	st. dev.	min.	max.
A: all lengths measured *in situ*, irrespective of pathological changes to stature					
males	32	158.4	8.9	142	172
females	42	149.2	9	121	172
B: lengths measured *in situ* of skeletons without obvious pathological changes to stature					
males	23	160.1	8.1	144	172
females	34	151.4	7.3	135	172

Table 14: The lengths of the identified skeletons (Series A), as recorded in situ.

are different for men and women, and that therefore first the sex needs to be determined from the skeleton. It should be remembered that a sex determination from metric traits is not independent of the length of long bones and hence will affect the reconstruction of the individual's stature. Further the research question plays an important role in the choice of method. In general the aim is to reconstruct the 'healthy' or 'potential' stature. Both with *in situ* measurements and with reconstructions from long bones, individuals whose stature is obviously affected by pathologies are omitted. This ídealised' stature is used for recognising long-term trends in stature.

The problem of the various formulas in circulation could easily be resolved by comparing not the reconstructed statures but the lengths of long bones. That anthropologists still work with reconstructed stature is because in this way a link may be sought with the documentary sources recording stature, such as military records or forensic evidence. If we are not interested in potential stature, but by contrast want a full picture of statures within a population, then we should not, for example, exclude hunchbacked individuals. Such statures affected by pathologies can be ascertained only by *in situ* measurements.

For the early 19th-century population of the Broerenkerk the average stature measured *in situ* was 158.4 cm for the adult men, and for the adult women 149.2 cm (Table 14). If we omit those individuals whose stature was clearly reduced through pathological changes, the average lengths are 160.1 and 151.4 cm, respectively. Yet among these 'healthy' skeletons we could rule out any taphonomical disturbance only in the case of three men and seven women, which means that we should reckon with a margin of error of +/- 5 cm.

For reconstructing the bodies' lengths in the Broerenkerk study, we used the formulas by Telkkä and by Trotter & Gleser. The latter are the most commonly used in archaeology. Trotter and Gleser in 1952 used bone material of American soldiers killed in World War II, supplemented with material from an anatomical collection so as to also have sufficient female material.[43] In 1958, they updated their formulas for men with the bodies of American soldiers who had died in Korea.[44] Archaeologists often use the more recent formula because of the misunderstanding that these were improvements rather than updates. In 1970

43 Trotter & Gleser 1952.
44 Trotter & Gleser 1958.

Trotter herself expressed a preference for the original formulas of 1952, because of their smaller standard deviations.[45]

Also from the perspective of mutual comparability of anthropological research results it would be desirable that only the older formulas of Trotter and Gleser are used. In the Broerenkerk study we have however adhered to common practice. After the study, doubts were uttered as to the correctness of the length measurements of the tibia that Trotter used for formulating her formulas.[46] Therefore most forensic handbooks warn against the uncorrected use of the formulas of Trotter & Gleser in which the length of the tibia features. Here the formulas and the outcomes however are represented in the uncorrected form as they were applied in the Broerenkerk study of 1988.

Telkkä's formulas are an important alternative for those by Trotter & Gleser, because they were developed on the basis of a European population, from Finland.[47] Because the formulas of Trotter & Gleser appeared soon after the publication of Telkkä, the latter have remained largely unnoticed. Only Telkkä's later formulas for children have seen some application in Germany.[48] Since the Broerenkerk study, a particular preference for the use of the formulas by Breitinger has arisen in the Netherlands.[49] Like our preference for Telkkä at the time, this preference too has been prompted by the European origin of the bone material. However, Breitinger's data derive mainly from young sportsmen and -women and students from an urban context, who cannot be considered representative of the general population. Moreover, Breitinger did not measure dry bones, but took measurements from living individuals.[50] This last point means that for Breitinger's formulas unconventional measurements must be taken (H2, R1b, T1b). Finally, Breitinger offers formulas only for men, so that for females we are obliged to fall back on Trotter & Gleser or the less commonly used formulas by Telkkä and more recent studies. In order to somewhat accommodate current practice in the Netherlands, we have here added the third formula of Breitinger, who uses F1, to the various stature calculations of our 1988 material.

The formulas for stature calculation used for the Broerenkerk material are presented in table 15.

The length of the long bones is measured both on the left and the right. In all formulas the average of these two should be used, but studies in the Netherlands often deviate from this practice. Only if the left or the right side could not be measured, most methods allow for the use of a single value. Yet Telkkä's method introduces a correction, because there usually are differences in length between an individual's left and right limbs. These differences have been calculated for the identified skeletons from the Broerenkerk (Tables 16 and 17).[51]

---

45 Trotter 1970.

46 Jantz *et al.* 1994.

47 Telkkä 1950.

48 Telkkä *et al.* 1962.

49 Maat 2005, 281-282.

50 Breitinger 1937; Wurm 1986, 164.

51 For every measurement, the recorded values have a roughly normal distribution (Shapiro-Wilk test and Q-Q plot, SPSS).

Breitinger		male
	Br3	94.31 + 1.645 * F1 ± 4.8 cm
Telkkä		male
	Tel1	169.4 + 2.8 * (H1 – 32.9)
	Tel2	169.4 + 2.1 * (F1 – 45.5)
	Tel3	169.4 + 2.1 * (T1 – 36.2)
	Tel4	169.4 + 2.5 * (Fi1 – 36.1)
Telkkä		female
	Tel5	156.8 + 2.7 * (H1 – 30.7)
	Tel6	156.8 + 1.8 * (F1 – 41.8)
	Tel7	156.8 + 1.9 * (T1 – 33.1)
	Tel8	156.8 + 2.3 * (Fi1 – 32.7)
Trotter & Gleser 1958		male white
	TG1	1.31 * (F1 + Fi1) + 63.05 ± 3.62
	TG2	1.26 * (F1 + T1) + 67.09 ± 3.74
	TG3	2.60 * Fi1 + 75.50 ± 3.86
	TG4	2.32 * F1 + 65.53 ± 3.94
	TG5	2.42 * T1 + 81.93 ± 4.00
	TG6	1.82 * (H1 + R1) + 67.97 ± 4.31
	TG7	1.78 * (H1 + U1) + 66.98 ± 4.37
	TG8	2.89 * H1 + 78.10 ± 4.57
	TG9	3.79 * R1 + 79.42 ± 4.66
	TG10	3.76 * U1 + 75.55 ± 4.72
Trotter & Gleser 1952		female white
	TG11	0.68 * H1 + 1.17 * F1 + 1.15 * T1 + 50.12 ± 3.51
	TG12	1.39 * (F1 + T1) + 53.20 ± 3.55
	TG13	2.93 * Fi1 + 59.61 ± 3.57
	TG14	2.90 * T1 + 61.53 ± 3.66
	TG15	1.35 * H1 + 1.95 * T1 + 52.77 ± 3.67
	TG16	2.47 * F1 + 54.10 ± 3.72
	TG17	4.74 * R1 + 54.93 ± 4.24
	TG18	4.27 * U1 + 57.76 ± 4.30
	TG19	3.36 * H1 + 57.97 ± 4.45

Table 15: The formulas for stature calculation used for the Broerenkerk material.

This clearly demonstrates that as a result of prevailing right-handedness the long bones of the right arm generally are a few millimetres longer than those of the left arm, whereas there is no significant difference between the left and right lower limbs.

In tables 18 and 19 the results of all applied formulas are placed together to show the considerable range in the calculated body lengths. The calculated average stature of men ranges from 170.7 to 175.2 cm, the lower value being achieved with Breitinger's formula. For the women, the values range from 157.7 to 166 cm. It is impossible to determine wich value most closely reflects reality. This demonstrates most clearly how problematic it is to compare stature reconstructions that have been achieved by different methods. Within the Broerenkerk population, the

	n	mean	st. dev.	min.	max.	t	p
H1	28	4.11	3.15	-2	11	6.889	0.000
U1	16	3.25	3.73	-1	12	3.483	0.003
R1	23	2.13	3.33	-4	7	3.064	0.006
F1	32	0.63	5.53	-10	20	0.640	0.527
F2	32	-0.13	5.25	-8	18	-0.135	0.894
T1	29	-0.17	3.69	-6	7	-0.251	0.803
T1a	30	0.40	3.54	-6	8	0.619	0.541
Fi1	6	0.50	2.51	-3	3	0.488	0.646

Table 16: The length of right long bones minus the length of left long bones of males in mm (Series A), and the degree of difference (t) between the distributions (paired-samples t-test, SPSS).

	n	mean	st. dev.	min.	max.	t	p
H1	32	4.31	4.14	-6	11	5.895	0.000
U1	13	3.23	2.83	-3	7	4.112	0.001
R1	19	2.47	2.44	-2	8	4.428	0.000
F1	39	-0.62	4.11	-11	6	-0.936	0.355
F2	39	-0.82	4.11	-11	5	-1.247	0.220
T1	36	-0.50	3.10	-9	5	-0.967	0.340
T1a	38	-0.61	3.25	-11	5	-1.148	0.258
Fi1	8	0.50	4.34	-4	9	0.326	0.754

Table 17: The length of right long bones minus the length of left long bones of females in mm (Series A), and the degree of difference (t) between the distributions (paired-samples t-test, SPSS).

formula	n	mean	st. dev.	min.	max.
TG1	17	173.6	5.9	164.4	184.0
TG2	33	172.9	5.7	160.1	185.2
TG3	17	172.6	5.5	162.9	181.6
TG4	35	173.2	5.9	159.5	185.2
TG5	35	173.1	5.4	162.5	183.8
TG6	29	174.0	5.2	165.7	185.5
TG7	29	173.2	5.4	161.7	184.3
TG8	35	175.2	4.8	164.8	184.5
TG9	32	172.6	4.7	165.1	184.8
TG10	31	173.6	5.1	162.8	185.0
Br3	35	170.7	4.1	160.9	179.2
Tel1	35	171.3	4.7	161.3	180.3
Tel2	35	171.3	5.3	158.9	182.2
Tel3	35	173.0	5.6	162.2	184.2
Tel4	17	172.5	5.3	163.2	181.2

Table 18: Estimation of stature from the long bones of the identified skeletons (Series A), early 19th-century males.

formula	n	mean	st. dev.	min.	max.
TG11	28	163.8	5.1	153.0	177.6
TG12	37	164.1	5.4	153.0	178.4
TG13	21	162.8	4.7	155.1	175.6
TG14	43	166.0	5.6	154.9	179.3
TG15	31	164.9	5.0	154.9	177.3
TG16	45	162.5	5.0	151.2	176.4
TG17	28	159.4	4.9	150.7	168.7
TG18	25	157.7	4.0	151.3	166.2
TG19	41	162.9	3.4	154.4	170.9
Tel5	41	158.2	2.7	151.4	164.6
Tel6	45	160.5	3.7	152.3	170.7
Tel7	43	162.3	3.7	155.1	171.1
Tel8	21	162.6	3.7	156.6	172.7

Table 19: Estimation of stature from the long bones of the identified skeletons (Series A), early 19th-century females.

differences in outcome in some cases even exceed the standard deviations. Thus it is not feasible to arrive at reliable conclusions about differences between populations and about any secular trend in growth. On the basis of the Broerenkerk study, we have therefore argued that for a study into secular trends as much as possible the raw data of the long bones should be used. This has also been suggested by other Dutch researchers.[52]

In 1992, the average body length (172.9 cm) calculated with Trotter & Gleser's second formula was compared with data from other studied populations to see whether they fitted into the secular trend as it was then understood.[53] But given the above, we have become more cautious.

In 1992 there was still no reference material for females. But recently a useful overview has appeared on the basis of research in Eindhoven.[54] Because for females there are barely any formulas available other than those by Trotter & Gleser of 1952, at least the results for females from various populations are somewhat better comparable; but as we already saw, even the nine formulas by Trotter & Gleser produce substantial differences.

Health

Numerous pathologies were recognised in the skeletal material (Series A and B): benign and malignant tumours, degenerative changes to the joints, inflammation, paralysis, DISH, osteomyelitis, rickets, fractures and spinal deformities. A recovered hernia truss points to a case of groin hernia. It was the second hernia truss ever excavated in the Netherlands. Since then, more specimens have been recovered.[55]

52 Maat 2005, 281; Baetsen & Weterings-Korthorst 2013, 158.
53 Aten 1992b, 81.
54 Baetsen & Weterings-Korthorst 2013.
55 Mulder 1981, 64; Aten 1992b, 86; Bitter & Goubitz 2001; Nijhof 2001, 118.

Most of the pathologies occur just once or a few times in the material. This is insufficient for reliably determining their prevalence or making claims about the general state of public health in Zwolle. Exceptions are the more numerous fractures and cases of rickets. Comparisons could be made with the populations from the Hooglandse Kerk site in Leiden and from the whalers' graves on Spitsbergen (Svalbard)[56]. These sites represent three different social classes. Middle-class people in the Broerenkerk, members of the elite in the Hooglandse Kerk, and the proletariat on Spitsbergen. The comparison shows that rickets occurred twice as much amongst the 17th- and 18th-century whalers (10.0 %, n = 50) as in the early-19th-century Broerenkerk population (Series A: 5.3 %, n = 95), and least of all in the 17th- and 18th-century elite in the Hooglandse Kerk (1.5 %, n = 531). As nutrition and exposure to sunlight are decisive factors for this condition, a social aspect is only to be expected.

A similar pattern was observed in the prevalence of bone fractures. Fractures occurred far more among the whalers than in Zwolle or Leiden. But even in comparing bone fractures between populations we should be aware of methodological problems. In the Broerenkerk study we already pointed out that after proper healing, fractures need no longer be obvious.[57] After long survival, fractures may be barely if at all visible even on X-rays. This means that the age distribution of the studied population affects the number of recognisable fractures. Also the variable expertise of limb setters affects the visibility of fractures: old ones remain visible especially when poorly set. And finally, the prevalence of fractures often is so low that differences between populations cannot be statistically demonstrated.

Baetsen and Weterings-Korthorst add to this that differences in recording fractures, and in the various ways of calculating their prevalence and the representativity of the sample may constitute further obstacles to comparative studies.[58]

As usual in post-medieval populations, very frequent pathologies were found in the teeth. Dental health in early-19th-century Zwolle can only be called deplorable. This is hardly surprising, because the middle class townsfolk of Zwolle were already enjoying the newly available refined sugar, but as yet gave little attention to dental hygiene. Besides, the general use of clay tobacco pipes was the cause of many additional problems.[59]

The Broerenkerk population displays a remarkably high number of serious disorders of spinal curvature, both scolioses and kyphoses. It is difficult to explain such a high incidence of severe scoliosis. Even modern medicine often fails to find a cause for the occurrence of scoliosis. Such cases are called idiopathic scolioses. In archaeological material it is even more difficult to identify causes of scoliosis, although presumably the poorer general state of health may have been responsible for an increased prevalence of pathology-induced scoliosis, for instance resulting from rickets. For a gradation of scolioses in the skeletal material we could not make use of clinical classifications, which are in part based on motor characteristics in the living individual.

56 Maat 1981; Maat *et al.* 1984.
57 Aten 1992b, 88.
58 Baetsen & Weterings-Korthorst 2013, 194-195.
59 Bouts *et al.* 1992.

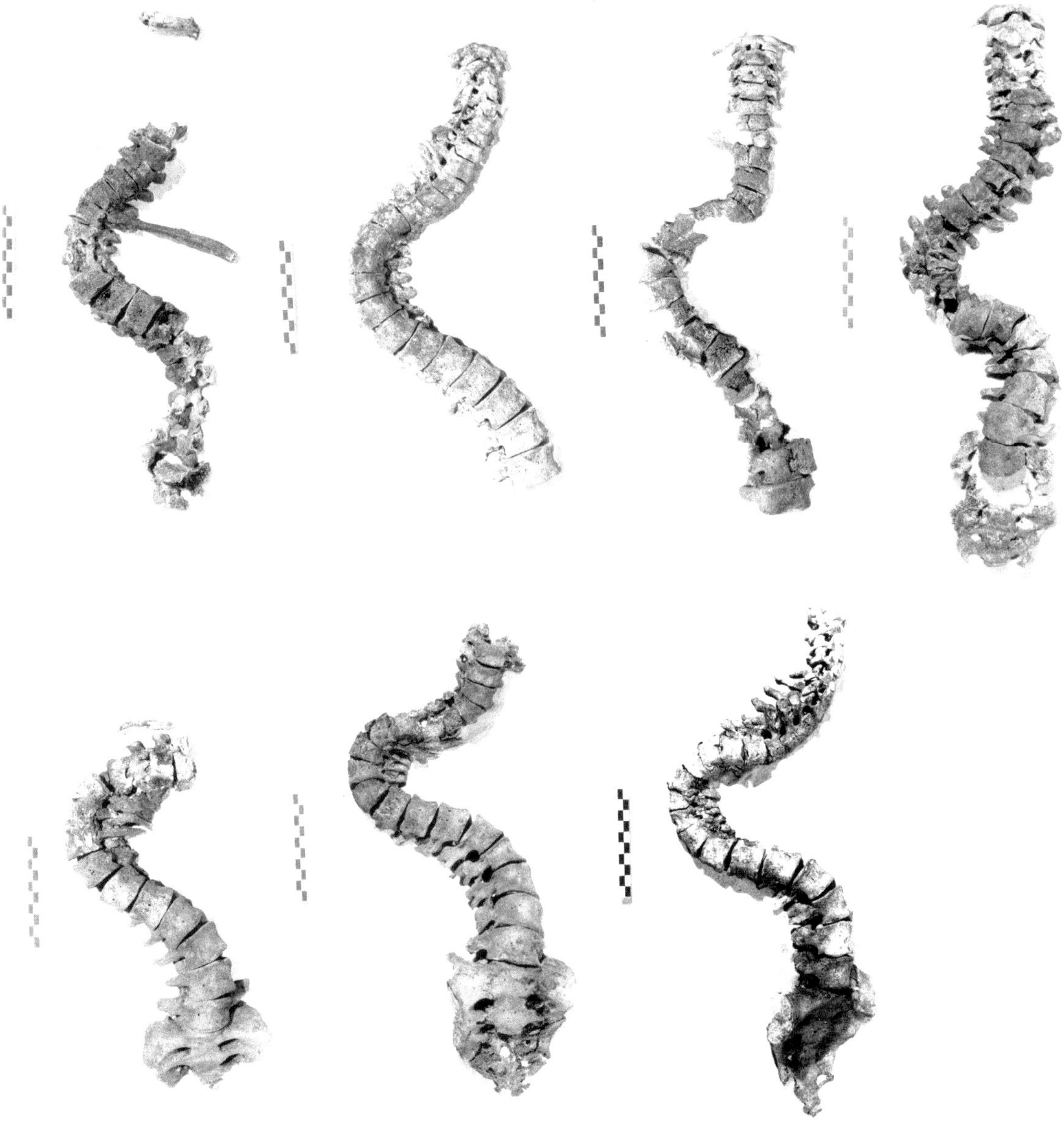

Fig. 9: Severe scoliosis in seven individuals of Series A, from top left to bottom right: female aged 48; female aged 46; male aged 73; male aged 23; female aged 60; female aged 60; female aged 40. An eighth case of severe scoliosis in Series A could not be depicted here owing to its poor conservation.

Therefore we made a classification in which only the maximum obliquity of vertebrae with respect to the longitudinal axis was decisive. An obliquity of up to 20 degrees was termed a slight scoliosis; an obliquity of 20 to 45 degrees a moderate one, and one over 45 degrees was called severe. The spines of 71 identified adults (Series A) could be examined. There were eight cases of severe scoliosis, a prevalence of 11.3 %. Besides, three moderate cases (5.6%) and ten light ones (14.1%) were identified. This implies an overall prevalence of scoliosis of 31.0 %. How much

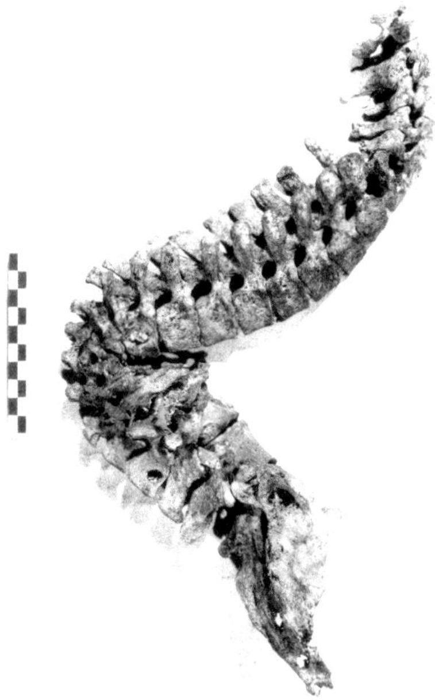

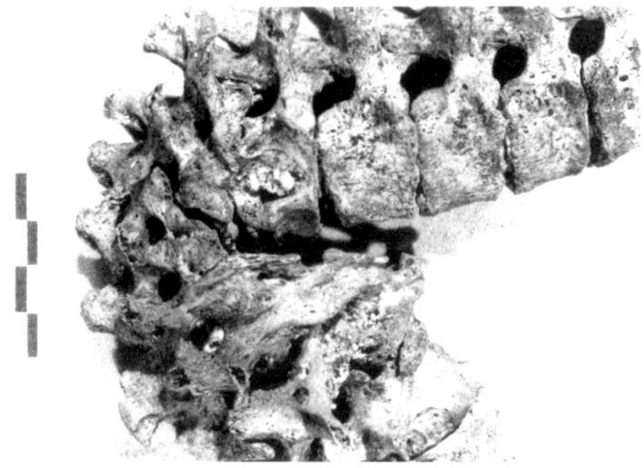

Fig. 10: A case of Pott's disease (tuberculous spondylitis) with typical kyphosis resulting from vertebral collapse in an unidentified individual from Series B. Note the complete obliteration of five thoracic and three lumbar vertebral bodies (left: total view; right: detail).

someone's stature might be reduced by severe scoliosis could be established from two females whose actual skeletal height could be reliably measured *in situ*. They were 132 and 136 cm tall. Given the lengths of their femurs, their 'healthy' stature might have been 166 and 157 cm, respectively.

Apart from scolioses, a case of serious kyphosis was observed, probably resulting from tuberculosis. Inflammation of the ninth thoracic vertebra led to the complete disintegration of the vertebral body and a marked kink in the spine. This led to the classical hunchback deformity of Pott's disease. Another case of Pott's disease was found in Series B and is depicted above. Here the inflammation probably started at the tenth thoracic vertebra, eventually leading to the total destruction of no fewer than five thoracic and three lumbar vertebral bodies. The white cheese-like dead cell mass, resulting from caseous necrosis, remained well preserved within the soil. Further three light kyphoses with unidentified causes were observed in Series A.

A poignant example of an all too common tragedy in those days was the skeleton of a woman who had died in childbirth (Series B). Her baby had fully engaged, but had lain in shoulder presentation. Apparently an attempt had been made to save the mother's life by forcibly delivering the baby. Only this can explain how the baby's articulated right arm came to lie beside the mother's right upper arm in the coffin.

Thirty years on

The excavation took place in the winter of 1987-1988, and the popular book "De doden vertellen" appeared in 1992.[60] Several things would be done differently today. First of all, there are the modern Health & Safety regulations. The way we

60 Clevis & Constandse-Westermann 1992.

Nederlands Dagblad Zaterdag 2 januari 1987 Streek/Binnenland

Wetenschap leert van skeletten van vorige generaties Zwollenaren

In de Broerenkerk in Zwolle wordt grondig gespit in het verleden

Zwolle graaft honderden skeletten op

Volkskrant van DINSDAG 22 DECEMBER 1987 BINNENLAND

SKELETTEN TONEN LEEFOMSTANDIGHEDEN IN ACHTTIENDE EEUW

Onderzoekers leggen botje naast botje

Honderden skeletten uit Zwolse kerk onderwerp studieproject

Trouw VRIJDAG 8 JANUARI 1988

Mensen

Kerkgraf geeft historie prijs

Bodemonderzoek in Zwolle naar gezondheid in late middeleeuwen

Zoeken naar gezondheid vroeger

ZWOLLE (ANP) - In de Zwolse Broerenkerk zijn 120 complete skeletten opgegraven voor een onderzoek naar de gezondheid in de 16e, 17e en 18e eeuw, waarover weinig bekend is. De skeletten verkeren in goede staat. Dit vergemakkelijkt volgens stadsarcheoloog Clevis het onderzoek. Het is de bedoeling aan de hand van de geraamten en gebit de sexe, lichaamslengte, leeftijd en ziekten vast te stellen. Over ziekten werd weinig geregistreerd. Als doodsoorzaak werd vaak pest genoemd, maar dat was een verzamelnaam. In de Broerenkerk zijn eenvoudige mensen begraven, meest gewone werklui, waardoor het mogelijk is een beeld van de gemiddelde gezondheidstoestand te krijgen.

Fig. 11: Some of many newspaper articles about the excavations in the Broerenkerk.

worked then would nowadays be quite illegal. Removing the tombstones would now be done mechanically; but then they were shifted by hand. Furthermore, we now have quality guidelines. Fieldwork headed by students is no longer permissible. The deployment of experienced specialists in fieldwork has become a matter of course. Besides, there have been technological developments. At the time, the ROB visited the site for just one day to try out a brand-new 'total station', which was said to be far too complicated for everyday use. Since then, digital surveying, the use of digital notebooks and of course digital photography have brought great improvements in archaeological practice. And although even then metal detection was used, this would now be done systematically.

But some things have not changed. Even 30 years on, there still is widespread use of methods for age assessment that remain untested on independent archaeological populations of known sex and age, and more often than not margins of error are ignored. And 30 years after the Broerenkerk study, the metric method for sexing is still considered subordinate or supplementary to the morphological method. Even today, comparisons of stature in life are made on the basis of reconstructive assessments made by differing methods; whereas for most research questions, comparing the lengths of long bones would be the most appropriate approach.

The Broerenkerk study is only rarely quoted. Because the project was largely conducted by students and was only published in Dutch in a monograph aimed at a broad readership, it hardly found its way into the academic media. Certainly the research had major limitations, for instance because it did not consider microscopic or destructive methods. Nevertheless, the Broerenkerk excavation was innovative in its testing of methods for age and sex determination on identifiable archaeological material, and thus in its emphasis on a broader archaeological perspective. It was not the first large-scale church excavation in which the skeletal material was the primary object of study rather than a secondary matter. Maat's investigations in the Pieterskerk and the Hooglandse Kerk in Leiden, as well as the research on Spitsbergen were important models for the Broerenkerk project. But at the same time, these actually provided almost all the material available for comparison. The results from the Broerenkerk threw a revealing light on the potential and limitations of physical anthropology in the context of archaeology, and recently the Broerenkerk study was described as 'trail-blazing'[61]. Owing to the great publicity generated by the project at the time, with 39,000 visitors looking down from wooden walkways on the skeletons being excavated, and with nationwide coverage in newspapers and on television, it sparked an interest in skeletal analysis within Dutch archaeology, and gave it a significant boost. The Broerenkerk excavation served as a model for other projects, such as that in the Grote Kerk at Alkmaar, and inspired young people to pursue careers in archaeology or physical anthropology.

Acknowledgements

Our recollections of the excavations in the Broerenkerk are vivid and positive, owing to the selfless commitment of dozens of volunteers who recovered the skeletons from damp trenches in the cold winter months. Many parties supported the project; but without the volunteers, who shared our love of archaeology and physical anthropology, nothing would have come to fruition.

We thank Xandra Bardet for the English translation.

61 Bitter *et al.* 2013, 12.

Bibliography

Arbeitsgruppe europäischer Anthropologen, 1979: 'Empfehlungen für die Alters- und Geschlechtsdiagnose am Skelett', *Homo* 30, Anhang 1-32.

Aten, N.A., 1992a: 'De opgraving in de Broerenkerk', in: H. Clevis & T. Constandse-Westermann (eds.), *De doden vertellen: opgraving in de Broerenkerk te Zwolle 1987-88*, Kampen, 12-29.

Aten, N.A., 1992b: 'Het onderzoek van de skeletten', in: H. Clevis & T. Constandse-Westermann (eds.), *De doden vertellen: opgraving in de Broerenkerk te Zwolle 1987-88*, Kampen, 66-97.

Baetsen, S. & L. Weterings-Korthorst, 2013: 'De menselijke overblijfselen', in: N. Arts (ed.), *Een knekelveld maakt geschiedenis*, Utrecht, 151-212.

Bitter, P., 2002: *Graven en begraven: Archeologie en geschiedenis van de Grote Kerk van Alkmaar*, Hilversum.

Bitter, P., 2018: 'Buried in Alkmaar: Historical and archaeological research on urban cemeteries', in: R.M.R. van Oosten, R. Schats, K.Fast & H.M.P. Bouwmeester (eds.), *The Urban Graveyard. Archaeological perspectives*, Leiden, 87-115.

Bitter, P., V. Bonenkampová & K. Goudriaan, 2013: 'Inleiding', in: P. Bitter, V. Bonenkampová & K. Goudriaan (eds.), *Graven spreken: Perspectieven op grafcultuur in de middeleeuwse en vroegmoderne Nederlanden*, Hilversum, 7-19.

Bitter, P. & O. Goubitz, 2001: 'Medische attributen', in: S. Baetsen, *Graven in de Grote Kerk: Het fysisch-antropologisch onderzoek van de graven in de St. Laurenskerk van Alkmaar*, Alkmaar, 106-111.

Black, T.K. III, 1978: 'Sexual dimorphism in the tooth-crown diameters of the deciduous teeth', *American Journal of Physical Anthropology* 48, 77-82, DOI: 10.1002/ajpa.1330480111.

Bocquet-Appel, J.P., 1986: 'Once upon a time: Palaeodemography', *Mitteilungen der Berliner Gesellschaft für Anthropologie, Ethnologie und Urgeschichte* 7, 127-133.

Bocquet-Appel, J.P. & C. Masset, 1982: 'Farewell to Paleodemography', *Journal of Human Evolution* 11, 321-333, DOI: 10.1016/S0047-2484(82)80023-7.

Bouts, W.H.M., T. Constandse-Westermann, T. Pot & H. Verhoeven, 1992: 'De gebitsresten uit de Broerenkerk, Zwolle, circa 1800 AD', in: H. Clevis & T. Constandse-Westermann (eds.), *De doden vertellen: opgraving in de Broerenkerk te Zwolle 1987-88*, Kampen, 99-141.

Breitinger, E., 1937: 'Zur Berechnung der Körperhöhe aus den langen Gliedmaßenknochen', *Anthropologischer Anzeiger* 14, 249-274.

Brothwell, D.R., 1981: *Digging up Bones*, Third edition, New York.

Chamberlain, A.T., 2006: *Demography in archaeology*, Cambridge Manuals in Archaeology.

Clevis, H. & T. Constandse-Westermann (eds.), 1992: *De doden vertellen: opgraving in de Broerenkerk te Zwolle 1987-88*, Kampen.

Constandse-Westermann, T.S., 1997: 'Age estimation by dental attrition in an independently controlled early 19th century sample from Zwolle, The Netherlands', *Human Evolution* 12, 269-285, DOI: 10.1007/BF02438180.

Ditch, L.E. & J.C. Rose, 1972: 'A Multivariate Dental Sexing Technique', *American Journal of Physical Anthropology* 37, 61-64.

Dittrick, J. & J.M. Suchey, 1986: 'Sex determination of prehistoric central California skeletal remains using discriminant analysis of the femur and humerus', *American Journal of Physical Anthropology* 70, 3-9, DOI: 10.1002/ajpa.1330700103.

Hagedoorn, J., 1992: 'Dood en begraven', in: H. Clevis & T. Constandse-Westermann (eds.), *De doden vertellen: opgraving in de Broerenkerk te Zwolle 1987-88*, Kampen, 31-65.

Hakbijl, T., 2000: 'Arthropod remains as indicators for taphonomic processes: an assemblage from 19th century burials, Broerenkerk, Zwolle, the Netherlands', in: J.P. Huntley & S. Stallibrass (eds.), *Taphonomy and Interpretation: Symposia of the Association for Environmental Archaeology*, 95-96.

Hinck, V.C., C.E. Hopkins & B.S. Savara, 1962: 'The size of the atlantal spinal canal: a sex difference', *Human Biology* 34, 197-205, PMID: 13954632.

Hirsch, R.J., 1921: *Doodenritueel in de Nederlanden vóór 1700*, PhD thesis University of Amsterdam.

Howells, W.W., 1973: *Cranial variation in man: a study of multivariate analysis of patterns of difference among recent human populations*, Harvard (Papers of the Peabody Museum 67).

Jantz, R.L., D.R. Hunt & L. Meadows, 1994: 'Maximum length of the tibia: how did Trotter measure it?', *American Journal of Physical Anthropology* 93, 525-528, DOI: 10.1002/ajpa.1330930410.

Katz, D. & J.M. Suchey, 1986: 'Age determination of the male os pubis', *American Journal of Physical Anthropology* 69, 427-435, DOI: 10.1002/ajpa.1330690402.

Lovejoy, C.O., R.S. Meindl, T.R. Pryzbeck & R.P. Mensforth, 1985: 'Chronological metamorphosis of the auricular surface of the ilium: a new method for the determination of adult skeletal age at death', *American Journal of Physical Anthropology* 68, 15-28, DOI: 10.1002/ajpa.1330680103.

Maat, G.J.R., 1981: 'Human remains at the Dutch whaling stations on Spitsbergen – A physical anthropological study', in: *Proceedings of the International Symposium Early European Exploitation of the Northern Atlantic 800-1700*, Groningen.

Maat, G.J.R., 1982: 'Boerhaave en zijn tijdgenoten, en de betekenis van hun lichaamslengte (een fysisch-antropologisch onderzoek van begravenen in de Pieterskerk te Leiden)', *Nederlands Tijdschrift voor Geneeskunde* 126, 705-712.

Maat, G.J.R., 2005: 'Two Millennia of Male Stature Development and Population Health and Wealth in the Low Countries', *International Journal of Osteoarchaeology* 15, 276-290, DOI: 10.1002/oa.785.

Maat, G.J.R, G.T. Haneveld, M.R.M. van den Brink & W.J. Mulder, 1984: 'A Quantitative Study on Pathological Changes in Human Bones from the 17th and 18th Centuries Excavated in the "Hoogland" Church, Leiden', in: G.T. Haneveld, W.R.K. Perizonius & P.J. Janssens (eds.), *Proceedings Paleopathology Association, 4th European Meeting, Middelburg/Antwerpen 1982*, Utrecht, 140-148.

Maat, G.J.R., R.W. Mastwijk & E.A. van der Velde, 1997: 'On the Reliability of Non-metrical Morphological Sex Determination of the Skull Compared with that of the Pelvis in The Low Countries', *International Journal of Osteoarchaeology* 7, 575-580, DOI: 10.1002/(SICI)1099-1212(199711/12)7:6<575::AID-OA308>3.0.CO;2-4.

Martin, R. & K. Saller, 1957: *Lehrbuch der Anthropologie in systematischer Darstellung*, Stuttgart, 1956-1962.

Mays, S., 2002: 'The Relationship Between Molar Wear and Age in an Early 19th Century AD Archaeological Human Skeletal Series of Documented Age at Death', *Journal of Archaeological Science* 29, 861-871, DOI: 10.1006/jasc.2001.0751.

Mays, S., 2014: 'Resorption of Mandibular Alveolar Bone Following Loss of Molar Teeth and its Relationship to Age at Death in a Human Skeletal Population', *American Journal of Physical Anthropology* 153, 643-652, DOI: 10.1002/ajpa.22465.

Meindl, R.S. & C.O. Lovejoy, 1985: 'Ectocranial suture closure: a revised method for the determination of skeletal age at death based on the lateral-anterior sutures', *American Journal of Physical Anthropology* 68, 57-66, DOI: 10.1002/ajpa.1330680106.

Meindl, R.S., C.O. Lovejoy, R.P. Mensforth & R.A. Walker, 1985: 'A revised method of age determination using the os pubis, with a review and tests of accuracy of other current methods of pubic symphyseal aging', *American Journal of Physical Anthropology* 68, 29-45, DOI: 10.1002/ajpa.1330680104.

Mulder, W.J., 1981: 'Cultuurhistorische aspecten', in: A.M. Luyendijk-Elshout (ed.), *Graven in de Pieterskerk*, Leiden.

Nijhof, E., 2001: 'Breukbanden', *Bossche Bladen: cultuurhistorisch magazine over 's-Hertogenbosch* 3, 118.

Perizonius, W.R.K., 1983: 'Closing and Non-closing Sutures in 256 Crania of Known Age and Sex from Amsterdam (A.D. 1883-1909)', *Journal of Human Evolution* 13, 201-216, DOI: 10.1016/S0047-2484(84)80065-2.

Rösing, F.W., 1983: 'Sexing Immature Human Skeletons', *Journal of Human Evolution* 12, 149-155, DOI: 10.1016/S0047-2484(83)80020-7.

Schutkowski, H., 1986: 'Geschlechtsdifferente Merkmale an kindlichen Skeletten: Kenntnisstand und diagnostische Bedeutung', *Zeitschrift für Morphologie und Anthropologie* 76, 149-168.

Schutkowski, H., 1987: 'Sex determination of fetal and neonate skeletons by means of discriminant analysis', *International Journal of Anthropology* 2, 347-352, DOI: 10.1007/BF02443994.

Stloukal, M. & H. Hanáková, 1978: 'Die Länge der Längsknochen altslawischer Bevölkerungen unter besonderer Berücksichtung von Wachstumsfragen', *Homo* 29, 53-69.

Telkkä, A., 1950: 'On the prediction of human stature from the long bones', *Acta Anatomica* 9, 103-117, PMID: 15403864.

Telkkä, A., A. Palkama & P. Virtama, 1962: 'Prediction of stature from radiographs of long bones in children', *Journal of Forensic Sciences* 7, 474-479, PMID: 13997454.

Todd, T.W., 1920: 'Age changes in the pubic bone. I. The Male White Pubis', *American Journal of Physical Anthropology* 3, 285-339, DOI: 10.1002/ajpa.1330030301.

Trotter, M. & G.C. Gleser, 1952: ‘Estimation of stature from long bones of American Whites and Negroes’, *American Journal of Physical Anthropology* 10, 463-514, DOI: 10.1002/ajpa.1330100407.

Trotter, M. & G.C. Gleser, 1958: ‘A re-evaluation of estimation of stature based on measurements of stature taken during life and of long bones after death’, *American Journal of Physical Anthropology* 16, 79-123, DOI: 10.1002/ajpa.1330160106.

Trotter, M., 1970: ‘Estimation of stature from intact long limb bones’, in: T.D. Stewart (ed.), *Personal identification in mass disasters*, Washington D.C.: National Museum of Natural History, Smithsonian Institution, 71-83.

Ubelaker, D.H., 1978: *Human Skeletal Remains*, Washington D.C.

Unselt, M., N. Aten, Y. Burnier & P. Kranendonk, 1995: ‘Archäologische Untersuchungen im Umsiedlungsstandort Inden/Altdorf: Die Besiedlung einer Kleinlandschaft’, in: Altvertrautes neu gesehen, Band 3, *15. Jahrbuch der Geschichtsverein der Gemeinde Inden e.V. 1995/96*; Jos. Fischer OHG, Jülich, 20-60.

Vallois, H.V., 1937: ‘La durée de la vie chez l’homme fossile’, *L’Anthropologie* 47, 499-532.

Van Spelde, F. & M.L.P. Hoogland, 2018: ‘A rural view of early modern mortuary practices. Context and material culture of the 18th- and 19th-century cemetery of Middenbeemster’, in: R.M.R. van Oosten, R. Schats, K. Fast & H.M.P. Bouwmeester (eds.), *The Urban Graveyard. Archaeological perspectives*, Leiden, 307-336.

Weaver, D.S., 1980: ‘Sex differences in the ilia of a known sex and age sample of fetal and infant skeletons’, *American Journal of Physical Anthropology* 52, 191-195, DOI: 10.1002/ajpa.1330520205.

Wurm, H., 1986: ‘Zur Geschichte der Körperhöhenschätzmethoden nach Skelettfunden: Vorschläge zur Körperhöhenschätzung nach Skelettfunden bis zur Mitte des 20. Jahrhunderts’, *Anthropologischer Anzeiger* 44, 149-167.

About the contributors

Nico **Arts** studied cultural and physical anthropology at Leiden University and pre- and proto-history at the University of Amsterdam. Since 1989, he has been employed as the urban archaeologist for the city of Eindhoven. Nico has published many studies about the stone age in the south of the Netherlands and medieval and early modern archaeology in Eindhoven. He has edited several volumes focusing on the urban archaeology of Eindhoven. Most recently he has been responsible for a major publication on the results and analysis of the excavation of the St. Catharine graveyard. Currently, Nico is finishing his archaeological synthesis of town and country in the Northern Kempen region in the period 1000-1650.

Nico **Aten** read physical geography and ecological pre- and proto-history at the University of Amsterdam, specialising in physical anthropology and medieval archaeology. His master's thesis was on the Broerenkerk project. In the 1990s he conducted large-scale, multi-season, urban-centre excavations, e.g., in Frankfurt (Oder), where he shed light on the evolution of medieval city defences, and in Cologne, where he was the first to demonstrate both Merovingian and Carolingian habitation and artisan activity in the city centre and hence the continuity of urban life. In addition, he has written about his analyses of human skeletal material from Inden, Wassenberg, Tell Sabi Abyad, Cologne, Neuruppin, and Wormerveer. In 2002 he was appointed an inspector in the State Inspectorate for Archaeology, now the Cultural Heritage Inspectorate.

Steffen **Baetsen** is a physical anthropologist and archaeologist at Steffen Baetsen Physical Anthropology. He studied archaeology and cultural history of Native Americans at Leiden University, focusing on osteoarchaeology in the Caribbean. For more than 25 years he has participated in Dutch research projects and archaeological excavations where human skeletal remains are involved, particularly in large-scale excavations (100+ burials). These include the Church of St. Catharine in Eindhoven and more recently the Eusebius Church in Arnhem. In February 2019, he started a position as senior specialist in physical anthropology at the Archeologisch Diensten Centrum (ADC), Amersfoort.

Hemmy **Clevis'** master's thesis was a historical-archaeological study of the counts of Kessel (University of Utrecht). His PhD at the same university was a historical-topographical study of the development of the lower town of Nijmegen 1300-1500, combining archaeological and documentary evidence. Employed at the ROB (now RCE, Cultural Heritage Agency of the Netherlands), he was involved in analysing the pottery and glassware from the excavations at Dordrecht, Deventer, and Nijmegen. Since 1987 he has been the municipal archaeologist of Zwolle, initially also of Kampen. Through various foundations, he has not only published aspects of his own research but also that of many colleagues. He was an initiator of the

Deventer System, a classification system of late- and post-medieval ceramics and glassware, which went online in 2019; also he is the godfather of the Belgian-Dutch Contact Days and of the Assembled Articles symposium. His publishing house SPA-Uitgevers has through the years issued many archaeological publications.

Tim **de Ridder** graduated from the Faculty of Archaeology, Leiden University in 1994. He has been working for the municipality of Vlaardingen since 1994 and since 1997 as the municipal archaeologist. The investigation of Count Dirk III's court in 2000 and the Gat in de Markt location were an incentive for him to set up a multi-year project entitled 'Graven in Vlaardingen'. The project resulted in, among other things, kinship research involving DNA testing of living Vlaardingers, in an effort to reach out to the public. He has published various articles and collaborated on books about the relationship of Vlaardingen with the Count's court, and in particular, the almost forgotten Battle of Vlaardingen.

Kerry **Fast** holds a PhD from the Centre for the Study of Religion at the University of Toronto. Her doctoral research was a historical-anthropological study of Canadian women's religious lives. In more recent years, she has focused her research attention on traditional, distinct Mennonite groups, which has taken her to Bolivia, Mexico, and across Canada where she has conducted ethnographic research in Mennonite communities. She has published several articles on aspects of Mennonite religious life and is co-editor of *Mothering Mennonite*. Kerry is also a full-time language and copy editor, specialising in academic editing in the humanities and social sciences. She lives in Toronto, Canada.

Michel **Groothedde** studied cultural pre- and proto-history at the University of Amsterdam, with an emphasis on the Middle Ages. In 1992 he was appointed municipal archeologist for the municipality of Zutphen, a position he still holds. From 1994 to 1999 he was also the municipal archaeologist of Deventer, and since 2007 he has been the archaeological consultant for the municipality of Doesburg. In all three cities he was involved in various excavations of historical graveyards and cemeteries. In 2013 he obtained his PhD at Leiden University, supervised by Frans Theuws. His research topic was the Zutphen gravenhof, a medieval centre of elite power, where a royal palace once stood.

Michael **Klomp** graduated in 1999 as an archaeologist from the University of Amsterdam with a specialization in the Late Middle Ages and Early Modern period. After working as an archaeologist in Nijmegen and Deventer, in 2002 he was appointed as municipal archaeologist in Zwolle. Through cooperation with other municipalities, his working area has been extended to the municipalities of Zwartewaterland, Kampen, and Hattem. He regularly publishes on topics related to the archaeology of Zwolle, Hasselt, Zwartsluis, Genemuiden, Hattem, and Kampen.

Jessica **Palmer** began her career with a Master of Arts in northwest European prehistory (with distinction) from the University of Ghent before transitioning to human remains with a Master of Science in human osteoarchaeology from Leiden University (cum laude). In 2014 she was appointed as stable isotope researcher, lab assistant, and lecturer/teaching assistant at Leiden University. In 2019 she defended her PhD thesis on skeletal evidence of physical activity in the post-medieval Low Countries. Her research interests include stable isotope analysis of human and animal remains to reconstruct diet and provenance, physical activity in human societies, and the spread and socio-cultural context of disease in past populations. She is currently combining existing datasets with new analyses to reconstruct the lives of people buried in and around the post-medieval town of Aalst, Belgium.

Roos **van Oosten** began her academic career studying medieval history after which she turned to archaeology, which culminated in a thesis on urban archaeology. Her PhD dissertation at the University of Groningen focused on sanitation management, which she successfully defended in 2014. In 2011, she was appointed as university lecturer in urban archaeology at Leiden University. In addition to undergraduate and graduate teaching responsibilities, Roos is working on her VENI-funded project entitled 'Challenging the paradigm of filthy and unhealthy medieval towns'.

Barbara **Veselka** studied Human Osteology and Funerary Archaeology at the University of Leiden in 2012. Recently she received her PhD on vitamin D deficiency in skeletal remains from 17th-19th-century communities from the Netherlands and has published several articles in international and local journals. She worked as a physical anthropologist at Stichting LAB from 2013 until 2018, during which time she excavated many human skeletal collections in the Netherlands and abroad. One of them was the collection of Hattem. Currently, she works in Brussels at the Vrije Universiteit Brussel as a postdoctoral researcher in the CRUMBEL project that studies cremated human remains and mobility in Belgium from the Late Neolithic to the Early Medieval period.

Rachel **Schats** studied archaeology with a specialisation in osteoarchaeology at Leiden University and University College London after which she was appointed as a research and teaching assistant for the Laboratory of Human Osteoarchaeology in Leiden. In her PhD (defended November 2016), she aimed at gaining a better understanding of the physical consequences of medieval developments, such as urbanisation and commercialisation, by comparing rural and urban skeletal populations. In 2018 Rachel was appointed as an assistant professor at the Faculty of Archaeology, Leiden University and is working on her VENI-funded project 'Mapping medieval malaria'.